NALANDA

NALANDA

History's Best-Kept Secret

SHIVANI SINGH

AMARYLLIS

AMARYLLIS
An imprint of Manjul Publishing House Pvt. Ltd.
• 7/32, Ansari Road, Daryaganj, New Delhi 110 002
Website: www.manjulindia.com
Registered Office:
• 10, Nishat Colony, Bhopal 462 003 – India

ISBN 978-93-90924-42-4

Cover Design: Kashmira Sarode

Printed and bound in India by Thomson Press (India) Ltd.

Contents

N
W
E
S
Observatory
itation Caves
Garden Of Austerities
Main Assembly Hall
Cotton Fields
Ten Wisdom College
Giant Buddha
Abbots White Palace
Honey Comb
Roofless Temple
Dragon Pool
san's Guild
Alchemy Lab
Tara Monastery
Nagarjuna Gold Mint
nadhi
rine
Brahmin Cook Tenements
Slave Quarters
Cowherd Gate
Sitavana
Baladitya Monastery
Ratnasagar Library
Royal Vihar
Monastery
Karmadana Offices
Seals Office
okiteshwara Sthrine
LibrariesRatna...
RatnaBodhi
Trader's Market
The dessicated pond
Admission Gate
Main festivities shrines
Reject's Colony
Pavilion
The Map of Nalanda

Prologue

A few kilometres shy of Bhutan's capital city Thimphu is an obscure nunnery perched on a mountain outcrop, like an exotic bird of the Himalayan paradise.

A row of Buddhist prayer flags marks its entrance. Within its gates, the low buzzing of prayers and the reassuring regularity of daily rituals keep its sixty-odd nuns in a state of constant physical and spiritual activity.

Today is a special day because Dorge Nhagmo Tulkuma from the Black Hat Monastery in Lhasa is passing through. She is the holiest female lama in Tibet and it is a matter of great fortune that the nuns have been allowed a special audience with her, even though it's just for a few minutes.

The small convent is weighed down by the auspiciousness of the occasion. The ceremony is so solemn that not even the air seems to move. The courtyard is small but clean. The bite in the cold Himalayan air is familiar to all present.

The Abbess and other convent functionaries move slowly through Dorge Nhagmo's hypnotic field like iron filings around a magnet. Ageless and unlined, she sits stock-still on her many cushions. She is the only one there who wears her hair long. She radiates an unsettling quiet. Behind Dorge Nhagmo, decorated with many scarves, hangs a tangkha painting of a naked Goddess engulfed in flames. The Goddess holds a curved knife in one hand

and a skull bowl in the other. Besides the tangkha, there are no other ritual objects.

Billowing maroon habits and tonsured heads make the nuns seem of indeterminate age, of uniform size. Even though they are everywhere, there is very little sound and very little movement.

One by one they have their private moment with Dorge Nhagmo. They take their blessings and the line moves quickly. Except one nun who slows the line down.

She looks up from her deep bow and, raising her boyish angular jaw in determination, she speaks. She does not look older than twenty years. 'Do I have permission to ask a question, Esteemed One?'

Dorge Nhagmo nods her assent, even as functionaries look about in startled dismay.

'I am compelled by an urge to write. There are voices in my head that whisper words and stories that I have never heard before,' the nun says. 'But I do not know whether I should write them down,' she trails off in respectful hesitation.

For a moment, all is quiet as Dorge Nhagmo stares into the distance, as if looking into the future. And then, to everyone's surprise, she bursts into peals of laughter. The Abbess is quite alarmed to see Dorge Nhagmo, usually so stoic and stern, so uncharacteristically animated.

'Very good, very good!' Dorge Nhagmo exclaims, and laughs some more.

The nun bows her head to the floor in deep gratitude and then shuffles away to make way for the others. The line moves on.

Later, Dorge Nhagmo is taken to the airport in the convent's battered old Maruti van. As they drive, the Abbess, her hands folded demurely on her lap, sits quietly next to Dorge Nhagmo. The vehicle lurches on a pothole. '2016, and nothing has changed. The roads are as bad as they always were.' The Abbess's small talk is polite and grave.

'Who is the girl who wants to write?' Dorge Nhagmo's tone is curt. It is very clear who is in command.

'Her name is Bilana.' Is there something special about the girl, the Abbess wonders. 'She has lived here all her life. She came to us from Mother Teresa's orphanage in Kolkata. She claims she gets lucid revelations of a monk's experiences from an ancient time—a time when the great university, Nalanda, was destroyed. As and when the revelations come, she says she feels forced to write them down.'

'She must write,' Dorge Nhagmo commands. 'And I want the books when they are finished.'

There is so much seriousness in the instruction that the Abbess cannot resist asking, 'Why, Dorge Nhagmo?' And to justify her question she continues, 'She is very ordinary.'

'Then you have not read the signs,' Dorge Nhagmo says looking straight ahead at the mountainous streets through the windshield. It has just started to rain when she says, 'She is a terton.'

The Abbess gasps. A terton is a great being incarnated to reveal sacred texts called terma or mind treasure. Both terma and terton are considered of deep significance to humanity. A hush descends inside the moving car, ensconcing even the driver. Not another word is spoken till Dorge Nhagmo breaks the silence.

'Keep her well,' she instructs.

'Guard her.'

Bilana's Revelations

Book 1

Benediction

Om mani padme hum.

I invoke blessings from the three directions throughout the three times.

If this book is open to public, it means a thousand years have passed and my master's prophecy has been fulfilled. The book has emerged from its burial place to a glorious time. A time when iron birds fly, horses have wheels and Dharma has come to the land of the red-faced man.

O glorious time! You are finally upon us. It is time to reveal the treasure. Treasure that need not be guarded any more, or hidden. All those who lay their eyes on it will be changed. They will be awakened.

I begin this story with the invocation of the three Buddhas. May the benevolent Gods bless my enterprise and may the malevolent Gods protect me. I invoke the Mother of the Universe, my chosen deity of worship.

I offer salutations at my master's lotus feet and also a fervent prayer that the creative act of writing is not besmirched by my petty conceit or deceit.

And last, my salutations to all those who read this. I honour you, the noble born in a wondrous age and glorious time, you who know nothing of the horrors of the past that have produced you. I salute your future.

May you read with a clear heart and a good mind, and thus may you learn the truth. Truth brings knowledge, and knowledge brings freedom. Freedom brings liberation from the sleep of ignorance, and causes the Great Awakening. This is how the Buddhas want it. This is how it will be written. This is how it will be done. Let not the sacrifice of your masters and ancestors go in vain.

Now, let the truth be told.

I live at a time when more than a thousand years have gone by since the Buddha's passing.

Like him, I too go by the name Siddhartha.

I live in a time when his spirit lives on in form.

A form that calls itself Nalanda mahavihara.

Nalanda, where stone walls are alive and minds attuned to every known frequency. A hundred larger-than-life Buddhas look down from invincible heights at Nalanda. Nalanda, where high-ceilinged corridors loom. Where garden lizards and trees look back at you with a mysterious awareness. Where the knowledge of the ancients is a great flame that has been kept alive since the days the Buddha walked on this blessed land.

It is a fire stoked every day, fed by the perseverance of its seers and by the endurance of time.

Nalanda is not just a form. It is a precious seat of scripture, probably the most precious in my world and time.

Nalanda is not just the most precious seat of scripture.

It is the fulcrum of many dimensions.

It is not just a fulcrum balancing the forces of polarities.

It is the centre of the universe that attracts all galaxies to itself.

In the hold of this centre, sways the history of mankind.

And the seeds of its own destruction.

1. *Leaving Home*

I remember clearly the day I first arrived at Nalanda.

Although fully ripened into manhood, I am still a boy. A boy raised to be a monarch, yet taking the vows of a monk. I see myself as a prince ready to pay a king's ransom for knowledge.

Our capital city Pataliputra still basks in the golden era of its previous Pala kings. Buddha's teaching, established by the Great Emperor Ashoka, is the religion of my land, and its prayer flags catch the wind of the Hindukush mountains in the north and the islands in the east, spreading across the deserts of the west, holding sway right down to the southern tip where the land meets the ocean of other worlds.

Or so it is said.

Though there are rumblings of Shankaracharya's rival Vedic doctrines ousting the keenest Buddhist dialecticians of my time in debate, non-Buddhist kingdoms are rare and far between. Which is what the Buddhists believed.

I have travelled all the way from Vaishali to Nalanda. My journey showed my inexperience in worldly matters. After a few hours, just like the Buddha did a thousand years ago, I sent my entourage back. Upon reaching Nalanda, I had to walk the last few miles on foot because my rented mule died on the way. I was penniless and starving, hungering more for food and a good night's sleep than all the knowledge in the three worlds. It shamed me because I was sure that was not how Prince Siddhartha had felt when he left home.

My mother had wept before my departure, exhorting me to do the duties of a first-born male and heir-apparent to the throne. But her tearful words had fallen on deaf ears. I was determined to join the Order and dedicate myself to a life of learning. I used to fantasise about manuscripts with my name emblazoned in golden letters in the hallowed libraries of Nalanda.

I had made my announcement before a full court, dressed in the regalia for my coronation. My father had looked at me with his sternest expression, but my resolve had remained unshaken.

The courtiers had responded with disbelief. Some had been apoplectic with rage, a few had staged a walkout, others had been bereft with grief. Only my brother seemed to be smiling through it all.

The court had quickly adjourned to my father's private pavilion and very soon only my parents and I had been left, locked in a fruitless argument for so long that the torchbearers had come when day turned to night and left when night turned to day again. My brother had been our only audience, nursing his goblet of wine, bemused but there, listening. Younger than me by only a year, he was larger than me in physique, ambition and worldliness.

'Please understand, my dearest first-born,' my father had agonised, 'that our religion is statecraft. Its purpose is to maintain our subjects in peaceful equilibrium. That is how it has been since Emperor Ashoka's time. Our priests help us rule. Our scholars seek out the knowledge of worldly affairs. Only fools try to emulate Buddha's life. They try to catch water that has already flown under the bridge. The Buddha's lifetime is over and long gone, my son!' My father was a stately, proud scion of the most illustrious Lichchavi clan. Not once had I seen him slouch or hesitate.

'You should never have named me Siddhartha, Father. Therein lay your mistake.' I reasoned as calmly as I could.

'It was a moment of parental weakness,' he had exploded. 'At your birth, the court astrologers read your horoscope and said that you will achieve greatness like the Buddha.'

I had not reminded my father that the court astrologers had prophesied that I would achieve greatness, but unlike the Buddha, *after* my death.

I had looked at his face, distorted with contempt now, tired and emptied of all his reasons. 'At the time I did not know that it would take you many lives to be worthy of a name like that.' He had hoped that berating me would work when entreaties failed.

'Prince Siddhartha left his father's throne in the search for Truth. You leave yours to join a heretical university,' he had thundered. His luxuriant moustache had bristled as he paced the pavilion, favouring the leg that he had almost lost during a battle with a neighbouring Lichchavi chieftain.

'Heretical!' it was my turn to explode. 'You call Sri Nalanda heretical? Great intellectuals cross the seven seas to study in Nalanda and you call it heretical? Such is the narrowness of your vision, Father.'

'You are still very innocent, my first-born,' my mother had said, her woeful entreaties gone, now as grim-faced as my other parent. She had looked beautiful, my mother. She looked scintillating even when sullen. Her eyes had been full of remorse. She had wrapped her shimmering stole, threaded by the rare beetle worm, more closely about, as if shuddering against an unearthly cold.

'Your notions about the path of knowledge are too romantic. The difference between reality and appearance is the difference between heaven and hell.'

'I know that, Mother,' I implored her. 'That is why I want to study in Nalanda. Only in Nalanda are the teachings so powerful that the veils of ignorance are quickly lifted. Do you know that the wisdom of the present Abbot of Nalanda has made him immortal? They say he is three hundred years old.'

'Nonsense, son,' my father retorted. 'You talk about these silly legends the way an infant babbles about magic. And this comes from a student who wants to learn the empiricism of logicians. Shame.'

My father had caught me out.

I had looked on defiantly as my mother calmly continued. Nothing is worse than two parents aligned against you.

'Nalanda is not a university,' she said. 'It is a colony of dissolute reprobates. They live off the fat of the land just like kings and landlords. They are a far cry from Lord Buddha's bhikshus who only ate what was dropped in their begging bowls. Their grandmasters live in obscene abundance. Yes, as kings, we too live in material opulence, but we suffer from worldliness. They suffer from moral depravity. Your chances of assuaging your thirst for knowledge are higher here, on the throne of our kingdom, than a place like that, where Kapalikas, skullmen, roam free, practising their charnel ground rites, desecrating all sacred things. I have heard women there are preserved in secret chambers. I shudder to think of the unspeakable slavery they are subjected to. Ghouls roam the lands of Nalanda,' my mother had tried to frighten me, 'and half-dead zombies and monsters who eat children!'

'Mother, I am not a child anymore,' I had said, hoping to impress her with my casual disdain.

'Don't try to scare me with Kapalika stories,' I had warned her.

'I know what they are. They are cannibals who only eat and drink from bowls carved out of the skull of a Brahmin. But they are only a small unseen minority in the university. Their presence in Nalanda is maintained in the spirit of egalitarianism. As for the throne of this kingdom, you are blessed with another son, who is waiting, I am sure, with much eagerness to take up the duties of kingship.' My brother, to my annoyance, had not once intervened. I could see him still smiling into his wine goblet.

'Stay,' my mother had implored. 'Or go to Taxila. Our personal retinue shall escort you. But not Nalanda.'

I had resorted to the famed melodramatic technique unique to my father's side of the family. I had torn a tuft of my hair and thrown it on the ground. 'I declare myself a renunciant from this moment on.' At that time I had not known whether I had been shouting out of a desire for renunciation or in defiance of it. 'I may no longer be bound to family ties,' I had screamed.

My last memory of home is that look of unfathomable sadness only mothers are capable of. *Oh Mother, Mother, do you not know that even motherhood is just another impurity? If we were truly pure, there would be no birth or death. No you, no me.*

I knew I had finally reached Nalanda when I caught my first glimpse of the Giant Buddha from over the horizon. It was hundred feet of pure gold and famous in the entire Buddhist world. As I neared the threshold of Nalanda's gates, my kingdom's feisty black-eyed maidens, the camaraderie of horseback rides, the royal hunts with my brother, the pomp of my father's court, all turned from burning cinders to cold ashes in my memory. I was finally going to shed all vestiges of who I was. I would finally become what I had always wanted to be. A monk, a mathematician, a logician, a seeker of higher truths, who had lived a life of opulence but had remained proudly indifferent to it. A true renunciant.

Soon the entrance gate loomed over me. Its mighty portals shone with the resplendence of wisdom, intimidating me, dwarfing me into inconsequentiality. The names of Nalanda's eighty-four grandmaster mahasiddhas inscribed in white on the admission gate sparkled in the dwindling light. But the gigantic candidate bell that hopefuls tolled to announce their candidature was ominously still. Night was falling fast. The torchbearer's flame flickered on the looming ramparts, engulfing all light in its coagulating shadows. As the sun dipped into the horizon, my heart sank. I would have to sleep hungry and wait for the first light of dawn.

Fortunately, I found an inn on the outskirts of the university, maintained expressly for the purpose of providing night lodging to wayfaring candidates. I took the unscheduled halt as a good omen because it was only now after seeing the forbidding portals of the university that the possibility of rejection dawned upon me. The inn was run by an old-timer who had retired from the smithies and gold mines of Nalanda. I wanted to ask him about Nalanda's legendary alchemical laboratories where it was said base metals were turned into gold. I wanted to know whether it was true that Nalanda's gold had made its Abbots richer than all the kings across the seven seas, but the man looked preoccupied and I was emotionally drained. The meal of coarse rice and bean curry was hot, well-cooked and of generous proportions. My straw pallet was dry and comfortingly warm. I slept as if there were no tomorrow.

As soon as I stepped out of the inn the next morning, freshly clothed and well-fed, I was surrounded by a bustle. It seemed that while I had slept, a little township of inns and shelters had sprung up. Everywhere, hawkers and vendors peddled their wares. There were candidates camped in makeshift platforms. Some of the beggars were aspirants too. They were a disgruntled lot, looking as if they had been waiting here for years. I approached the entrance gates with a mixture of confidence and trepidation.

Unnerved by their appearance, my gaze turned away and fell on yellowing parchments. Written in many languages, they were stuck to the admission gate's temple pillars. I asked a groundnut vendor passing by what they were.

He shrugged, 'Rival doctrines, petitions for entrance, announcements and news from within, deaths, births, lost and found.'

After a point I could not hear the street cacophony any more because of the pounding of my heart. A slight monsoon drizzle had dampened my clothes, but I did not care for it, as I saw the rain as a propitious sign. Looking up at the ramparts, I could see sentry monks intoning the virtues of Nalanda in a monotonous rhythm.

Stone walls rose high and towered over and behind the ramparts. A small mob, curious about the fate of my candidature, had collected around me. From them I learnt that gruel was served at all the gates at intervals. Sometimes, lectures were given by senior monastics through holes in the walls, encouraging a crowd to collect around the niches.

I looked around me and took a deep breath. It seemed candidates toiled tirelessly within the gates and without. Above us we could see the master acharyas walking the high walls of the gateways, gazing down on us, deciding our fates.

I finally separated myself from the crowd and walked to the candidate bell. It was many times my size, standing in our midst like an anthill among dung beetles.

According to procedure, any candidate who wanted admission rang the bell and waited for one of the masters to come out and take an interview. On an average, there was one candidate every day, and the acceptance rate was one a week. The maximum rush was during the annual monsoon retreats.

I stood paralysed before the bell, surrounded by a veritable township of rejects. They watched my plight with interest. I looked at the bell but could not reach out for it. It shone from the nervous sweat of a million aspirants.

Finally, I stepped forward. My arms felt puny as I shook its giant dome. I imagined the sound reverberating in the deepest recesses of Nalanda as I waited for my destiny to unravel.

In the endless interim, I listened to the chatter of the others. I heard how sometimes candidates were given preparatory work before admission. They were made to till land or rear cattle. Or sent to other monasteries. But in general, candidates were treated well. Because the next great scholar might well be amongst us.

Those turned away could come back and try their luck again and again. Sometimes, due to this, specially worthy candidates who were denied admission repeatedly became accomplished on their own. However, not all news was encouraging. A bitter reject spat betel juice from his blackened mouth and said that Nalanda's discipline was so strict that there was even a protocol on how to dream.

After a while, a small side door opened and I separated from the chattering group. The bored expression of a tonsured monk with a clean unlined face and slanting eyes presented itself. He looked singularly unmoved by me. He brusquely ushered me into a dark, airless room and made me sit on a stone bench facing a wooden window. I knew this was the admission window because it had graffiti scratched on all sides. Names, sutras, obscenities, images of the Buddha distracted me, but only momentarily. The bench was the only furniture in the room.

The walls stank of urine. And the nervousness of many like me.

'Subject?' he enquired, without looking at me.

'Pratityasamutpada,' I said. Pratityasamutpada was a popular doctrine of Buddhist ontology, with its own epistemological system, ethics, logic and theism.

'The master you would like to acquire?'

I was taken aback by this question because I had not given it any thought. My aim was to get into Nalanda. It did not matter who my master was. 'Shilabhatta,' I blurted without thinking. He raised his eyebrows and made a face that could have meant that I was presumptuous to choose the Abbot of Nalanda himself.

'Let me confer,' he said, and disappeared through a door.

I waited for a long time in that room. It looked like a tunnel to the netherworld. I waited so long that my wet clothes dried up. From a small adjacent window I could see a little patch of the rolling greens of the Nalanda gardens beyond. I gazed upon it the way a prisoner gazes upon the freedom of nature.

Presently, movements and the rustling of robes in the adjoining room got my heart pounding again. The wooden slats of the admission window in the wall opposite my bench opened noisily and through the vertical iron grills my anxious gaze met the most remarkably intense pair of eyes I had ever known. I was taken aback by their colour and intensity. They were grey, like the early morning sky.

Not once did his eyes leave my face throughout the long interview, not once did his expression change.

'What is your name?' he asked.

'Siddhartha, heir apparent of the first Lichchavi kingdom in Vaishali,' I said, as clearly as I could.

'How many collections of sutras and shastras do you know?'

'Ten,' I said proudly.

'You are young to know so many,' he remarked.

'They have still not slaked my thirst for knowledge,' I said, and stopped myself from saying more, so as not to sound unctuous.

'Is it knowledge you seek, or the truth?' he asked after a grave pause.

'Pardon me, Sir, but I do not see the difference between the two.'

Again that charnel ground silence. I fought against its unsettling effect. He proceeded with his interview with questions from the Mahaparinirvana Sutras that I answered easily because of the disciplined tutelage of my royal teachers. Memorising the Buddha's quotes in the Mahaparinirvana Sutra had been a morning ritual throughout my boyhood. It taught about the substance the Buddha is made of, the Buddha nature and how all conscious beings could achieve it.

I kept my confidence while speaking about the intricacies of Nyaya and floundered but only slightly on Panini's grammar. Luckily, though, I answered quite successfully his questions on the four Vedas.

Just as I was bracing myself for his next question, he looked at me for a long solemn moment and said, 'I am sorry. You are not for me.' And he was gone from the window.

The first image that flashed in front of my eyes was the humiliation I would suffer before my parents. His announcement had taken me completely by surprise. I felt my face crumple like a dry prune. I suddenly wished that I was out in the rain, so the tears coursing down my cheeks would be unnoticed. Presently, the doorkeeper returned to the window. Seeing my condition, he used a gentle tone.

'The esteemed Abbot says that you are worthy, but not meant for him. He says you are meant for Aryadatta. Brother, is that all right by you?'

Stunned by this miraculous turn of events, I joyously exclaimed, 'The Great Aryadatta! Yes, brother, a thousand times yes. It is the master I seek. What greater fortune than being sought by him.'

I whooped in delight and the doorkeeper's weary face broke into a sympathetic smile.

At this time I was too ecstatic to ponder over my drastically fluctuating fortune. Only later would I know why the Abbot had declined my tutorship. Just like the wombs we are born in, we carry the imprints of our masters at birth. So also with our spiritual initiations. The number, degree and level of our initiations and the conductor of our initiations are predetermined.

The Abbot could see through my soul and tell that I was not appointed for him. Such is the mysterious nature of the true master-student relationship. But I was ignorant of all this then.

All I knew then was that the doorkeeper was jangling his heavy iron keys with a broad, friendly smile. I would later learn that he was called Sakya, the Monk Who Never Sleeps.

'Come, Nalanda brother,' he said, his eyes crinkling with a gentle friendliness that I would later grow to love. 'Let me show you in.'

2. *Inside Nalanda*

Nalanda's colleges, streets, markets and hostels were a self-contained township, nay, a whole independent world. A world created by knowledge, for knowledge, of knowledge.

All buildings, the college chaityas of halls, monasteries, the observatories conjoining with the clouds, the viharas and stupas, demanded this knowledge. Even the limpid lotuses in pools and garden paths weaving through the university seemed to exist for the sole purpose of aiding the process of contemplation. I remember when I first came, how enamoured I was of the fairy turrets reaching the clouds, the splendour of red kanaka blossoms, the blue lilies in the university ponds and the rolling fields of the best and most scented kusha grass.

When you looked up at the ceiling, the huge domed arches were of such magnificent and luxurious design that they inspired awe. Awe not only for their superlative architecture but also for what they represented. The religious empire of Buddhism. Throughout the kingdoms in the East and the West, coins and seals carried Nalanda's emblematic definition—'Charity without intermission'.

Eighty-four monastic colleges and eighty-four shrines glorified the might of Nalanda. The souls of the greatest kings rested in the palms of Nalanda's eighty-four mahasiddha grandmasters. We call the ability to create miracles siddhis. The siddhas are miracle makers, and the mahasiddhas the great miracle makers. The mahasiddhas are the kings of kings. It was a matter of great pride for me that one such mahasiddha's name, emblazoned in pure white, was of my master, Aryadatta.

Truly, Nalanda turned out to be more than I had imagined.

Aryadatta, a man of giant stature, hailed from Uddiyana, the mythical land of magic, east of Nalanda. He was of fierce demeanour but had been surprisingly gentle when he received me, almost like a mother. Clad in silken robes and bejewelled sandals, his hair in a lustrous topknot, his overwhelming smile and words had immediately put my nervous apprehensions to rest, but the manner in which he spoke made my skin erupt in its pores.

'So, finally,' were his exact words, 'You are here.' As if he had known me for a long time, and had been waiting for my arrival.

Our first meeting had occurred immediately after entering Nalanda. He was waiting at the rear entrance of the admission gate temple with three other new entrants. As Sakya, the Monk Who Never Sleeps, walked ahead of me, the jangling of his iron keys like music to my ears, I saw them from a distance. They stood under a red pavilion overlooking the immense green of kusha grass. I must have been the last to arrive because it seemed they had been waiting for a while. Before I could look askance at the Monk Who Never Sleeps, he explained the protocol.

'This is just a preliminary introduction. Your ordination will take place during the next ekadasi, a fortnight from today. You should be well settled in your monastery by then.'

'What am I supposed to do now?' I asked with mounting urgency.

'Follow the others,' was his flippant reply.

When we reached the pavilion, I followed the monk and reverently took off my slippers and lined them neatly along with the other pairs of sandals. Like him, I followed the conscious two-step walk up the three stairs of Dharma, Sangha and Buddha.

As soon as we finished climbing, my master took out a conch from his robes and blew it three times.

'We can begin,' said the Monk Who Never Sleeps. The three new entrants who had been there before me, I don't know for how long, turned to face the master. They all looked roughly my age.

The prostrations began.

'I am Bilwa, I forever cut my ties to my homeland, the island of Sumatar, many leagues south, to seek your refuge.'

'I am Asita, prince of a Kingdom in Kamboja, a hundred yojanas north of here. I forever cut my ties to my homeland and seek your refuge.'

'I am Tarpa. I come from the land of snows, many leagues north of here. I forever cut my ties to my homeland and seek your refuge.'

It was now my turn. With much emotion I prostrated full length before my master.

'I am Siddhartha, prince of Vaishali, a few yojanas east of here. I forever cut my ties to my homeland and seek your refuge.'

That is when my master said those words.

'So finally,' he said, 'you are here.'

His gaze was so intimate that it bore through my soul and I knew immediately that the person I faced was not just a grandmaster but a mahasiddha, a fully enlightened being.

At our very first lecture, I had watched a flower bloom in my master's hand, unbeknownst to him, even as he spoke. It is said that enlightened beings do not exhibit miracles but endeavour to move like ordinary men in the company of common people. For a logician like me, therefore, this was epistemological proof of his enlightenment.

There were many similarities between the Abbot and my master. Both had striking physiques, the Abbot more so, since he hailed from the land of Gandhara, whose people are known for their physical beauty. The two of them, even though they were of differing schools, were the two greatest intellects of renown in my time. Yet my master reminded me of an effulgent volcano, forever giving of itself, in spite of its smoke and fire, its sound and fury. His temperament was plain to all.

The Abbot was more like Nalanda's legendary Dragon Pool. Mysteriously dark, of fathomless depths. He was of many colours and myriad reflections. One look into his intense grey eyes and one could wonder whether he was the mythical Naga serpent transmogrified into the form of a human.

To close our preliminary introduction at the pavilion, our master again blew his signature conch three times. This was instantly echoed by three resonating conch calls from the ramparts at the entrance gate. It was followed by the concatenating beat of a drum roll that announced to all that four candidates had gained entrance to Nalanda.

We were led to the Bhaumakara Monastery and shown our cells. It was the smallest and newest of all the monasteries. All four of us had adjoining cells at the fourth stage. We climbed the staircases in single file. My only constant objection to Nalanda's architecture was that the doorways and staircases were too small for larger men like Asita and me.

In the cells too the beds were too narrow but in the spirit of the Sangha, the bigger men slept with their feet dangling from their beds with nary a complaint.

On each narrow bed lay our monk robes, made of hemp, that would scratch my spoiled skin for many months. We were also given wooden sandals, a begging bowl and a staff. For a few years, we would not be allowed to wear our sandals, except on ceremonial occasions. Until then we would walk barefoot.

After a ritual bath at the bathing lakes, the barber waited for us at the monastery courtyard. Shorn of our lustrous locks, nails clipped, dressed in hemp, we looked at each other, a riot of emotions flitting across each face. We rubbed our hands against our raw scalps and laughed, and were immediately admonished by a venerable old monk who came out from the second stage balcony and told us to stop behaving like a bunch of washer girls.

Before our ordination, Asita and I had to undergo a special renunciant ritual to wash off any psychic obscurations of princedom.

And then on a balmy ekadasi morning, our ordination ceremony took place in the green field before the Giant Buddha.

A Vigrahapala senior from the Abbot's office conducted the solemnities. The Vinaya sutras, the sutras of right conduct, were read out to us and we took our monastic vows one by one. The ceremony was fairly simple. At the end of it, the Abbot's ceremonial diamond dagger was used to make a notch on each of our staffs to mark our first chronological year at Nalanda, and our first ordination. Our first alms, a fried plantain, was dropped into our begging bowls as we were shown the strictures of bhiksha, begging. The exhaustive difference between Vedic begging and Buddhist begging was clearly and vehemently outlined. Any breach in our bhiksha conduct, we were told, would throw us into the lower hells.

As we rose from our final prostrations, a karmadana notary from my master's office had news for us.

'Grandmaster Aryadatta wishes all of you to take the tour of the Ten Wisdom Colleges in case you want to reconsider your choice of subject. The final decision, however, is yours to make.'

I joined the tour with Bilwa, Asita and Tarpa. A venerable monk from the Sthavira village of old retired monks conducted the tour. We followed his bent frame and rasping voice with much reverence.

He led us away from the busiest and most popular colleges dedicated to metallurgy, artisanry and statecraft. These subjects were the most sought after because of their high career prospects.

Behind these colleges, the alleys opened out to an amra

grove beyond which the first deity of the Ten Wisdom Colleges became visible.

At the entrance of the front academic courtyard, in the extraordinary maze of intertwining courtyards, was a gigantic statue of the Dark One, the great and terrible goddess frozen mid-step in her classic dance of cosmic destruction that contained all the elements of cosmogony. It was a statue of exquisite beauty.

'When some of these old monasteries fell into decrepitude or were raided by the White Huns,' the Sthavira's voice rasped, 'the royal patrons did not destroy the buildings but built around them, in concentric circles, like the bark of an old tree.'

That explained the confusing labyrinth before us, I thought. These older colleges were completely empty, save for a few sweepers brooming the corridors. It seemed today was a study holiday and every one was away at the ekadasi celebrations.

'These, you see,' the old master pointed in the eastern and western directions, 'are where the lecture rooms are situated.'

He took us to every college chaitya encircled by a row of classrooms. Each chaitya had at least one statue of a Wisdom Goddess symbolizing some aspect of the science and arts studied there.

'When I was a young monk like you, this is where I studied Aryabhatta's Mathematics.' His bent frame moved as if in permanent supplication. Inside, the room held an intricately designed panel of the eternal serpent Adishesha reclining in the posture of the leminiscate, the horizontal eight, symbol of infinity.

'Aryabhatta taught the close links between zero and infinity,' the Sthavira explained, with just a hint of nostalgia for his lost college days.

'From the Isavasya Upanishad,' he propounded like a military commander.

'*Poornasya poornamaadaya poornameva visish-yate*'. To mathematically explain this, we have to assume that the first poornam represents infinity and the second, zero. In Sanskrit, as you all know, *poornam* means both full and zero. We have to distinguish between these two notions which are mutually contradictory and follow Aryabhatta's most profound law of inversion. Following this law, both quantities become the inverse of each other. The division by zero gives infinity.'

This was the first time I had heard of the law of inversion. As I walked through the empty corridors, I did not know that the law would become a lifetime mission.

Further on, we walked through interlinking courtyards radiating from one another. The Wisdom statue here symbolised benevolence. We looked about us in awe, not daring to speak even in hushed tones. How many other young novices before us must have looked around as wide-eyed as us, I wondered.

'There in those rooms are taught *sabda vidya*, the science of linguistics, and Panini's grammar. Medicine and Ayurveda are taught in the adjoining colleges.' He pointed in the direction of a stone installation of the Wisdom Goddess, the humped and ugly Crone. How ignorant I was, that I did not contemplate even for a moment the correspondence of her cryptic imagery with subjects taught under her hawkish eye. Only much later would I understand how the law of inversion escapes the most accomplished.

The Sthavira elder took us to an outer courtyard and pointed a gnarled finger at a tower in the distance, enclosed by walls. It too had a high pinnacle but not as high as the pinnacle of the building we stood in. 'There, see that large herbarium? Behind the herbarium, on its west side, is the Vimana tower, where studies based on the texts of Vimana Shastra, on flying vehicles, are implemented.'

I walked in mesmerised silence with my companions around the larger-than-life vision of the Wisdom Goddess, who signified the Earth. She looked down at us, smiling like a mother about to offer a tasty treat.

The portals of the upper stories were guarded by a terrifying Wisdom Goddess, the Headless One. We walked around her naked form as she held her severed head aloft, blood spurting from her neck in three different directions.

From here we proceeded to a large hall that contained the mechanical implements for the study of natural sciences, my favourite subject.

'Let me recount the precise directions for constructing man-made lightning, from the Agastya Samhita, which have been followed in the making of these chambers,' our Sthavira croaked.

'Knowledge of man-made lightning is much sought after.' Finally one of us had spoken. We all turned to look at Bilwa. He spoke with great confidence, and did not seem at all overwhelmed like the rest of us. 'Especially by Muslim traders who are taking this knowledge to their alien yavana lands.' We now turned to the Sthavira for his reaction, expecting a stern admonishment for speaking out of turn. But ignoring Bilwa, the Sthavira continued as if he had not been interrupted. We muffled our laughter in our robes. The old man was probably blind and deaf!

'Place a well-cleaned copper plate in an earthenware vessel. Cover it first with copper sulphate and then moist sawdust. After that put a mercury-amalgamated zinc sheet on top of an energy known as the twin compound Mitra–Varuna. Water will be split by this current into Upwind and Downwind. A chain of one hundred jars gives a very active and effective force,' he rattled on.

Next, he took us to the lecture halls for the studies of astronomy. It was completely bare, except for the statues of Aryabhatta and Brahmagupta. They stood sentinel on two sides of a raised teacher's platform, keeping watch on the earth rotating on its axis. 'Brahmagupta said,' I recited, eager to show off my learning, 'all things fall to the earth by the force of the laws of nature. For it is the nature of the earth to attract and keep things.'

This time the old master's wrinkled face broke into a toothless smile of indulgence.

Asita nudged me in my ribs.

'You brought him back from the land of the dead.'

'He smiles because he knows it is quite fruitless to stem my vast flow of knowledge,' I retorted.

Seemingly deaf again, the Sthavira continued his monotonous intonations.

'Beyond, to the north, are the laboratories for the study of celestial bodies.' He pointed at the pinnacle and, clasping his hands, went into raptures about Aryabhatta's powers of contemplation.

'Aryabhatta was a great astronomer of remarkable originality.' The Sthavira closed his eyes as if in prayer.

'Again, his knowledge is highly sought after by the Afghan traders,' muttered Bilwa under his breath.

But the Sthavira's practised chant of Aryabhatta's eulogy was in full spate, and he ignored Bilwa.

'World-renowned is he for his discovery of the diurnal revolution of the earth on its own axis. Another important conclusion was the apparent motion of the sun and the moon. The starry vault is fixed! It is the earth which, moving on its own axis, seems to cause the rising and the setting of the planets and the stars. He also gave the most accurate account of cosmic time, the kalpas. In my time I have taught many niggardly idiots how each kalpa was worth one day in the life of Brahma, the God of Creation. In other words, the four ages of the mahayuga must be repeated a thousand times to make a "day of Brahma", a unit of time that is the equivalent of 4.32 billion human years, doubling which one gets 8.64 billion years for a Brahma day and night. The cyclical nature of this analysis proves a universe that is expanding to be followed by contraction. An ever-expanding cosmos without any end.'

The flourish of his lecture stopped our wandering minds and

we quietly followed his dried frame. The clattering echoes of our new sandals resounded in the corridors, echoing the contemplation of lives well spent. The mysterious imagery of the iconic Wisdom goddesses we crossed in each department was not lost to us. The Bird-Beaked One, the Common One, the Smoky One, the Virgin, all seemed incongruous in the portals of high science. But it did not pique our curiosity.

'In the observatories above,' the Sthavira's misshapen finger went up again, this time to point at a tower visible across the courtyard high above us, looking quite unreachable, except to the finest minds, 'you will find the astrolabe, an instrument devised to measure the positions of heavenly bodies, to determine the angle of altitude of the eclipsed body and, possibly, the time of the phase of the eclipses.'

Then he pointed below to a sandstone panel stretching across the entire entrance of the Astronomy College. It depicted Surya, the Sun God hurtling across the skies on his chariot, pulled by seven horses reined by seven snakes. This time I listened carefully to the scintillating concepts of Surya Siddhanta. How light breaks into seven different colours of the prism, and how the nature of a ray of light is curved like the snakes wound around the horses.

'In these rooms here,' the master continued his tour, stopping by a row of lecture rooms that lined a spacious inner courtyard with an old shady Adumbra tree in the middle, 'are taught Vaisheshika atomic theories.'

He momentarily turned his milky rheumatoid eyes towards me but I could not be sure he had seen me. Without speaking he turned and walked up to a handsome stupa at the entrance with a small altar for ritual offerings. Some students had placed fruits and a butter lamp to propitiate the Wisdom goddesses and seek their blessings. But I was more drawn to an imposing yet benevolent figure in the corner of the room, his hand raised in granting the boon of fearlessness, the Abhay Mudra.

'This is Kannada,' our Old One said by way of introduction, 'a great master of masters. How can reality be predicated on what is subject to change and reassumes no more of its original character?' he continued in the same vein, till I realised he was asking us the question. It was rhetorical, but I knew the answer.

'Earth is fabricated into a jar; the jar is divided into two halves; the halves are broken to pieces, the pieces become dust; the dust becomes atoms and so forth,' I said.

For the first time since the tour, the Sthavira fell silent.

'So Siddhartha,' he said, his voice strangely deep. 'What do you choose? Are you attracted to Cosmology? Does it interest you?'

My hesitation, like youth, was too brief.

'Sir, they say Cosmology requires too many hard hours of deep meditation. I still choose, instead, the logician's doctrine of dependent origination.'

The Sthavira paused for a long thoughtful moment before asking the others. If the Sthavira was disappointed with my choice, he did not let it show.

'Cosmology,' said Tarpa.

'Cosmology,' said Asita.

'And you,' the Sthavira turned to Bilwa with a sudden penetrating stare. 'Choose Sabda Vidya.'

'How do you know?' Bilwa blurted, and in immediate regret, pursed his lips at his impudent response.

'That,' the Sthavira gave a short raucous laugh, 'is a question all masters are used to. And one you will be asking them all the time.'

Four years have gone by since the day of my admission, and even today, I am not quite inured to Nalanda's grandeur. The magnificent resplendence of the gold statue of the Lord Buddha conspicuously placed at the centre of Nalanda has never ceased to be a source of wonder. Sometimes when I emerge from my fourth stage room and behold the clouds, I still feel as though I have been transported to a celestial abode of learning. And when, on pleasant days, students rush out to play water games in the bathing kunds, or gambol in community competitions in their eternally monochromatic robes, orange or maroon or white, I think of Nalanda as a valley bursting with blooms.

My closest friend and confidant is Rahula the Artisan. His own features are as chiselled and beautiful as his artistic creations. He lives in the cell next to mine and was the first monastery inmate I met. Initially, he took great pleasure in ridiculing my inability to wash clothes, cook or even pour drinking water for myself; I used to have palace slaves to do these things for me. But gradually, he started helping me and we became friends. He taught me how to fold my robes and cook the morning gruel in the monastery kitchen.

He is the son of a Brahmin priest who teaches Yogashastras in the neighbouring University of Vikramshila. He is of keen eye and sharp intellect and always ready with an observant remark. Rahula is an artisanry apprentice and I deeply respect him for this.

Artisans are in great demand and he never forgets to remind me how rich and illustrious his future will be. Nalanda is not only famous for craftsmanship and metallurgy, but also sixty-four kinds of arts. He has already specialised in stone, metal and bronze. He never tires of telling me how stupid I was for renouncing my kingship because, as Rahula says, I would still have to make a living by teaching Dharma.

Artisans have immense opportunity and benefit greatly from royal patrons, temples and wealthy people. The acquisition of a sculpture is mandatory even for the mildly wealthy, and artists are handsomely paid. My discipline, on the other hand, is so austere and rigorous that it can only end in penury. But I never take his jesting seriously.

My monastery named me Siddhartha the Doubter. Considering that doubt is an authentic practice in the Logic discipline, I was pleased with this name. At least it was not Siddhartha the Mongoose, or Siddhartha the Smelly.

There are a hundred lectures in Nalanda every day, on as many different subjects, with participants from as many different lands. I had come across some aliens in my father's kingdom. This is because Vaishali, my homeland, has always had close contact with travellers from the deep West. The aliens, or yavanas as we call them, came with the great King Sikander, or Alexander. They settled in Vaishali and married into our Lichchavi clans. I was told that the Lichchavi republic, a mode of government I had earlier thought unique to us, was also practised in the lands of the yavanas.

I was used to yavanas, but never had I seen so many as in Nalanda. Their skin tone varied from the very dark to the very fair and many shades in between. Some even had fair eyes and fair hair. Their eyes varied from slanting upwards to downwards to the big and the narrow. Their hair could be straight as a cascade of water, or wound in tight curls. I looked at them and marvelled at nature's creation. And all of these people from so many different lands had converged here to receive the wisdom of Nalanda, like great rivers reaching out to the sea.

In four years I mastered twenty collections of sutras and shastras. It was of course extraordinary for my age, but not once did I let myself get into the quagmire of competition because I realised that if I did, I would be a dwarf among the giant intellectuals surrounding me.

All I knew was that my memory and intelligence had stood me in good stead, allowing me to make consistent progress in my studies in Grammar and Logic.

Eventually, I would learn how young and immature I am. I would also learn that though Nalanda was home to nine million manuscripts... *its real knowledge was the teaching of deep ignorance.*

On that fateful and benign Nalanda afternoon, I looked at my life and was content. I was my master's favourite student and had been allotted a master's service of high esteem. Master's service was a mandatory activity for all students, even ordained monks, whereby they spent one-tenth of each day in the service allotted to them. I was not condemned to the kitchens, or the gardens, but had the honour of assisting in the prestigious Seals Department.

I was content to enjoy the respect of my peers and the fondness of the elders. I was living out my life in the abode of my dreams. The great halls, the pulpits, the intricate designs of the interior chambers, the revered artistry evoked in me a sentiment that my father's palace had never inspired. I had come to realise with much relief that my mother's fears were nothing more than a horror tale wet nurses narrate during bedtime. All I saw around me were examples of academic excellence, nothing else. Every day, I exulted over the precision of the varying logical schools and the rigours our masters put us through. Every day, in the debating pits, I discovered new revelations and scaled new heights of intellectual perfection. Indeed, life was good.

Then, why was it that as I stood on the balcony and looked about at the strange afternoon light so typical of Nalanda, an unease like I had not experienced in four years, pervaded through me? Many said that the ethereal light found in Nalanda, described in the scriptures as prevailing only in extra-terrestrial worlds, was because of Nalanda's perfect alignment between the sun and the moon. It rendered a mystical glow on Nalanda—from the lakes and pavilions to the amra orchards and the monasteries.

Why was it that the same light seemed to bear down on me and fill me with sudden foreboding?

I found my mind reverting repeatedly to a disturbing incident that had occurred earlier that morning.

I had set out, as usual, to the neighbouring village, with my begging bowl and staff. Three times a week, the students, and sometimes even masters, set out mid-morning, according to the age-old bhikshu tradition started by Lord Buddha, to beg for food. It was not as if the Sangha needed to. The revenue of three hundred villages was more than enough for the upkeep of Nalanda's monasteries. There was sometimes, I think, too much food in Nalanda. There was so much wastage in the common dining halls. At times, the granaries rotted with overflowing grain. My friends say that the coffers of Nalanda were full of precious gems and priceless relics. Some of the panditas and grandmasters ate the Mahashali rice that only kings and emperors could afford. On numerous occasions, we had feasts in the dining halls that I greatly enjoyed but was slightly embarrassed by because of the richness of the meats and the grains. Even the important laity in the neighbouring villages took but an excuse to throw a big feast on our behalf, and sometimes the grandeur of its scale was shocking.

Begging thrice a week was done more out of respect for Lord Buddha's tradition than the mandatory need to fill our overfed bellies. But I enjoyed my little sojourns into the villages. It was a good distraction and gave me an opportunity to sort out my thoughts and also meet new people.

So when the karmadana official in charge of the alms walk looked at his roster and announced my name during the morning assembly, I was pleased.

Only a few days had passed since the full moon of Shravana and the weather was good. There were large throngs at all the entrance gates because of the ekadasi festival, so I avoided them. I left instead through the little used Cowherd Gate just beyond the slave quarters.

I always wondered why this area saw such little traffic. Maybe because the ugliness of its surroundings went against Nalanda's preoccupation with beauty.

Mentally, I started creating a logical treatise on how ugliness is equivalent to falsehood. Wrapped up in the elegance of my theories, on that bright balmy day, I unconsciously ventured too far out and beyond a village west of Nalanda towards a tall bluff hill called the Cockfoot Mountain. As I walked down a goat-track of a hillock, I noticed a modest but substantially large house nestled below, secluded from the rest of the neighbourhood. I tried to remember whether this area fell on the list of approved households for begging. There were certain households that were not approved for begging; I could not, however, recall whether this was one of them and decided to take my chance. I never did understand why there was a list of unapproved households. Maybe the university administration did not want unsuspecting bhikshus to be subjected to political antagonism in certain Brahminised households. There were so many strange Nalanda regulations that were completely illogical, but like the rest of my Nalanda brothers, I never questioned them.

I had felt good and pious that day, walking down that hillock, imagining that I was walking in the footsteps of Gautama Buddha, and since that was too presumptuous, in the footsteps of one of his more enlightened bhikshus. I did not know that a rude shock awaited me.

I reached the empty courtyard and stood at the prescribed distance from the entrance. According to calculations of the Vinaya, our textual codifications of monastic discipline, six feet was a respectable distance. I adjusted my upper robes to check that my chest and shoulders were properly covered. And then I waited for the scheduled period of time with my eyes downcast. Unlike most Brahminical sects who beg for alms with specified words, we are meant to beg in silence.

Since nobody came to the door and my prescribed time was lapsing, I coughed. Presently, a girl-woman appeared. I say she was a girl-woman because she was neither a girl nor a fully grown woman. To my consternation, she was luminously beauteous and when her lips brought up a sudden image of the red kanaka flower, I was thrown into a terrible confusion. My first instinct was to leave, but nervousness kept me rooted to the spot.

'Wait,' she said; it was almost like a command.

She returned shortly with the ideal food of bhikshus. Sugar, honey, milk and clarified butter. She clearly displayed knowledge of religious matters. Norm demanded that the bhikshu lift the fold of his robe to disclose the begging bowl, take the bowl in both his hands and receive the food in it without looking at the face of the giver if it is a woman. For some reason, I fumbled with my robe. Perhaps it was her proximity and the heady scent emanating from her body, perhaps I was being clumsy because I was trying so hard to avoid her gaze.

Whatever the reason, she gave a taunting laugh and reached her hand out to help me with my robe.

I immediately raised my hands in forbiddance and said, very sternly, 'Stand back, woman.'

The mockery in her laugh had stung me to the quick. My own ineptitude angered me. But most importantly, by attempting to touch a bhikshu, she had broken the bounds of propriety. 'Keep your distance,' I said in a more conciliatory tone.

Brazen that she was, my warning made her desist but did not affront her. She looked closely at my averted face and asked as if she were interviewing me, 'What is your name?'

'A bhikshu need not tell you his name.'

'Yes, but what is your name?' she repeated in a stubborn manner.

After a moment's hesitation, I told her.

'How old are you?' she demanded.

'How old are you?' I snapped back, imitating her.

'Three hundred years,' she replied, her eyes suddenly very dark and fathomless, like the new moon. I steeled myself against an involuntary fear creeping through my bones, for I suddenly remembered nighttime stories of Dayani witches. I made light of her statement, dismissing it with a condescending smirk, 'Then the Abbot and you must be colleagues.'

'Maybe we are,' she said, her voice slow and sinuous, like a tongue creeping down my ear. She was so close I could feel her breath. I shuddered.

'Whose student are you?' she asked in the same tone.

This time, I involuntarily returned her impertinent gaze. 'The great Sri Aryadatta.'

My words did not have the desired effect on her. She smiled, 'I need keep no distance from a student of Aryadatta.'

And then, to my shock, she walked up to me, wrapped her leg around my hips and planted a kiss deep inside my mouth. And then she calmly went back inside the house.

Norm demands that after receiving alms, the bhikshu should cover the bowl and walk back slowly and carefully. But I, with an empty bowl and a burning sensation in my innards, my throat, every fibre of my being, did nothing of the sort. I fled up the hillock as fast as my feet could carry me.

3. *The Heretic's Challenge*

'I *need keep no distance from a student of Aryadatta.*' For many days her mocking words echoed in my head like an incantation.

However desperately I wished to take this matter to my master, I couldn't do it. It would have been improper, throwing doubt over the master-disciple relationship. I feared that a candid discussion of the topic might demean me, or worse, him, and I did not want this to happen over a promiscuous and silly village girl.

I thought of discussing it with my friends, but they would have reduced my worries to ribald tomfoolery or turned to idle university gossip. So I decided to tell only Rahula. As I recounted the incident, I unfortunately confessed to him the image of the red kanaka flower evoked by the village girl's lips and he did not let me go beyond that point.

'Red kanaka flower, eh,' he started to jibe. We were sitting on a garden wall that connected up to the ornate stone arches of the university gate. As I looked at the vast expanse of well-maintained bowers and flowerbeds, ponds and swans, I remembered the time that I had seen only a patch of it from across the university admission gate.

'Really, Rahula, you are as bad as the rest,' I complained.

Uncustomary raised voices reached us from the admission gate. Today seemed like a busy day for the Candidate Admission Department.

'No, Siddhartha. It is much better for us to release our sexual tension in verbal frivolity than behave like many others who become so desperate that they commit forbidden acts on each other.'

'So you believe that scurrilous gossip passing around from monastery to monastery?'

'Don't be such a shrinking lily, Siddhartha. Everyone knows it's true.'

'Well, if it is true, it is disgusting. It is a reflection of the corruption of our times. I am sure this never happened in the days of the Buddha.'

'If Buddha's time had been so perfect, he would not have needed to take birth to redeem us.'

Rahula's argument annoyed me and I turned on him. 'I do not think the world is as black as you think, Rahula. I do not know what sexual tension you speak of. For I have not felt any. But I can see all the manifest symptoms in you, brother.'

'You lie, Siddhartha,' his candour was taking severe advantage of my patience. 'If not to me, then definitely to yourself. If you did not feel it, you would not be human. And if others did not feel it, the Order would not need to design so many lengthy vows of celibacy.'

I turned to him to let loose a fitting reply. We found ourselves standing in the combative debating posture. We were about to launch into a wordy duel when the raised voices at the main entrance turned to pandemonium. Gate sentinel ran helter skelter in the gardens and some people rushed towards the admission gate. From their hair ornaments and elaborate robe embroideries they looked like karmadana notaries from the high offices. Monks were suddenly everywhere. The laity of the university too was moving in great agitation from one whispering monastic group to the other.

'What happened?' Rahula shouted a question to a lay student running frantically to the gate. He was a boy from one of the eastern villages. We called him Broken One. Abandoned as an infant at the admission gate, the university had adopted him. Though slow in speech and some mental faculties, he had an astonishing aptitude for Mathematics.

'There's a letter posted at the gate. It's the end of Nalanda, Sri Rahula, the very end,' he said, weeping and stammering at the same time.

'Hush, boy,' Rahula admonished. 'You could never put that tongue of yours to any good use.'

But that didn't stop him or me from jumping off the wall and joining the crowd running towards the gate. Outside, in the Nalanda square, we saw a jostling mob kept at bay by a tight cordon of stick-wielding sentinels. Startled, we stopped in our tracks and looked around for the incriminating document. And sure enough, there it was. Next to the giant candidate bell that the aspirants tolled. On a pillar, pasted over encrypted royal inscriptions, we glimpsed a parchment. And I came face to face with the darkest of my nightmares.

'The monks of Nalanda,' the letter said in Pali, in neat legible writing, *'practise the doctrine of heresy. Their sky flower doctrine is the same as the deplorable Kapalikas. Our refutation thesis is here for you to see. We come in forty days. If the heretics of Nalanda cannot defeat us in debate, they must die.'*

And pasted on the front gate, all over the names of the eighty-four mahasiddhas, like dirty smears on the face of Nalanda, were pages of their thesis. An indignant rumble coursed through the monks as they scattered and huddled around each page of the thesis.

'Curse Nalanda!' A screech rose from the throng and a few voices added in chorus. The throng became louder as they were beaten back by the sentinels.

'Blood suckers of the poor!'

'Sodomisers!'

'Reprobates!'

A few stones were thrown. They landed innocuously a distance away from us, preoccupied as we were by the thesis.

The sky flower theory of Mahayana, the first parchment read, *self arrogated as the Greater Vehicle, is opposed to Hinayana, which is derogated as the Smaller Vehicle. For many centuries, it is Hinayana that has adhered closely to Buddha's teaching whilst Mahayana has not. Its latest claim, that all phenomenon is empty and imaginary like the sky flower, was never taught by the Buddha. The abominable Kapalikas, who haunt cremation grounds drinking blood from skull caps and smearing their bodies with the ashes of burnt corpses, also preach the exact same theory. Therefore, the priests of Mahayana are no different from the Kapalikas.*

This was their first premise.

While most of us crowded around the pages of the rival thesis like flies around putrid food, Asita stepped away to confront the hostility rising around us by the swelling mob of disgruntled bystanders.

'Hah!' Asita said. He was now called Asita the Great by the entire monastery. He brandished his fist at the crowd, veering dangerously close to them, from behind the protective cordon of sentinels. His wiry physique was well-muscled and oiled in the wrestling pits and, for a moment, the throng was taken aback by his booming voice.

'These are Brahmins!' He roared, pointing at the parchment. 'This isn't the first puny dog that has barked at Nalanda's glory. Hiuen Tsang, the Great Master of Law, had defeated a similar lunatic Brahmin in a most erudite debate.' Asita, though still a monk, was already being championed as the next mahasiddha. For some reason, I was skeptical of his spiritual promise. Maybe as a Bengal prince, from a background similar to mine, I could see through the shine of his exterior. He did not inspire in me the admiration and envy he did in Rahula.

'I remember,' Tarpa, now called Tarpa the Gentle, joined the confrontation of the malevolent at the Nalanda square. Rotund, jolly and always smiling, he and Asita had become close friends. Maybe because they attended the same lectures, they were never seen apart. 'And the ignominious Brahmin did not cut off his own head as he had promised to do if he was defeated. He chose shame instead.'

The crowd slowly dispersed in the face of the violent beating of sticks. A few stragglers stood their ground staring and hissing at us, weathering the blows. Dry dust billowed around them, changing the light, filling me with dread. Slowly, as we repeatedly read page after page of the voluminous thesis, even the stragglers left.

'Look,' I said, still reading a page pasted at the corner of the Admission Temple wall.

'They keep repeating their premises that Buddha never sanctioned the Mahayana teachings.'

'Hinayanists,' said Bhim the Burly, the youngest, most intelligent and handsomest of all of us. A blue-eyed, straw-haired yavana, we had named him after the mighty Pandava brother in our famous epic Mahabharata. 'It's a political conspiracy hatched by Hinayanist kings.'

He sat down at the foot of the admission gate with the Broken One and some other monks from the Vaibhashika Monastery. They looked like disheartened malcontents from the Rejects' Colony.

'Till the day I die,' Bhim said, his chin sinking into his chest, 'I will not understand why our great religion was divided into Mahayana and Hinayana.'

'And why Dharma brothers must oppose Dharma brothers,' came a voice from behind him. 'And I,' the Broken One said, a tear rolling down his cheek, 'will never understand this devastating difference between Mahayana and Hinayana.'

Rahula walked up to the Broken One and put his arms around his shoulders. 'Hinayana is the root and Mahayana the fruit of the

Buddha's tree. They are only divided by the passage and effects of time. That is the difference.' A pause ensued and the only sound we heard for a while was the Broken One sniffing and crows cawing on the Nalanda ramparts.

'But Nalanda shall never be conquered,' Bhim the Burly finally said. 'Nalanda has existed for centuries, it was conceived in the golden womb of the cosmos, survived the corruption of time and the collective pettiness of many kings. Nalanda is blessed by all the Buddhas of all the realms.'

This was true, quite literally. It had been rumoured that in certain pavilions, bodhisattvas from other dimensions emanated from the fourteen elements in a temporary body and walked the monasteries, blessing the chosen ones. Sometimes openly, sometimes secretly. I had never been witness to this and never believed in the rumours. Maybe because, unlike the eye witnesses, I was not a chosen one, I liked to say. This was just one example of the many cryptic dimensions ascribed to Nalanda. In the debating pits I denied them all, adhering to my foundational belief in objective reality. This put me in the precarious position of the vilified Hinayanist minority, but try as I might, I could not accept the magical realism of Mahayana doctrines. Even though it was the prevailing trend, I found it logically untenable. While many masters and monks alike claimed bodhisattva sightings, I rejected the science of dimensional overlap.

'We shall see who these enemies of Nalanda are,' came a voice from behind me, and a heavy hand fell on my shoulder, in reassurance. I winced under its weight. I did not need to turn around to recognise Vallabha the Long Nose.

A yavana like Bhim the Burly, he too belonged to the Sarvastivadin Monastery. He stood so close to me I could see inside his flaring nostrils. 'Let them come. We shall see.' He talked as if he would meet them on the battlefield rather than with a verbal duel.

Now, as these words emanate from me, with full knowledge of how Nalanda was destroyed, my heart wrings at his words.

But I was silent during the furious confabulations that ensued, wondering how our masters would react to this challenge. The word Kapalika kept ringing in my head, like a warning bell, evoking after a long time the image of my mother's sad eyes. She had accused Nalanda of harbouring the charnel ground ascetics who wore human bones around their neck and ate faeces. And also, some said, the flesh of newborns. At that time I had defended their presence in Nalanda because I had been led to believe that they did exist in the university. To my relief, though, I had found it to be every inch the rigorous institution that I had imagined it to be. There were no Kapalikas here. Their presence would have shocked and dismayed Nalanda's inhabitants.

Yet, the repeated reference to this scandalous cannibalistic sect disturbed me. I found this recurring motif to be uncanny and not coincidental. But I could not explain why.

Presently, the doorkeeper, Sakya, the Monk Who Never Sleeps, appeared, wearing his permanently impassive face. He blew the doorkeeper's horn to get our attention.

'The panditas and acharyas have asked the laity, monks and students alike to go inside and maintain the decorum of the university. Seven lectures are going on, and one conference. You should not be indulging in idle chatter here.'

Rahula and I were the last ones to leave. Even though the sun burned brightly over us, a pall of gloom seemed to hang over the deserted Nalanda square. Only a lone sentinel stood guard. That and the watchful goddesses at the Admission Temple.

4. *Dragon Body*

All the ten thousand students in Nalanda, I can safely assert, were exceedingly conscious of their university's reputation of intellectual seriousness. Like one organism harbouring one intention, the entire chattering body of monks adjourned to the great halls. I too, somewhat absent-mindedly, sought out the company of my master and joined him in conference on a topic that had little hold on my interest. I had been ignorant of his interest in it too, and struggled to understand the lecture, so alien to the schools of logic that I had so far been accustomed to.

The high timbre of a Chinese accent carried across the pillars and ornamental balustrades, its tinkling cadence at contrast with the forbidding severity of the gathering.

On entering, I saw grandmaster Siroha sitting with his followers next to my master. He was a small lean man with an immense beard. Always visible in small and large assemblies, Siroha was considered one of the most influential panditas of Nalanda. He had many names, including 'Great Debater' and 'Siroha the Unconquerable'. He had never lost a debate, a feat even my master could not boast of. His followers said the God Maheshwara Himself entered his body to help him speak. Magical parrots whispered in his ears. Goddess Saraswati wrote on the sky for him. His predilections were Brahminical, something reviled and ridiculed by the staunch Buddhists in the university.

The conference was well attended with many masters of repute present with their disciples. There was a generous sprinkling of silken white, pleated grandmaster robes throughout the hall. I wondered at the importance of the occasion.

We the students either sat on hemp mats or stood around our masters, fanning them and shielding them from the prying eyes of the sweating and shouldering general public. We were separated from the laity and the general public by a ceremonial fence that circled the inner Great Hall. A lattice of bright sunlight from the stone meshes of the ceiling domes fell on all of us, like equality over hierarchies.

Through the mesh of the ceremonial fence, the outside public was allowed to press its ears and listen. This was a chance for them to catch snatches of the great debates taking place in the illustrious halls, like managing a drop of elixir from the gods. Today, even the outer halls were packed with hot, heavily breathing faces. They held the same collective expression of disbelief I saw reflected in all faces around me inside the Great Hall.

Something was definitely different about today's conference. And upon moving closer to where the Chinese scholar sat, I realised what it was. Like some incredible, unfathomable miraculous freak of nature, the Chinese scholar was, indeed, a woman! And she had everyone in thrall.

My jaw slackened as I stared at her. Nalanda had witnessed lectures by many strange masters. There were legends of two-headed panditas and an acharya with a monkey face and tail like Hanuman, but I had never ever heard of a female master!

The immobility of the air seemed to have permeated the outer halls, making not a single body twitch. The wind stayed, not one leaf in the trees beyond moved, as if they were the Bodhi tree itself, and every piece of stone in the hall was listening to words that were not words but keys unlocking the secrets of the universe.

As for me, I did not know whether it was her womanhood or the words she spoke that were having a mesmeric effect on me. In all ways she looked like any other shaven-headed Chinese monk. Only her face was soft and her skin supple. Never before had I listened to a woman imparting knowledge, and that too with so much confidence.

She spoke in Sanskrit, with the lucidity only Sanskrit can render, her enigmatic face not betraying the slightest passion.

'Fellow scholars, my studies over many years show that the Great Goddess power inside the human body, and its subsequent awakening, was not known only to those of this land of Jambudvipa. Here some call her Candali, and some call her Kundalini.

'I have learnt from other scholars, during the course of my travels, that her secrets have been known and practised in many different countries. In my land, the power is known as *chi* and in neighbouring lands, it is known as *qui.* In a dark continent many leagues west of this land, and across seven oceans, this power is also known, and the natives call it the *feathered serpent.* In many countries, it is simply known as the dragon, and in some as the thunderbolt.'

My mind strayed. I looked about me. A thick stucco depicting the Buddha's life separated the monks from the laity, and a further ceremonial fence separated the laity from the general public outside, yet all classes and ranks of men were staring at the woman with one singular malevolent eye. I also noticed that sitting below her teaching platform and surrounding her in a protective circle were the monks from the Vaibhashika Monastery. They seemed to be there to protect her. *Why are the masters allowing such blasphemy,* I wondered with a sharp pang of alarm. But her voice dragged me back to her words.

'However, only in *this* land,' she said, 'the Buddha's birthplace, has this power been harnessed to its maximum capacity and created the greatest siddhas known to mankind. O learned men and astute students of this august assembly, it is my contention *that no number of noble virtues and purity of heart and mind can make one a Buddha*. A Buddha is one who has transcended the limitations not only of body, mind and intellect but also the limitations of virtue and goodness itself. A Buddha has the capacity to become one and also to become many. He or She contains the knowledge of all the three worlds within Him or Her. He or She is capable of miraculous acts outside the realms of possibility for an ordinary mortal. He or She has conquered death. He or She enjoys powers that all categories of beings like the gods, devas and bhutas envy.

'All this cannot be achieved merely by understanding the scriptures and committing virtuous acts and harbouring pious thoughts. Buddhahood can only be attained, without any exception, through the process of metamorphosis. The analogy is not metaphorical. It is physical. The act of a human metamorphosing into a Siddha is a biological one, a physiological one, much like a caterpillar into a butterfly.'

'Blasphemy!' Rang out a voice near the barricades, the face unseen, lost in a sea of angry expressions. 'She ridicules the Buddha's Virtues.' In no time my beloved Nalanda had turned from a peaceful university into a bristling hornet's nest.

My heart contracted in fear for her. If I had been her, my voice would have quivered. But it seemed she had not heard.

'A woman cannot achieve enlightenment!' rang out another voice in unprecedented fury.

'Does the Kundalini even exist in women?' another question arose from the faceless crowds.

'No, it doesn't exist in women.' This was the only question I remember her replying to, calmly and without a trace of rancour. 'It is the woman! Every particle of the female body is a manifestation of the Great Goddess.' This comment, heretical in all dimensions, did not go down well with the inflamed crowd.

'To achieve enlightenment, a woman needs to be born again in a man's body,' continued the symphony of rage. 'The Buddha said so!'

Cries of 'Witches have infiltrated Nalanda!' and 'Hang her!' rang out as many accents united by a similar sentiment exploded across the gathering.

Still she continued, without a tremor.

'This physiological metamorphosis takes place only when the Great Goddess—in the form of subtle energy unseen by the human eye and unfelt by the human senses and coiled like a serpent three and a half times in every living man's spine—awakens. I repeat and cannot stress the fact enough that She, the Great Goddess, lies dormant in *every* living breathing man. When She is awakened, the mahasiddha's Dragon Body takes birth.'

She is every woman, but only exists unseen in a man. I couldn't help mutter under my breath.

A low rumble rose in the outer halls, like cavalry at a distance, full of impending danger, as if it would burst upon us any moment. Amongst the woman's protective cordon, eyes followed the rumble, but not a muscle moved in the faces of the ones guarding her.

Seemingly oblivious of her surroundings, the woman continued.

'When the Great Goddess awakens, she makes a difficult and arduous journey up the spine till she reaches the crown of the head, where she merges with the Absolute. Thus she awakens the man to Buddhahood. During her journey, she pierces the five subtle, invisible energy wheels aligned in a central channel inside the spine. These wheels are situated at the navel, the heart, the throat, between the eyebrows and the crown of the head. As she makes her journey upwards from the navel, she purifies the physical body of psychic impediments that the man has collected over thousands of lifetimes. With each cleansing, the man experiences new powers till the culmination in the Absolute. Let it be known, my Learned Gathering, that though the Great Mother's path spans but four feet, it takes a millennia of perseverance to traverse it.

And when it is traversed, an etheric Dragon Body is created. A body capable of flight, magic, levitation and many other siddhis or powers.'

The rumble was rising and rising outside the Inner Hall, like a wave preparing to hit the shore. From the corner of my eye I saw that the Abbot had quietly appeared. His presence certified the seriousness of the conference. He stood partially in the shadow of the stone panel depicting the Buddha's life. She noticed his presence and they exchanged a small smile. From his giant magnetic frame his intense eyes pierced the gathering. Across the sea of celibate monks, he then caught my master's eye. They both shook their heads in regret. It looked to me that I was the only one who saw the glances exchanged.

'Do not think,' the scholar's soft voice wafted to all present, 'that your mind resides in your skull, and can be controlled by reining in your thoughts. Your mind resides in the rhythmic movements of your lungs and the beating of your breath. That is why when you refer to yourself, you involuntarily point at your heart and not your head. The mind is controlled not by your thoughts but by your breath. Because it is the energy residing in the breath that rustles up thoughts in the subtle energy petals near the heart. You would have noticed, my esteemed Nalanda Brothers, that when the breath is slow, the mind is calm. And when the space in between the breaths is extended with practice, the Great Mother enters the central spinal channel we call the 'sahaja' and starts the journey upwards. This is the only way to enlightenment.

'Two channels run alongside the sahaja. The 'prajna' or 'ida' channel on the left is governed by the biorhythms of the sun. The 'pingala' or 'upaya' channel on the right is governed by the biorhythms of the moon. These are male and female energies also called yin and yang in my country. They are two equal polarities of the union causing nirvana. During 'brahmamuhurta,' or the time of early dawn when the sun conjoins with the moon in the outer world, in the inner world, the male and female energies concentrate near the opening of the sahaja at the base of the spine. At this important junction, when union between male and female is achieved, higher states of consciousness become accessible.'

Could she be talking about sex? I looked in shock about me. Faces were darkening in anger all around. Many of the interrupting questions were increasing in vigour, but her serene voice overrode them all, like the even eye of a cyclone.

In four years I had heard many esoteric doctrines expounded from the pulpits of Nalanda, and I had learnt to accept them with monastic equipoise. One had to. It was a minor hazard of being born in my land. Esoterism was in the air. God was in the air, even though the Buddha had admonished us to stay away from God. And there were so many mystical doctrines that it was impossible to keep count of them. One had to eat it with one's food, cross it in the street, drink it in the taverns, and take it to bed. I have often heard it said that one needed to accumulate many lifetimes of merit to be born in my land because my land is the land of spiritual endeavour.

Godhood not only came easy here, it was free.

But I was a modern logician. My sole objective was academic. I wanted to write a more sophisticated thesis on the Theory of Dependent Origination, propounded by the great masters Dinnaga and Dharmakirti. And even though I knew that the prevailing doctrine in Nalanda was that of polytheistic Mahayana Buddhism, and I had by now become quite inured to its polymorphic images of divinities overpopulating the university, and all the accompanying rituals and rites that the university performed, so antipodal to the Buddha's initial teachings, now degraded as Hinayana teachings, the passion lurking in the Chinese scholar's voice annoyed me.

Though I confess that all the sutras and shastras that I had learnt and intellectually debated smacked of the same uncerebral passion and professed the same annoying universality of their one and only Absolute Truth, this scholar's claim that this was the only way to Buddhahood angered me greatly. Her making light of the Virtues also seemed to me a direct insult of the Buddha's Eight-Fold Path, but I held my tongue because my objection was clearly Hinayanist, and it was becoming apparent that they were not only unacknowledged outsiders, but maybe even enemies of this hallowed institution. Moreover, I had only a layman's passing acquaintance with her subject, knowing it vaguely (and wrongly as it now seemed) as some form of the New Science I could never specify, primarily because of a complete lack of interest.

I admit I also suffered from a certain disdain against the New Science as an anti-intellectual and anti-scriptural practice. The New Science was cryptic and spoken about in hushed whispers in secret conclaves as Tantra. Its practices were supposedly unconventional and heretical. Rahula said it imploded the constructs and boundaries of the known human mind and intellect. To me its mention always brought up the image of the Kapalikas and their execrable practices that no sane person, let alone a person of intellect, would give a second thought to. Surely the grandmasters, 'arhats' as we also called them, must know the similarities between the New Science and the Kapalikas. Could they not see that both were as abhorrent as their perverse existence merited?

A fresh recollection of the letter posted impertinently on the Admission Temple gate raised another bout of anxiety in my heart and I could not prevent myself from whispering fiercely into my master's ear: 'What she speaks of is New Science! Just like the Kapalika heresy!'

My master, his prodigious beard resting peacefully on his chest, was looking on at the Chinese scholar with a whimsical half-smile on his face. I could do nothing but look on in utter trepidation.

Directly opposite us, beside Siroha, sat Master Dharmapada with his school of followers. Dharmapada the Logician, many in the university believed, would have acquired a status equal to my master had he risen above his jealousy. He was more famous in the university as my master's rival, than for his logical treatise.

My master oft repeated that contrary to popular belief, if a seeker could save himself from the two traps of envy and pride, namely debating and teaching, he would reach the highest state.

Unfortunately, Dharmapada expended more energy striking down my master in fruitless debates and stealing his followers than focussing on his studies. What was interesting was the expression on Dharmapada's face today. He sat on his cushions just a few feet ahead. His eyes danced over his hooked nose and his fingers tapped his bony knee. His presence in the lecture halls was always accompanied by much sound and fury, and his ferocious and passionate interjections usually carried out into the gardens. And as usual, he did not augur well.

'Quiet!' He raised a bejewelled hand to quieten the audience. My heart sank. I knew that tone. It was primed for a verbal bloodbath.

'My Esteemed Colleague,' Dharmapada said, turning to the Chinese scholar, 'I don't know what else to call you,' and a titter passed through the front rows.

He raised his lanky body from the cushion facing the raised dais where the woman sat. Cushions were reserved only for the masters, the number of cushions allotted for each master signifying the level of his competence, reputation and intellect. It was a matter of pride to me that my master, a certified arhat, grandmaster of high standing, was allowed the honorific title 'The Great Aryadatta,' and his cushions were two more than Dharmapada's and equalled those of the Abbot's. Everyone knew that the relationship between the Abbot and my master was special. In senior assemblies, it was noticeable to all how they communicated telepathically through a nod and a gesture, and finished each other's sentences.

'The scriptures,' Dharmapada said with stentorian authority, 'say that there are a thousand and eight ways to attain siddhahood. Some scriptures have, and very liberally so, enumerated that an intense hatred towards God is *also* a way to reach God. You describe what aboriginal moolanivasis and heretics here call Kundalini Yoga. It is *one* way. But according to the logical laws of universal quantification, one cannot become many. Therefore, one is not many. Therefore, Kundalini Yoga is one but not only. Therefore, the fundamental premise on which Kundalini Yoga rests is wrong. Therefore, the whole doctrine is wrong. Therefore, there is no Kundalini. Therefore, the Dragon Body does not exist.'

'So be it. So be it.'

'Hear, hear.' He had used the trite laws of logical syllogism. I exchanged glances with my master and we both smiled in condescension. But Dharmapada's sycophants flapped about like one headless organism.

'Encore!' They repeated. Many such voices emerged from the galleries and balconies, from the laity and students. Also, more ferocious contradictions came towards the Chinese scholar from the outside halls. However prejudiced I was against the woman and her theories, the learned audience seemed to me like dogs nipping at a bhikshu's heels.

'Order and decorum!' My master was now standing on the cushions, cutting a splendid figure, his voice booming across the hall in magnificent confidence and authority. My master, he stood like a lion among men.

But Dharmapada was not to be silenced.

'It is not one colour but seven that make the rainbow,' he shouted, trying to take full control of the debate.

'But, my Respected Colleague,' the Chinese scholar calmly intoned, 'that is precisely so. You do not break my argument but make it. The silliest novice knows that the seven colours he draws on his pennant, when moved in high speeds, becomes one colour, white. Thus, it is also so with what you dismiss as Kundalini. She is the basis of all praxi. Be it the path of devotion, or knowledge, or action, it is only the awakening of the Great Goddess that takes the particular path to its destination. Achieving siddhahood, or sainthood as my yavana brethren call it, without awakening the Great Goddess, is simply impossible.'

The fact that Dharmapada was sputtering and had sat down on his seat spurred the scholar on.

'The union between the male and the female can be seen in many ways. The merging of polarities can be emotional, mental, spiritual, social, or even political. But it is known to all that it is in the physical act, the biological aspect, that this union is best understood.

'It is in this primal aspect that we understand the begetting of progeny, the most fundamental act of creation. Thus also understand the Great Goddess. Her process too is the most primal act of esoteric creation. The union of one with the Absolute, of the particular with the Universal, of man with Buddhahood, of prajna with upaya, of male with female, of yin with yang creates the siddha.'

A hush fell on the audience, whether out of affirmation or dissent, I could not tell.

'I must add here a word of caution. The way of the Great Goddess is to remove all traces of arrogance from Her path. But there are many driven by arrogance who try to control her through the force of their passion. Many such succeed temporarily and acquire great power too, even a type of siddhahood. But the ultimate goal of enlightenment is denied to them. And she makes sure that only death and destruction ensues to those who wrongly try to yoke her.' And then to stress her point, she raised her voice and her statement rang through the hall, and into the future.

'Those who walk the sacred path with arrogance will be destroyed.'

Dharmapada rose slowly from his seat and spoke in an exaggeratedly grave tone. I could tell that he was apoplectic with rage, a purple blush staining down to the back of his fair neck.

'My Learned Colleague,' he said, 'it is clear to me that the Great Goddess you speak of with such erudition in this august assembly is none other than the daughter of Mara. The demon Mara who sent his daughters to tempt the Buddha away from the path of righteousness with their evil sensual temptations. The same Mara that Buddha subjugated beneath his thumb to attain enlightenment.' He rode a wave of accusatory glances directed to the sole woman in our midst and under its onslaught, it seemed that she was finally, perceptibly, beginning to wilt.

'It seems to me,' Dharmapada continued in cold deliberation, 'O Alien One, that heresy is practised in your land. Are the people of your kingdom barbarians or simply beasts of passion that they use such gross analogies as the sexual union between man and woman in monastery lecture halls to explain the objectives of sainthood?'

'That was not my intention,' the scholar placated. She had broken down after all. Tell-tale sweat stood out clearly on her hairless skull. I could sense the wave of antipathy rising against her was reaching a dangerous level.

And then Dharmapada delivered the final blow:

'The mistake,' he said, pointing his finger at her as if it were a deadly sabre, 'lies not in you, but your perception.' But it was also a strike that saved her. I heaved a huge sigh of relief. Because at the mention of the last word, there was a collective intake of breath, as if the word perception was not a word but a juicy beast brought in for a feast.

I sighed and sank back on my mat, preparing for a long and fruitless debate. Presently, I spotted Rahula in the orange, red and maroon crowd behind the balustrades and sidled up to him.

'Sometimes,' Rahula said, staring at the quarrelling masters, 'all our great intellectuals do is raise a dust storm and then complain they can't see.'

And we watched, our arms crossed across our chests, 'perception' receive a flogging from our grandmasters and arhats till it was as dead as the mule that tried to bring me to Nalanda.

'Time for the snake and rope,' I whispered to him.

And so it was. Even as I spoke, a Vedic scholar from a Rashtrakuta kingdom tried to quieten the din in a loud voice by starting to say, 'Just as when a man mistakes a rope lying in the dark to be a snake and lives in momentary fear of the snake that doesn't exist...'

Rahula and I tried hard to smother our giggles, covering our faces with the edge of our robes. Soon, all I could see of the Vedic scholar in the melee was a wild eye and a finger making circles in the air.

'So too is the very nature of cognition flawed. We live in a state of ignorance because of the veil of illusion that drops in our limited powers of perception. It creates duality when in fact there is none. All is one.'

That was like the crack of a whip in a chariot race. The followers of Sankhya, Mimamsa, Nyaya, Vaisheshika, Vedanta and the six disputing schools of Buddhism were in battle array. They jumped into the fray amid much dispensation of energy and I swear by the Rajgir Stupa, if they had had swords in their hands, much blood would have been spilt that day. There were even some visiting yavana scholars from the land of Plato, and some disciples of Sucrat and Aristu from Bactra, called Socrates and Aristotle in their lands, who were attending the conference. Unable to keep up with the steady spate of the Sanskrit language, they quarrelled with each other.

Some said that neither the snake nor the rope exist, and cognition by the very nature of maya is flawed. Some said that both the snake and the rope exist, the mistake is an error of cognition. Others said that besides the snake and the rope, there is a third object that has both the qualities of the snake and the rope. Some said that neither the snake nor the rope exist, but the act of cognition existed independent of the two. Others said that the act of cognition was not independent but dependent. Some went about expounding the various categories of the cognition of matter that greatly annoyed the others. In all this, some tried hard to expound the nature of the Buddhist Void or Shunyata that tremendously incensed those who were already annoyed. And when others tried to classify the Void in different categories, some Vedic scholars and Buddhists stormed out of the hall together, only to realise that they were arch enemies.

I noticed that Dharmapada's behaviour had become altogether peculiar. He suddenly lost his customary incisive argumentativeness. His rebuttals became disjointed and incoherent. And then all of a sudden, he confusedly started taking sides, first of the Advaita and then of the Sautrantik schools, both completely opposing. I was surprised that nobody but me seemed to notice that his speech was slurred and his lanky frame was unsteady.

Meanwhile, all were unaware that the Chinese scholar had disappeared. And with her, the ring of protective monks. But I noticed. Only because I was following my master's gaze as he watched the woman leave. Again I caught him muttering under his breath.

'This was a mistake,' he said, 'Nalanda is not ready.'

We left the Hall deep in thought. Much as my head was spinning, I tried to mentally recollect the various arguments because I knew that my master, tough disciplinarian that he was, would make many riddles out of the conference and expect me to come up with points of refutation from the reference point of pratityasamutpada. Inadvertently we walked to the Dragon Pool, where the mythical naga serpent was still meant to be resting. As I wrestled with differing concepts, I looked at the reflection of my perplexed face on the pool's quiet surface. I thought I saw a snake slither past my reflection and smiled.

'How deceptive the mind is,' I said to Rahula.

He did not reply, combating as he must have been his own enemies. And sitting by the silent pool, I felt the balminess of the air, so different from the cacophony of the hall. I couldn't help agreeing with the Vedic scholars, however opposed I was to them.

The power of illusion, or maya, was truly all-encompassing. Things are never what they seem.

And then, in a moment, I had an epiphany. A series of visions passed in front of my eyes. In snatches, my future flashed by in lightning speed. It was so fast that I could not see images but the hint of a sensation of what was to come. They were unformed inceptions arising from my gut.

For my greater good, my time of unravelling is at hand.

I had been handed over to the full force of the law of inversion.

Therefore, reality will be the opposite of appearance.

So instead of life, teachers will take me to death's door.

Kings and institutions, politics and religion will show their inverted nature.

The treasures of Nalanda will be the inverse of what they seem.

Knowledge for the masses will not be the same as knowledge for the elite.

In a flash, that moment was gone.

I got up from the Dragon Pool and put my arm around Rahula's shoulders.

And I walked away from the moment as simply as reality from appearance.

5. *The Palace Officiates*

The daily debating regimen had turned into ugly wrestling pits after the Chinese conference.

Was age finally catching up with our three hundred-year-old Abbot, was one topic. What were the masters thinking when they took the preposterous decision to allow a woman in the hallowed corridors of the Great Assembly Hall?

It must be a conspiracy, was another. It had to be a plot hatched by warring master factions. Some debaters declaimed that at the root of this factionalism were the wretched Kapalikas. From the debates I learnt that the first Kapalikas were banished to the fringes of Vedic society for twelve years for the crime of killing a Brahmin. They had to carry the Brahmin's skull wherever they went and eat and drink from it. They smeared their bodies with ashes from the cremation ground they were forced to inhabit because they had become execrable to human society. From their seat at the funeral pyre they evolved secret and utterly deplorable methods of enlightenment, including sexual congress with low-caste women. And thus the necromancers formed a sect. This sect was infiltrating every establishment created by Brahmins and Buddhists alike and eating it inside out. Brahmin and Buddhist, both had a common enemy—the Kapalika scourge.

Has the scourge reached Nalanda? Was the woman a sign?

What was at stake was not just monastic tradition but the

future of Nalanda itself. In corridors, temple courtyards and kitchens, the nature of the crisis was discussed.

Many generations of kings had wasted their life's mission to patronise and increase the stature of Nalanda, but it was clear that it was no longer a celestial abode where the Great Learned Ones resided. Nalanda was now tainted.

All the stories set in stone in the eaves and porches were no longer a celebration of the material and immaterial wealth of knowledge. The lofty stone lions standing on Emperor Ashoka's victory pillars could no longer majestically roar at heretics. Because they hung their heads in shame. Shame that a woman was allowed to give a lecture to celibate monks in its sacred halls.

The debates went on and on, the extent of the catastrophe increasing with every win.

All doctrines expounded from the great pulpits of the Great Assembly Hall were now doubtable. The liberal spirit of intellectual enquiry and accepting contesting doctrines was destroying Nalanda. The woman's lecture brought to question the sutras and shastras filling to the brim the three great libraries, Ratnasagara, Ratnadodhi and Ratnaranjika. The knowledge collected here, meant to last the test of thousands of centuries, now lay to waste.

What then of our grandmasters, our mahapanditas, our arhats? Nalanda had not only produced some of the greatest scholars of all time but some of the greatest siddhas. Siddhas, as the Chinese scholar explained, were self-actualised beings. Beings who had achieved the ultimate goal of human birth, Buddhahood. Nirvana, or moksha, or sainthood.

In truth, it was not just scholarship but the names of the eighty-four mahasiddhas that had also been besmirched. Nalanda's head, that had been soaring in the clouds and the unified spirit aloft so much that even the Gods in heaven envied us, had been lowered by that woman.

Only Asita and Tarpa contended that none of the eighty-four

mahasiddhas were products of Nalanda's monastic establishment. That the mahasiddhas were Nalanda outsiders. But their debates were routed by sheer loudness of numbers.

The bed rock of every disputing doctrine, the ultimate, ultimate goal it rested on was nirvana. The affirmation of nirvana was the bed rock and the desire for it, the goal. This too, Nalanda debated unilaterally, the woman had destroyed.

As for me, I listened to the swell and ebb of the debates raging in every corner with aplomb. Because however bitterly my teachers disappointed me, I never took it to heart, or lost fundamental respect for them, respect being a cornerstone of the culture of my land, Vaishali. All of us, after all, were moving towards the same goal. And always the elegance and beauty of some logical treatise would rescue me from the moroseness of intellectual quagmire; the sparkling clarity of the mind that created the treatise would bring me peace and repose. I tried to keep my focus on that.

These were some of my thoughts as I wended my way to the Abbot's residence. Rahula had informed me that my master was with the Abbot, discussing finer points of the lecture and needed me there, to act as a scribe for his notes.

I thought this a good opportunity to seek my master out and mention to him my concern about Dharmapada the Logician. Even though a week had gone by after the conference, and Nalanda was consumed by the furore created by the lecture and the letter posted on the wall, Dharmapada prevailed in my thoughts, nagging me. He had been absent during some of our common lectures and convocations, making his followers fear that he had taken unwell. Some monks from my monastery who were his students were worried about his absence. A rash of diphtheria was spreading in neighbouring villages. We had initially thought of enquiring after his health in his quarters, but afraid of his foul temper and that he might consider our solicitations rude, we decided that on behalf of Dharmapada's students, I would speak to my master, without further delay.

The Abbot's court within the White Palace was nestled under the loving shade of two massive Bodhi trees and opened out to a beautifully maintained garden replete with flowering creepers, doves and lily pools. The porches were richly designed and studded with many life-size statues of all the Tara divinities renowned for their incredible beauty. The walls of his mansion were inlaid with gems. There were rumours that inside the White Palace was a magic mirror that could see every part of Nalanda.

The Abbot, and my master too, had a bodyguard, elephants, elephant trainers, many chariots, litters and palanquins.

The Abbot was also feared and revered for his magical powers.

His receiving chambers were highly frescoed with images of the greatly historical Buddhist Councils, and many tapestries made of rich fabrics of silk and other gossamer material I am unfamiliar with trailed from the ceiling to the floor. Religious artefacts abounded in the niches of the room, lending an atmosphere of pious opulence. There was a rumour that the Abbot had in his possession a lock of the Buddha's hair, though I had never seen it.

And there was something else in the air, something that had always made me uncomfortable in the Abbot's residence. Whenever I walked into the Abbot's house, I felt as if I was walking into the eerie brink of the unknown.

Maybe this was because of all the rumours and legends surrounding our Abbot, the Precious One. Every legend and rumour was as rich as the tapestries in the inner chambers of his White Palace.

Medicine pellets made of his shit were sold in markets far and near. After each visit to the White Palace, the young ones would ask me, 'Did you really see the Precious One? How many faces and hands does he have?' There was a high price for his bath water. His hair was worn in amulets.

There were rumours of a flying tigress who lived inside the White Palace. The Abbot supposedly dotted the night sky flying on her back.

What was more disconcerting was that the Abbot's physical presence blended with the clandestine air of his residence. After our first dramatic encounter at the gates of Nalanda, I had got to know him better in a much more informal setting because he was a close friend, almost the confidant, of my master. He was a mountain of gravity, with a belly to match his magnitude, and as dark and enigmatic as the night sky. While I was quite used to my master often smothering me with filial affection that even my father was not capable of, the Abbot's rare and grave reference to me as 'his son', was enough to transport me into realms of ecstasy.

As I wended my way through the Abbot's private garden leading to the inner courtyard, I did not know I was heading towards the biggest shock of my four years of peaceful monastic life.

From afar I could tell that my master and the Abbot were in serious conversation with a man dressed in kingly apparel. I received the intrusion with some indifference because royal patrons were a common presence in the university. It was only when I was in close vicinity to them and the outsider turned to face me that I stopped in my tracks and almost dropped my writing material. I realised the injustice of the situation—that he had had enough time to prepare for my presence while I had none. In fact, it was he who received me with more Buddhist composure than I. All I did was stare at him with my mouth open. A stifled exclamation rose involuntarily deep within my throat.

'Aditya Raj!'

'Yes, my brother,' he said, showing a perfect set of teeth and drawing me into a warm embrace. 'It is good to see you after such a long time.' My brother had always been taller than me. It seemed that he had grown taller still since I left home.

I am ashamed to say I went unwillingly into his embrace. I had received news from my mother once, apprising me of domestic developments. I knew that my brother had made a very important marriage alliance with the Princess of Bhojpur. Her father, the Bhojpur King, was King of Magadha, Mahipala's brother, a strong ally of the Magadha kingdom and generous patron of Nalanda for centuries. I knew that his marriage had made him next in line to the Bhojpur throne because the Royal Prince was afflicted by a deadly disease, rendering his limbs useless and his brain reduced to pulp. And even though he was presently the acting Minister of Bhojpur, he was already rumoured to become one of the most powerful men of Pataliputra and Magadha soon. I remember that this news had evoked disturbing emotions within me. On much soul searching and introspection, I had realised that though my mental makeup precluded the possibility of my becoming a successful man of the world, and though I was wholly devoted to the intellect, I could still be intimidated by worldly power and prosperity.

My brother stood in front of me, full of easy confidence and superiority, and I suddenly felt like a poor relation condescendingly invited to a lavish wedding feast.

'What brings you here?' I blurted out, abashedly realising that these should not have been my first words. Rather, I should have profusely proffered felicitations on his marriage.

'Are you sure that is what you want to discuss first? It is a rather delicate topic.'

How easily he smiled these days. How quickly the boy I had left behind had reached the full stature of a man, a Prince, a King. So tall too.

'What delicate topic?' I stuttered, looking about in confusion from one to the other. What a sorry, ignorant figure I must have cut before my younger brother.

This is when my master and the Abbot intervened in an exceedingly sombre manner. I felt that all three of them were towering over me.

'We think that it is best that you, Siddhartha, aid your brother in the king's investigation of this most unfortunate matter,' the Abbot said.

'Investigation?' I blustered on, amazed at this most disarming turn of events.

'Yes, brother, investigation. Are you not aware of the gruesome killing of Pandit Dharmapada?'

6. *Investigation*

The ground shook beneath my feet! At that moment I hated my brother for his knowledge over my ignorance, about a university where I and not he had studied for four years. Was it not enough that he was to be king of two kingdoms? Why did he have to come to my hallowed ground, all that I had? Suddenly, Nalanda seemed so small in comparison to him. Why was he sullying my sacred territory with his power-hungry arrogance?

'Well now, my young Minister,' the Abbot was saying in his grave voice. The Abbot too unnerved me, sitting on his marble perch surrounded by peacocks, their feathers trailing the floor, making me imagine them as tiger tails in my nervousness. My master stood grimly by his side, his hands clasped behind his back, looking as if he had never seen me before.

'Calling it a gruesome killing may be slightly premature at this stage of the investigation.' The Abbot pointed a bejewelled finger at my brother. 'In all my years of experience in Nalanda, I can safely certify that in all probability the "gruesome killing" was really an accident.'

'That, our esteemed Abbot, truth and the light of investigation shall soon reveal,' my brother retorted.

It was insolent of my brother not to use the honorific O Precious One. What was even more irregular was how quietly the Abbot tolerated this insult.

'His Highness King Mahipala has been concerned,' my brother began his diplomatic sophistry, 'about the affairs of Nalanda for many years now. Not only has the actual esteemed Abbot still not returned from the Land of Snows as he should have, you have been forced to discard your role as Abbot of Vikramshila to substitute for the responsibilities here. This has left an unhappy state of affairs in both Vikramshila and Nalanda. And now this unfortunate incident. His Highness Mahipala is deeply saddened and concerned. He presumes that this must be the preoccupation that prevented you Sir, the esteemed Abbot, from attending the Royal Newborn Prince's naming ceremony?'

'What happened?' I enquired in complete bewilderment, feeling much like the only child among grown-ups.

My master frowned at me, indicating that my question had put them in a diplomatic predicament. Seeing my masters so compromised, some deep-seated mental reflex went into motion to protect them and I found that I quickly regained my composure.

'Come now, Aditya Raj. Whatever the issues may be, I am sure we need delay my masters no longer. They are men of the intellect, of the spirit. I am sure mundane matters such as this are best handled by people inhabiting grosser levels like you and me.'

I detected that my masters looked on in some relief as I tried to lead Aditya Raj away from them. Aditya Raj resisted the insistent pressure of my hand on his shoulder, and displayed a steel in his voice I had never known before.

'This is not a mundane matter, brother,' he said. 'This is a political murder, the first of its kind in a sacred institution, none less than Nalanda. Conflict has been simmering amongst rival master factions in Nalanda for too many years now. And this is ample proof that things have gone much too far. It has reached the throne of Magadha.'

'Come, brother,' I said, putting a friendly arm across his shoulder as I led him away. 'What news of our poor mother? How bereft she must be losing one son to the search for spiritual posterity and one to material prosperity.'

And so I, taking the excuse of my poor mother, the Buddha forgive me for my duplicity, steered my brother out of the Abbot's garden and the Abbot out of my brother's reach.

At that time, naïve novice that I was, I did not realise I had performed a diplomatic coup. In becoming the principal university aide to the investigation, I had successfully trivialised the issue by bringing the matter down to the university's junior-most level. And by making Aditya Raj succumb to it, it became a tame domestic affair, where filial compromises were sure to follow, if necessary. I had won my beloved Nalanda diplomatic immunity.

But my brother was not so simple. Like in the royal game of shatranj, he had thought four moves ahead.

As soon as we were out of sight, Aditya Raj fiercely shook my hand away from his shoulder. He frightened away a row of parrots sitting on the palace wall chirping scraps of sutras.

'Don't you *ever* try to act familiar with me again in public! I'm on the king's mission and this is a royal investigation.'

'I am sure,' I took my distance and the liberty to present him a laconic smile. 'Only the king here is your wife's uncle.'

'That may be,' he shook his shoulders, as if trying to rid his body of my touch, 'but I never let that get in the way of my duty,' he finished in icy contempt. 'Remember, unlike you, I learnt statecraft from our great republic of Vaishali.'

I too wanted to get over the family charade. My mind felt like a boiling cauldron. I remembered the last time I had seen poor Dharmapada. His lanky frame had been swaying in a fugue state at the Chinese scholar's Dragon Body conference. Maybe her words had poisoned him, I thought in my agitation.

I sat down on a bench planted near a stone nymph and tried

to evoke whatever vestiges of elder-brotherly seniority there may be. 'Sit and tell me what has happened. Don't keep anything back.'

Aditya Raj sat down, looking relieved to unburden himself. Whatever it was, it had deeply disturbed him. 'The official story given by the Nalanda authorities is that Dharmapada drowned.'

I shut my eyes to banish the images that sentence evoked and mentally sent him protective sutras for his journey beyond.

'But the message we received in Pataliputra a day after he died, a week ago, was of an unnatural and sinister death. The letter was anonymous and hinted at murder and conspiracy. I reached here within a day.'

I sucked in my breath. So, my brother had been in Nalanda for a week unbeknownst to me. An unnatural death had occurred more than a week ago, and my masters had kept the matter secret. *What else was kept secret here*? It was a stray thought that I quickly erased from my mind.

'Brother, your masters are perpetuating a sinister atmosphere of secrecy,' he said. 'Everything is kept shrouded in a veil of ignorance. Nobody knows what's going on. Dharmapada was already buried when I arrived. And nobody knows that he is dead! I wonder when they plan to inform the public.'

'Buried?' I winced. 'That's unusual. Why wasn't he cremated?'

'The Abbot quoted some spurious sutra and said that it was best for Dharmapada because he was on the path to siddhahood. And siddhas, according to some death ritual, are never burnt, they are buried. His remains are in the samadhi shrines somewhere on the outskirts of Nalanda.'

I did not believe for a moment that my masters deemed Dharmapada capable of siddhahood of any sort. Something was deeply amiss.

'Only siddhas who have voluntarily given up their bodies are buried,' I explained. 'And the reason for that is to benefit other sentient beings. The atoms of their bodies are charged with high vibrations which purify the environment where the siddha is buried. If Dharmapada died of a sickness or committed suicide, it would be highly irregular to put him among the samadhis of the siddhas. The siddhas, after all, are accomplished saints,' I argued, quite unable to quell the doubts that were springing up one by one.

My brother's eyes shone at my presumed sign of complicity. It was just as well. It was important that I comply with him as far as I could. But the truth of the matter was, I too wanted to get to the bottom of this.

'My thoughts exactly, elder brother,' he said flicking off from his robe a wide-eyed mantis that had landed on it. From a distance, the young voices of novices learning verses by rote floated towards us.

'I suspect that the rites were conducted in a hurry to keep the matter under wraps. A cremation would have attracted attention. Nalanda has very detailed cremation rituals for a master. Right down to inscriptions, royal decrees and invitations to seven generations of the deceased family. This way all the formalities were avoided,' he said.

'Yes, but how did he die?' I asked with some impatience, wanting to know as much in as short a time as possible.

'They say he drowned in a well,' Aditya Raj said. 'That's all very plausible. But he drowned in a well in the Slave Quarters situated at the most distant Cowherd Gate.'

My eyes widened. 'The masters never ever go to the Slave Quarters.'

'Not only that.' He brought his face close to mine. 'He drowned in a well that only had enough water to cover a sitting man.'

That was grim news. 'He was a tall man. A head taller than me,' I remembered.

The understanding was implicit. We both got up simultaneously from our seat and moved silently in the direction of the village called the Slave Quarters. None of us spoke during the trip, beset by our own buzzing thoughts.

In Nalanda, there was protocol for everything. Even the shade of the robes monks wore were categorized and regulated. Red for one year of ordination, orange for two, and such. And since the highest panditas and arhats wore white, their accessories were categorised. The length of the top knot, height and colour of head dress, and suchlike. Wealthy students underwent a renunciation ritual that Asita and I undertook after an exhaustive consultation with the Vinaya rules of monastic discipline. There was even a ritual to sever your psychic umbilical cord with your mother that I had undergone. I also knew there were complicated rules for interaction inside the university between blood brothers. *So why were neither of us being informed of the necessary protocol required for the diplomatic conduct between a palace and a university official, especially considering we were so closely related?*

When we reached the village, unfamiliar even to me, I couldn't help thinking that no master in his right mind would have voluntarily ventured into so much squalor. Most of the residents were moolanivasis, natives of the forestland. Many were slaves, but some worked as menial labour in the Nalanda colleges. They were a primitive lot and shunned by monks. Dark-skinned and uncouth, they parted ways, averting their eyes and moving into their shabby hutments on seeing us approach.

Aditya Raj and I walked through the narrow paths between rough makeshift shelters made of hemp, mud and straw, holding our noses against the overpowering stench of extreme poverty. Some moolanivasi women, naked till the waist, were drying pickled amra in the sun. Unaccustomed to nudity, I averted my eyes. We were crossing a dirty courtyard littered with discarded terracotta pots around an old potter's wheel, when an unusual movement caught my eye.

I kept my banter with my brother going while I surreptitiously turned around to see what it was.

It was the brazen girl-woman who had kissed me! She was standing behind a broken hut with three other women, one of whom I certainly recognised as the Chinese scholar!

My throat went suddenly dry. The village obviously also had quarters for women slaves of some sort. This was possible, though women were not allowed in the monastic precincts. So much so that even bitches were not allowed inside the monasteries, only dogs. All menial labour was done by male slaves. All servants were either acolytes in service or pageboys. The Chinese scholar was most definitely not a slave. Who she was, was still a mystery to Nalanda.

I quickened my step so my brother would not notice.

We crossed another dirty courtyard where some elderly moolanivasis in the sparest loincloths sat in a huddle, impervious to the filth around them. They were not surprised by our intrusion. Many important personages must have passed here. Only the moolanivasi children, kicking around a ball of straw, dirty-nosed and unwashed, stared at us in impertinent impunity.

We finally reached the well. It was a medium-sized one, about eight feet in diameter. It stood in seclusion from the village and it was apparent that it was not frequently used because another larger well was placed more strategically at the centre of the slave community. A stone slab covered the well, easily removable by an able-bodied, adult man. On the stone slab was inscribed the Abbot's prohibition seal, the Dharmachakra. All of Nalanda knew that you stayed six feet away from a seal like that. Except my brother who carried a royal seal that gave him access to some prohibited areas.

When we peeked into the well, it became obvious that the water was not very deep below. Only about ten feet.

'See those rungs?' Aditya Raj pointed to small iron rungs on the sides of the well. 'One can easily climb out of the water, if one wants,' he said.

'Or climb in.'

'Notice that though it is dusty, the middle of the rungs are clean. Somebody has stepped on them recently.'

'Certainly,' I said. 'Many people must have descended to extricate the body.'

'Mistaken judgement, brother,' my brother said. 'The body was discovered at dawn and the well immediately sealed. The corpse was extricated with ropes within an hour and buried by noon. I know this for a fact because I conducted the investigation myself. All concerned were intensely interrogated and some were tortured. So that part is true.'

'Then who went down or up the well?' I wondered aloud. 'And we can definitely eliminate Dharmapada from the list of probables. If he went into the well...'

'He could easily have climbed back up, and been alive to tell the tale!' Aditya Raj said in triumph.

'Your brilliance dazzles me, brother,' I said, peering into the well. My words echoed back at me. 'I am presuming the well was open when the body was discovered.' I frowned in concentration.

'No. It wasn't. The stone slab covering was in place. Thus precluding the possibility of Dharmapada falling accidentally into the well. And even if an unknown person threw him down the well and covered the slab, Dharmapada could easily have climbed up, pushed the slab aside and walked out. But Dharmapada did not do that. So who climbed up and down the well is the crucial question.'

'There is one possibility,' I hesitantly postulated. 'The unknown murderer pushed Dharmapada over and covered the well with the stone slab. Injured by the fall, Pandit Dharmapada lost consciousness and drowned. It explains how he died in so little water.'

'Most Esteemed One,' my brother said in withering sarcasm, 'Nalanda has not sharpened your wits but dimmed it. Did I not mention the used rungs?'

'How was the body discovered?' I asked, changing the topic.

'Some moolanivasi children,' my brother replied, 'from the slave quarters were playing by the well. One of them noticed Dharmapada's sandals placed outside the well. They moved the slab and saw his corpse inside.'

'So very interesting!' I exclaimed. 'As if Dharmapada was prepared. He left his sandals by the well, slid aside the cover, then slid it back in place before climbing down the rungs.'

'And proceeded to drown in the least amount of water possible?' my brother finished.

'Was the corpse floating on the water?' I asked.

My brother was impassive and studiously silent. But he finally relented with the most curious news. 'Here is the interesting piece of information,' he said, turning his face from me, maybe because he did not want me to see his expression. 'He was found in the sitting position.'

'This surely is a most surprising mystery.' I stared at my brother in complete capitulation.

'I do not know what to make of it.'

'There is only one way to shed more light on this curious case,' Aditya Raj said in resignation and paused. In the hiatus, I could make out that within him a battle raged between trust and a hundred reasons not to trust me. When he first started speaking for a brief moment, I felt that trust had won the battle.

'The Raj Vaidya of Pataliputra rests in secret in a guesthouse in the city. He is not only the king's doctor, he is renowned in the science of anatomy. Tonight, you must help us gain him entry into the samadhi shrines and exhume the body of Dharmapada, so the Raj Vaidya can study the symptoms that led to his death.'

I smiled at my brother in derision. So, I was mistaken after all.

Rationality had not lost the battle to trust, but won it. What an obvious ploy to make me an accomplice in the royal investigation!

'Listen,' I pointed in the direction of Baladitya College, where the bells tolled at a distance. 'It is time for the mid-day meal. Come brother, let us eat and rest awhile. Give me some time to consult my master and I shall surely do your bidding.'

'For sure,' came his cold reply. 'Take your time.'

We made our way out of the Slave Quarters. I steered him away from where I had seen the brazen village girl. It was not just mid-morning hunger that made me hurry. The Slave Quarters felt sinister to me, like another Nalanda threshold to the unknown. Just as we turned to the main Nalanda path, a moolanivasi boy with a straw ball left his companions to bar my way.

'So have you come looking for your real master, like Dharmapada?' he said. His orb-like eyes reminded me of smelted iron, implacable and very, very still. Not like a child at all.

My brother laughed at him.

'He already has a master, boy. And a very good one, they say.' And then indulgently, 'I know you. You are the one who found the corpse. I tortured you. With fire and iron.'

The boy continued to bar our way. He looked back once to face his tense knot of friends watching him, then burst out in his surprisingly, still childish voice: 'I am asking you for the last time. If you so desire, I shall take you to your real master.'

I let loose at the boy a string of expletives, mostly concerning his parents and certain parts of the boy's anatomy. Thus I made it obvious to all that this extraordinary situation had finally frayed my nerves.

The boy fled to his companions and we made our way to Baladitya College in silence. When we reached the dining hall, the meal had not yet started. We were early. We had to wait for the noon chants to get over. I tried to overcome the jumpiness that had suddenly besieged me. Wherever I turned, I felt I was stumbling over a Nalanda mystery.

Besides being the oldest of the Nalanda colleges, Baladitya College had another strange reputation. There were whispers of a secret society here, whose members could be identified by their garb. It was supposedly a unique white with spun gold motifs that I had never espied anyone wear. As we waited at the Meals Courtyard, I noticed that the robes worn by this oldest monastic college were a different and definitive hue of yellow, orange, maroon and white.

'So?' I broke the silence, looking suspiciously at the robes the monks reading the noon day chant were wearing. 'What else have you found in your investigation?'

The tinkling strains of chants and deity bells for the noon worship emanated from every direction, enveloping us in their sweet rhythm. Singing and the sound of cymbals were punctuated by the low piercing calls of the conches, indicating the progress of another day of contemplation in the university. The animals, the birds, the deer, the peacocks too, made their presence felt in the congregation. But unlike them, we, the monks, could not seek a mate. Clothed in lonely monochromes, we took our eternal refuge in the Buddha, Sangha and Dharma. So went the chants the chorus boys sang.

'Any enemies? Any past vendettas?' I repeated when my brother did not answer.

'Only two worthy of mention,' my brother said, looking visibly moved by the serenity of the monastic setting. The dulcet melodies seemed to affect him in some deep way, probably instilling a peace hitherto unknown to him, given the stressful life of palace intrigue he must lead.

Maybe my life of contemplation had finally impressed my brother, I thought. Maybe this was the transformative instant that would make my brother, like Emperor Ashoka, take the path of non-violence. Then again, knowing my brother, maybe not. This was just me and my wishful thinking.

'One of his students, Bilwa by name, did not want to work under him anymore and had applied for a change of tutorship. There are rumors of a very intimate relationship gone sour.'

I pondered this information. An intimate relationship between man and man was not uncommon but frowned upon by the university authorities. Though I knew that some students and even masters indulged in this practice, I had never heard of it spoken of Dharmapada. And I knew Bilwa the Lazy. We were admitted into Nalanda on the same day, with Asita and Tarpa. Bilwa and Rahula had recently been shifted to my master's service. They worked as his translation scribes. And though we had different subjects of study, all of us were from the same monastery.

'I have heard that Bilwa considered Pandit Dharmapada incapable of taking the responsibility of stewarding his intellectual and spiritual growth,' my brother said.

'Your sources are unreliable, Aditya Raj,' I warned my brother. 'None of this is verifiable.'

But I did not tell Aditya Raj other thoughts that were teeming in my brain. Our monastery judiciary karmadana had filed a case against Bilwa the Lazy. He was on trial for sexual misconduct. Rahula and I had both signed the petition. But it was on an entirely different matter. I was filled with fear for Bilwa, and did not want him to get into any more trouble than he already was.

'Then the only other enemy,' my brother was saying, 'is Vishnu, the washerman pimp. Dharmapada had him whipped once.'

'Why?'

'Vishnu was a known pimp, soliciting his own wife as well as others. He had infiltrated all the monasteries, in the pretext of his laundry business. On being questioned by the Abbot, the washerman brazenly took the name of some masters. Dharmapada was one of them. Dharmapada had him whipped for tarnishing a master's reputation. Vishnu spoke against the injustice of the whipping. He said, and I quote, "Everybody knows that the masters and some students use the workers' wives and women for prostitution. If I should be whipped, then so should many of the esteemed alumni."'

I instantly recalled the girl in the village and recoiled at the statement, indignation boiling within me. 'And how reliable is this information?'

'Oh, come now,' he teased, just as he used to during our childhood days. 'You do know how much the university keeps under the wraps of its sanghati?'

7. *Midnight Oil*

I left Baladitya College knowing I had to find my master as fast as my feet would allow. A murder! A royal investigation! My head swarmed with questions like angry bees. Why was I chosen for such a high-profile affair? Was it because I was Aditya Raj's brother? What did my master want from me? Was Nalanda on the verge of some terrible calamity?

I decided to run towards my master's residence. His pageboys would know his whereabouts. The clepsydra showed that I must hurry.

But on the way, I found him sitting under a parasol by the Dragon Pool. Rahula and some other classmates were inscribing his lecture in parchments. How leisurely and focussed their pace, and how stormy and disjointed the thoughts in my head.

Seeing my condition, my master asked the rest to leave. With complete trust in my master I wanted to bare the entire burden of my thoughts in one long disjointed stream.

But I didn't.

Instead I said what was farthest from my mind. Maybe because I did not really have the courage to bare my thoughts that in all honesty were too unsavoury in nature. Maybe I did not have the confidence to face reality. Be that as it may, this is what I said:

'Doomsayers predict that Buddhism is at its sere, O my master,' saying so, I collapsed in a heap before him. 'A dry autumn leaf about to fall. In some sections of the Nalanda city quarters, monks are pelted with stones. Malevolent forces are inciting the masses against us.'

My eyes filled with tears. My master was staring at the dark depths of the Dragon Pool. And though the page boy held the parasol aloft at the correct angle, a slight breeze from the Dragon Pool ruffled my master's robes which had been folded perfectly to accommodate his most accomplished sitting position, the Padmasana.

He turned to face me. 'You must have heard the burning tallow story, the one that has made me famous in monastery courtyards?'

'Yes, my master,' I sighed. *So we will be talking in riddles today,* I resigned myself.

'What is the story?' he enquired.

'Legend has it,' I said respectfully, 'that in your younger years, you had once been driven to such a frenzy for liberation that one day, you took a burning tallow and glued it to the crown of your head. You sat down to meditate and swore that before the tallow reached the hair of your head, you would either get moksha or be burnt to death. Of course, you neither got liberation nor death,' I stopped.

'And?' my master gently enquired.

Even though I knew what was coming, I said, 'And what, my master?'

'What does the story teach you?' he asked with his characteristic patience.

'That such was the religious fervour of your time?' I offered.

'Not the response I was looking for.'

I lapsed into silence and waited. After a suitable pause, my master would give the answer. And so he did.

'Liberation is true knowledge. It cannot be achieved. It can only be revealed. It cannot be willed, or thought, or contemplated. It only comes through waiting. As you wait, you climb the steps to its secret sanctuary. And this is how the Bodhisattvas achieved Sunyata, the Void.'

I understood very clearly what my master was indicating. He was saying that I needed to wait and be patient. The truth about Dharmapada's murder investigation would be revealed in time. It also meant that I was not allowed to ask him questions. I too would have to speak in riddles. Dejection overpowered me. It demanded a certain diplomatic duplicity that I had forsaken a kingdom to avoid.

'How then,' I made a clumsy effort, 'does one explain the interweaving *web* of schools and counter schools, sub-schools and off-shoots of the religious dogma of our time? Sometimes when I am bewildered I see them as intricate *webs* of deceit to mesmerise the impressionable devout. Sometimes, I imagine that they accrue from the political exigencies of our time. Sometimes, I see not only deceit but also the conceit of those who want to stamp their individual seal on the intellectual map of our era. Sometimes, I think that the real truth is so deep, so mysterious, so hidden, that few would ever know, let alone understand, it.'

'Words of wisdom, my son. For it is true.' My master smiled. I felt the warmth of filial affection between us. 'Sadly, it is this *web*, this weakness that is gradually slowing the heart of this moment where Nalanda stands.'

Relieved to see that we were in accordance, I went on.

'I wonder whether we are too spellbound by fallacies. Are we not engaged in trickeries of conversion, too childishly preoccupied with creating counterpoints for our Vedic rivals?'

My master, the great Aryadatta, slouched a little from his perfect sitting position, and his chin sagged ever so slightly to his chest. 'Your words are harsh but true.'

'I fear,' I compulsively pressed on, unable to stem the tide of unnameable worry rising within me, 'that my beloved Buddhism will not die. It will be swallowed by the Brahminisation of our brothers.'

Without taking his eyes off my face, my master reached within the folds of his silk sanghati and placed his seal in my hands. 'You will need this to gain access to the samadhi shrines,' he said. My eyes flew to his face. *How did he know?*

My master smiled in mischief. 'Are you listening to too many stories of Nalanda Magic?'

I looked at my feet in embarrassment.

'An application for the exhumation had already reached us through the karmadana of the Royal Vihara, where your brother is staying,' he clarified.

'Yes master,' I meekly said.

'We are aware of everything that is going on. And every move you make,' he said. 'It will be dusk soon. You are falling behind in your lessons. Finish your pending assignments before it gets dark. It would be better than paying expensive cowries for midnight oil at the trader's market.' I bowed out three times without showing my back to him. He was alone now, staring silently at the Dragon Pool.

As I left, one sentence repeated itself in my head in concatenating rhythm. *Web* was the synonymous definition of the New Science.

Almost like a divination, I heard a commotion in the temple kitchen the moment I entered the monastery. I found Rahula bargaining loudly with other cell mates for midnight oil.

'What do you need midnight oil for, O great artisan?' I teased Rahula. 'You who never falls behind the lesson schedule.'

'By some terrible accident in the Scheduling Department, my service has been transferred to your master,' Rahula said, not quite meeting my eye. 'And he is a hard slavedriver indeed. I am not getting time for my studies.'

All the monks enjoyed his predicament. There was much jibing and friendly banter as the sellers counted their cowries and Rahul tied the midnight oil in a leather skein to his sanghati.

We walked out of the kitchens together, and as we crossed the monastery courtyard, Rahula and I fell behind to talk.

'Gossip of Mahipala's anxiety that the Nalanda grandmasters are giving Buddhism a bad name is reaching unprecedented proportions,' Rahula hissed, his carefree demeanour gone. He was sweating profusely, making his beautiful features look almost ugly.

'Calm down, Rahula,' I said. 'What are they saying?' *Did he know about Dharmapada's death? Did he suspect my role in the investigation? I had not mentioned a word of my brother's presence to anyone, not even him.*

'Your master may be one of the six gatekeepers of Vikramshila and Nalanda,' he started cautiously.

'All gatekeepers are considered great seers of our time,' I admonished, lest he speak against my master.

'But,' Rahula continued in his hissing whispers, 'please understand that the presiding deity of Vikramshila and Nalanda Mahaviharas is Pala King Mahipala. Mahipala is our Dharma Protector, regarded by tradition as the incarnation of Avalokiteshwar.'

'Come to the point, Rahula,' I said threateningly.

'Choose your loyalties well. It will be foolhardy to go against the king.'

So he had heard about Dharmapada's death. What else did he know? I wondered.

As we crossed the outer courtyards of the hostel, I peripherally registered some monks calling out to us. But we remained preoccupied in our animated discussion.

'You give too much credence to idle courtyard chatter,' I said. 'Obey the logic of your own intellect.'

'That is exactly what I am doing,' he retorted.

'Well, I am painfully aware, if you must know, that a rift between Nalanda and our Dharma Protector will destroy Nalanda and a millennia of its knowledge and history,' I said. Through the corner of my eye I noticed that from the group of monastery brothers that were shouting our names, one had fallen into a mud puddle in his frenzy to catch our attention.

'Siddhartha! Rahula! Come back fast. You've been summoned. We need your vote for the monk-on-trial,' came a series of voices thick and fast.

'Not now. Later,' I shouted back. 'I am on official duty.'

'This cannot wait,' a hostel fellow shouted. 'You two are the only ones missing.'

'Buddha's tooth!' I swore. I was swearing, uncharacteristically, a lot lately.

Begging forgiveness from the Buddhas, I joined my hostel mates and fell in line with them.

The trial did not take place at the hostel courtyard but in one of the Main Assembly halls meant for important public functions.

The hall was oval in shape and arranged in concentric circles. For larger assemblies, huge stone archways between the big and small halls were opened out. The laity and monks attended these assemblies. For public assemblies, even the fencing between the big and the outer halls were removed and in such gatherings, the monks, the laity and the general public attended in thousands. This trial was taking place in the small assembly in the outer ring of the big assembly in the main hall.

This meant that in the hierarchy of Nalanda's scheme of things, the trial was not insignificant but of middling importance.

When we reached the small assembly, the officer in charge of the proceedings, the Viharapala, had already started the trial rituals.

All the resident monks of my hostel sat in a perfect circle. Some monks from neighbouring monasteries sat in the audience gallery to watch the proceedings.

Under the giant vaulted ceiling, a standing divinity of Padmapani in black stone had been executed with great finish. The reading master listed out the charges against the accused monk. One of the novices held the reading master's embroidered parasol aloft. Before greeting the reading master, I fell in and bowed to him first. After quickly turning the dharma wheels, I took my place. And listened.

According to the rules of monastic conduct codified in the Vinaya, if the monks in a monastery had any business, they first presented the case to the Viharapala officer. The Viharapala was then ordered to circulate the report, with folded hands, to each of the resident monks in their cells. With the objection of even one monk, the trial would not take place. I remember perfunctorily declining when the Viharapala had addressed me, although I do not remember why. Maybe it was simply to give a fellow monk the benefit of doubt rather than a dishonourable discharge.

My disapproval had turned the business into a disputed matter and it took many months for the issue to be raised again. But the second time, I did not oppose the trial and the matter came to a unanimous conclusion. The rules forbid coercion or force to impose an issue, but now that all the monks in our monastery had approved the business, the reading master read out the report.

The case was against Bilwa the Lazy.

It was I who had gifted him this sobriquet, since he was always late for his debates. My heart wrenched looking at his downcast form standing at the centre of the circle.

Bilwa was from Sumatar, one of the islands across the ocean, and he was far away from home. He was being accused of bringing women into the hostel at night. He denied this, saying what the other monks saw as women were actually the emanations of a female deity and her retinue of dakinis. The proof that they were not physical women, Bilwa said, lay in the fact that their feet did not touch the ground. They glided one hand span above earth the way the sky-farers, dakinis in the local dialect, did.

Ever since I was a child, the word dakini had caused in me a vague discomfort. Nalanda lore defined a dakini as the divinised female form, the sky dancer, the enlightened Buddha. But I was unfamiliar with this lore rampant in Nalanda's inner echelons. Maybe deliberately so, I preferred the understanding of the common people. This defined dakinis as dayanis, or low-caste sluts. As dombis or witches who led depraved and obscene existences I did not want to know about.

Some monks believed Bilwa. The majority did not. I was part of the rest who were suitably and righteously disgusted at his inability to accept that he had broken his vows. We believed that whoever these women were, they were Mara's temptresses. And though amorousness was not uncommon in our time, it was uncommon in monastic life. And we intended to keep it that way. I had also freshly heard my brother's views about Bilwa and his unnatural relationship with Dharmapada.

Resident yavanas or aliens from far-off lands spoke of the power sexual freedom had given to women in our land, as was evident even in some of our temple architecture. These yavanas were shocked to hear that Amrapali, one of the most powerful historical figures in my country Vaishali, was a courtesan. Many aliens believed that we had made a mistake in civilian life by treating women as sexual equals. They thought it had made us a weak and primitive civilisation. Many of our elders, however, held on to the older beliefs of sanctifying womanhood. They said that old times were changing for the worse. My master, who hailed from Uddyana, the mythical land of magical hetera women, believed that the influence of the yavana invaders had imposed the orthodoxy of their ignorance on our enlightened people. Every time an invader or trader made our country his home, he taught us how to segregate the sexes a little more.

Be that as it may, it was still an implicit code among all faiths, that however licentious our civilian life may have been since the time the Buddha walked on our soil one thousand five hundred years ago, there had never been room for sexual permissiveness amongst celibate monks in the monastery. Ever. Celibacy for the monk has always been paramount. And we would make sure that this is how it remained for all time to come.

While the report was read out, Bilwa the Lazy, tall with a sunburnt face and enormous eyes, stood in a corner, his head hanging lower still. All present voted that he be expelled from Nalanda.

Eventually, he was given a chance to defend himself.

'Forsooth, brothers, this is how it must be.' We had to strain to hear his voice. Still, it seemed he was beaten but unbowed.

'The time has come for me to conduct my practices alone, away from the society of men. In the forest it must be, the Vedic way.'

There was an angry flutter in the group.

'Vedic? Hark!' Vallabha the Long Nose, from the Vaibhashika Monastery, spoke out from the outer circle of listeners. He got up from his seat, pointing a stubby accusatory finger at Bilwa.

'He blasphemes!'

'Punishment!' Bhim the Burly, sitting next to Vallabha, screamed.

'Another trial!' Rahula joined in.

'Send him to the chambers of solitary confinement! At least for a year,' I said.

Amongst all the shouting voices, Bilwa's voice was the calmest. 'Ignorant you are,' he said. 'And naïve. Obviously none of you have seen Nalanda at night. When Kapalikas dressed in bone ornaments go out hunting for female flesh.'

'Desist!' came Vallabha's loud voice. 'A debate. I challenge you to a debate *right now*. The loser shall give his head. He shall be hanged from the Banyan tree yonder.'

'The sky dancers speak to me,' Bilwa's voice was so soft that everyone quietened down. He spoke in a silken whisper and nary a sound broke the silence that followed after what he said.

'Souls of dead women are used to guard the library of secret books.'

'Cut off his tongue.' A voice finally came from the periphery of sound and went unheard in the spellbound crowd.

'Sacrificial fires are built by their burning flesh.' Bilwa scanned the rigid faces before him. He was beginning to look like a haunted spectre.

'Cut off his tongue,' the quiet whiplash of an old master sitting at the back became noticeable. All eyes turned to notice the Sthavira for the first time.

'The sky dancers speak to me,' Bilwa whispered. 'I have received great instructions and great initiations from the dakinis.'

The old master, fierce with age, raised his voice, his shriek ringing across the hall. 'Do not forget how the Buddha became enlightened,' he screamed. 'How the diabolical female tried to obstruct his goal. With one finger pressed to the earth, the Buddha subjugated the daughters of Mara. The demon Mara. Evil sinful temptresses were the daughters of Mara.'

The old master's voice was drowned by a thunderous charge of accusations read against Bilwa. Unlawful indiscipline, lack of celibacy, spiritual weakness, intellectual dimness, lack of respect for the Sangha, evil, disrespect of the Buddha, depravity, turpitude, wickedness, possession by malevolent spirits were some of them. With each accusation, Bilwa made a petition, and each time his plaintive voice was drowned out by a more stentorian one.

'Listen to me!' Bilwa pleaded. 'The dakinis guard the consciousness treasures.'

'Lack of celibacy!' we shouted in chorus.

'The only way we can get to the treasures is by supplicating the dakinis,' Bilwa begged us.

'Unlawful discipline!' rang out the accusation like a death knell.

'Can you not see why the ghosts, banshees and sirens haunting the centuries are all women? Women were always the easiest to sacrifice!' Bilwa raised his voice just a little.

'Moral depravity!' beat the judgement drum.

'Can you not understand what the outcasts are telling us! Please! Open your minds!' he sobbed.

'Turpitude!' The crowd kept ringing out verdicts, like whiplashes flaying skin.

'The beer seller, the princess, the hag, the crone, the cemetery dombi are trying to make you understand!' Bilwa's big round eyes brimmed over with tears. In the briefest moment when a pause interspersed the shouting, only Bilwa's breathless whispering could be heard.

'Follow the law of inversion!' he cried.

'Wickedness!' The mob finally responded, rousing to greater fury, ready to kill him.

'Listen to me! We cannot rewrite her history anymore,' Bilwa wept, his tears staining his sanghati like patches of blood. 'She will not allow it!' he said, crumpling to the floor.

'Disrespecting the Buddha, Sangha and Dharma!' rose the bloodlust against Bilwa the Lazy.

And we led Bilwa away in a public procession of shame because he had been found guilty on all counts. According to the rule of law, the extent of punishment was decreed by monastic peers and a fierce debate broke out amongst us on whether Bilwa should lose a limb. Bhim wanted castration, Rahula wanted his eyes gouged out and Vallabha wanted Bilwa to lose his tongue. But it was finally decided not to dwell on unnecessary complication.

So he was pelted with stones and evicted from our precious university with all the necessary prescribed humiliation. All of us took turns to lash him five times with our staff and blacken his face. And because he had blasphemed by using the Vedic word, we tied Vedic texts around his neck and made dogs chase him down the street. When the catcalls had receded and the others had sauntered off, I was the last one left behind, watching his sad, muddy and bloodied apparition staggering down the street. While I was watching him with mixed feelings of regret and retribution, an odd incident took place. When Bilwa turned the corner of the mud path, I recognised Asita and Tarpa waiting for him at the corner. Each took him in a tight embrace and hooking their arms under his shoulders, they supported him as he limped away. None of them turned back to see that I had seen them walking off together. Were Asita and Tarpa protecting Bilwa? I wondered at the incredulity of such a possibility with much alarm.

As I was about to turn away from the scene, I saw that Rahula had been watching across my shoulder the whole time. He had seen them too.

'The poor man is female obsessed,' I exclaimed, returning my gaze to the retreating figures. 'Rumours about Bilwa's unnatural relationship with Dharmapada are obviously not true.'

'Dharmapada was definitely coercing Bilwa,' Rahula's words were close to my ear, hot with breath. 'But it was not for a homosexual relationship.'

I stared ahead, still riveted by the now empty street, darkening in the gathering dusk.

'You are hinting at the warring master factions, are you not?' I said.

Rahula didn't reply, nor did I persevere. We walked back to the monastery in silence, each wondering how much the other was withholding. Both of us knew that our friendship had lost its innocence and in all probability would never be the same again.

I still remember Bilwa's words as Rahula and Vallabha had tied Vedic texts around his neck. His words had lingered in the air, like acrid smoke or the smell of sharp incense.

'The doomsday mare at the bottom of the ocean stamps her hooves for retribution, apocalyptic fire streaming out of her nostrils.

Her time will come.
She will wait.'

Maybe it was Bilwa's last words, or the sharp recall of the brazen village girl's unusual presence at the slave quarters, or the moolanivasi boy's impudent enquiry about my real master, or maybe it was to find more clues about Dharmapada's death. Something made me involuntarily turn my steps towards the Slave Quarters.

I retraced the path that I had taken through the moolanivasi village towards the well where Dharmapada had died. I crossed the hutments and saw a few moolanivasi men sitting quietly in a huddle outside their huts, smoking cannabis.

They did not look up when I crossed them. Questioning them would be pointless, for they looked too intoxicated to give coherent answers. Was their intoxication habitual? Were they trying to forget the reality of their existence? Or were they deliberately drugged into silence, were some thoughts that came up as I looked at them, stupefied in a huddle, oblivious to my presence.

I looked around for the moolanivasi boy, meaning to ask him to take me to the real master, whatever that was, but he was nowhere to be found. I missed his precocious presence, his little form had left an impact on me.

When I reached the quarters where I had seen the brazen village girl, I found it deserted. There was no sign of habitation. There was no life in the courtyards, whatsoever. I peered into the hutments. They were empty. The stoves were cold, all the cooking utensils had been removed. There was no one around, and not a sound. Overnight, all the villagers had disappeared. Rarely have I seen an entire colony suddenly depopulated like this.

They had only left behind a broken potter's wheel, lying forlorn in the middle of the village yard. And a vague stench of misery.

8. *Dharmapada*

That evening, I joined Aditya Raj as he took a walk with Pataliputra's Raj Vaidya in the Royal Vihara's pleasure park. The Raj Vaidya came from the same lineage as Sushruta, the famed Nalanda master of surgery. I recalled statues of Sushruta in the Medicine departments. His stone image looked every bit as sullen as the man standing before me.

'We were unable to get permission to exhume the samadhi shrines,' my brother informed me. *And yet my master Aryadatta had quietly handed me his seal of permission.* I stared at my brother in confusion wondering at the new quandary my masters had put me in.

'You are our only hope,' my brother was saying.

I digested this information. It was evident to me that my masters expected me to proceed with the investigation unofficially. Thus making it very clear that if the investigation did not progress as planned, it would be easy for me to take the fall. And even though this filled me with dread, I did not for a moment think of letting my masters down. 'Let us still make an attempt then. I shall help you,' I said.

For the first time I smiled at my brother in compliance. And it was a deceptive smile.

We met in the shroud of darkness for our midnight rendezvous, the Raj Vaidya looking every bit like the cadaver that he was intent on excavating. His crooked nose, his long fleshless face would have frightened me if it had not held within its wrinkles the gravitas of a skilled academic. Robed in a black cloak, like my brother, their hoods cast ominous shadows on their faces in the light of a pale repentant moon.

I offered to undertake the task of bribing the doorkeeper of the Cowherd Gate at the North Wall. The Cowherd Gate, I told my guests, was the busiest gate after dusk in Nalanda and the doorkeeper probably richer than the Abbot.

I had chattered on about how it was the least protected and most accessible of all the gates, the most discreet, and how a nefarious entry or exit could be made with a subtle bribe to the doorkeeper.

I was wrong.

When I told the doorkeeper that I was going into the neighbouring forest to look for a medicinal flower for my master, (I, like most other disciples who perforce needed to play truant once in a while, was skilled in the art of subterfuge) and it must be plucked on the sixth day of the moon's wane, which was tonight, the doorkeeper said, 'By any chance is the medicinal flower in the samadhi shrines, next to the forest?'

Word of the investigation was spreading fast within the university.

I surreptitiously showed him my master's seal. I did not want my brother to know that I had it.

The doorkeeper looked at me with the indifference of the ferryman who transports souls across the River of Death.

'I have only one rule,' his eyes looked murderous in the moonlight. His moustache drooped in soulless melancholy as he spoke.

'That you don't tell me where you are going, or who you are bringing in.'

'Of course,' my rejoinder was hasty. I quickly ushered my guests through the gate before he could say anything else. The faster we finished this business, the better, I thought. I mentally crossed him off my list of people to be investigated. I knew he would tell me nothing. Not even the location of the samadhi shrine. I had not seen it even once in my four years of ordination, nor had I passed through the gates of Nalanda under the blanket of night.

Luckily it was not difficult to find; it was located in a clearing, behind the cowsheds at the back of the Brahmin cooks' tenements. I have often been questioned by many yavana students about this royal and Vedic tradition of eating only the purest food cooked by Brahmins. It was true that though my religion had become egalitarian since the time of the Buddha, many Nalanda rituals, practices and most of its panditas and mahapanditas were still of Brahmin origin.

It was with relief that I saw five royal guards trailing us in the distance. My brother had brought them for digging. It was a wise decision, otherwise we would surely have been discovered over a half-dug grave in the early light of dawn.

We reached the Nalanda samadhis in complete silence. The guards found Dharmapada's grave under the samadhi shrine with his newly inscribed name in Sanskrit. Like the well-trained slaves they were, they fell on it without delay and we decided to bide our time in the slightly distant Tara shrine.

As we sat at the steps of the pavilion, looking about us silently at the enchanting spell starlight cast on Nalanda, I could have enquired more about the current affairs of the state court of Pataliputra. I could have made discreet forays into the intrigue that had suddenly beset my beloved university. But I sat dumbstruck, my head limply hanging from my shoulders, awestruck and unaccustomed to the almost feminine splendour of a beautiful night and the overwhelming presence of the people sitting around me.

My brother finally broke the silence. 'She wept bitterly, Siddhartha.'

'Who?'

'Our mother. When the Nalanda karmadanas came to the palace to hand over your last hair tuft cut during ordination to her.'

I was quiet.

'You know what it symbolises, of course?' he asked.

I was still unable to reply.

Officials make personal visits to the mother after the ordination so she knows that her son is now dead to her. The shaven hair tuft is the last reminder of what she carried in her womb.

Aditya Raj too became quiet, lost in thought. After a while he said, 'I have never seen her weep so much.'

I would not have been able to speak even if I wanted to. My tongue was swollen and a thousand needles pricked my eyes, but I would never weep before my brother.

She swam before my dampening eyes. My mother. Her face when I was young, her face when I was older. Her face as it must be now. A face that I would never see again. A teardrop escaped my eyelid and I flicked it away in annoyance.

In the distance, the incessant chanting and recitations at Nalanda were still audible like the humming of bees. The karmadana at our ramparts beat the drum of the last watch of the hour. The hour when mind demons infiltrate weak skulls.

When a soldier told us that the corpse had been exhumed and ready, I thought that I had finally swallowed my tongue. Though my mind told me that it would be exceedingly obscene and vulgar to watch the prodding and poking of the remains of a great scholar unearthed from his resting place, a macabre fascination drew me to the ghastly scene at the samadhi.

Pandit Dharmapada was not lying prostrate in his grave on the samadhi slab, as I had expected; he was sitting cross-legged, in the posture of meditation, in the posture siddhas are buried in. Seeing him like that made my heart beat without restraint, and I was driven by an irrational desire to laugh. The glow of heavy torches around him brought out the hollow cheeks of death in sharp relief. Though caked in mud, he looked as if he was in deep study and had forgotten to bathe and brush his hair. I had expected an expression of horror on his face, but there was none of that. He looked as if he were mulling over some intricate philosophical quandary.

'His body is surprisingly well preserved,' the Raj Vaidya sounded surprised. It was the first time I had heard him speak. His voice matched the funereal atmosphere of the samadhi.

'Well, it's only been about two weeks since his interment,' my brother spoke, his voice intruding into the silence of the night. His composure made me pull myself together to make a pithy observation of my own, but at that time the Raj Vaidya commanded Dharmapada to be placed on his back.

The soldiers wrestled with a corpse stiffened by lifelessness and when they finally succeeded, Dharmapada's skull cracked against the concrete slab. I winced. More at the thought of a human head that would never feel pain than the thought that it might. Seeing the indignity of Dharmapada lying supine in the cross-legged lotus posture on top of a samadhi slab with a small smile on his face, I let out a hysterical laugh and broke away from the sombre gathering to spray my vomit on the mulberry bushes.

I braved a return, still gagging into my sanghati, while the others looked on as if it was a part of their quotidian existence to watch a hook-nosed Raj Vaidya gnaw and poke a thoughtful scholar with evil-looking implements that made unearthly and bloodcurdling sounds. The Raj Vaidya spoke his observations aloud for all our benefit.

He held up Dharmapada's hands and observed that they were neither shrivelled nor bloated—the effects that long exposure to water have. His fingernails were clean, showing no signs of struggle. There were no bruises on his body, no injury to the head. No bones were broken, all his internal organs were intact.

At last, beyond the threshold of my endurance, the Raj Vaidya turned away to wash his hands that were soiled with unnameable substances. Leaving the soldiers to guard the corpse, we returned to the Tara pavilion to confer.

'Your man was drowned, all right,' the Raj Vaidya let out a deep sigh and I seethed at the derogatory appellation of 'your man.'

'How do you say?' inquired Aditya Raj.

'There is foam in the mouth and the windpipe,' explained the Raj Vaidya. 'Though that is extremely unnatural considering the man has been dead for a couple of weeks, it is still nevertheless a clear symptom of drowning. And his lungs have ballooned. The veins in his eyes have hemorrhaged and the bones in his ears have broken. These are the classic signs of drowning. Of a person who has struggled for air in the last stages.'

'So it precludes the possibility that he was killed first and then thrown in the well,' I said.

'Yes,' he said very politely, turning to me for the first time. 'Neither could he have jumped or been pushed or thrown into the well. There are no marks of external injury. He was not beaten, there was no strangulation, no knife wounds, no broken bones, nothing.'

Aditya Raj and I were silent. He too was probably picturing the murderer going down the well with a conscious Dharmapada who must have descended quite patiently to be politely drowned in a few feet of water.

'Can you tell whether he struggled during his moment of death?' I asked the Raj Vaidya.

'Yes, I can,' the Raj Vaidya said, 'he didn't. You can observe his fingers. They are not clenched. No clumps of hair or grass or mud in his fists. Not only did he not clench his fist, even his fingernails are not dirty. They are clean, as if the last thing he did was write a letter.'

'Maybe he was unconscious at the time of drowning,' I said. 'Maybe he was taking a walk in the Slave Quarters. Maybe the well was uncovered. Maybe he had a fainting fit, he was known to be unwell the last few days, maybe he fainted and slipped into the well. And drowned. We are making a really big event of nothing. To me it's quite obvious this was an accident.' I raised my voice during the last sentence, and remembering the indignities Dharmapada had just been subjected to, I smashed my fist into my palm.

The Raj Vaidya and Aditya Raj exchanged looks.

'In that case there would be some kind of external injury from the fall. But there is none,' the Raj Vaidya said. 'And he would be wearing his sandals.' When I did not reply, he added another question. 'Moreover, what was Dharmapada doing in the Slave Quarters?'

But I would not succumb to the Raj Vaidya's gravitas. 'That is an irrelevant question,' I replied.

'The well was an unused one, always kept covered. So accident is unlikely,' the Raj Vaidya was unrelenting.

'If it was murder, then why is there no plausible way in which it could have been done?' I countered. 'And would it not have been easier to just smother him with a pillow at his home than carry him through a busy colony to an unused well, where the chances of discovery are very high?' I finished.

'And lest we forget,' Aditya Raj said with exaggerated slowness, 'Someone climbed up or down the rungs of the ladder in the well. The well had busy traffic.'

'I have examined him,' the Raj Vaidya said, as if consoling me that murder was somehow better news than death by a natural cause. 'He shows no signs of a heart attack or a stroke or any obvious sign of fainting or unconsciousness. What is bewildering,' and here the Raj Vaidya's voice became a whisper, as if he were amazed by a profound discovery, 'is the mint condition his body is in. I cannot understand why there is so little decomposition.'

Here they paused and exchanged glances again.

'Should we tell him?' Aditya Raj asked the Raj Vaidya.

The Raj Vaidya shrugged. 'This is your investigation,' he reminded my brother. I looked from one to the other in increasing alarm.

'Something came to light while you were irrigating the mulberry bushes,' my brother said turning to me.

'What?' I demanded, very suspicious.

We walked back to the samadhi slab where Dharmapada still sat cross-legged, surrounded by Pataliputra's soldiers, waiting for instructions. The Raj Vaidya had stitched up his body and in the torchlight, Dharmapada looked dishevelled but ready for a class lecture. I noticed a small towel had been discreetly placed on his private parts. Aditya Raj removed it with a flourish and I sensed vomit gagging my throat again.

I had never seen the male private organ, except in statues or images. Even during the daily community bath at the pond, I always kept my eyes averted and chaste. Definitely I had not seen one that looked like this. It had swollen to an impossible size. It was monumentally erect and blackened with dried blood. It too was in mint condition. It was diabolical.

My impatience found the breach it was looking for.

'Enough conjecture. Enough. I should never have allowed this indignity to be heaped on a great scholar of Nalanda. I cannot understand how the cleverest minds of the land cannot see what happened. To me it is quite clear. Pandit Dharmapada was taking a walk in the colony. He had been unwell for a while, one of his disciples told me that he had been complaining of violent headaches. Maybe he had come to the Slave Quarters to clear his head. Maybe he did not even realise that he had ventured into an unfamiliar area. We scholars are absent-minded sometimes you know, we don't always have a clear focus regarding our self-interest. He reached the well and felt thirsty. Wanting to slake his thirst immediately, he took off his sandals and climbed down into the well, explaining why the rungs have been used. Maybe the physical exercise and the closed spaces of the well made him dizzy. He fell into a fainting fit and drowned.

'Why do people from Pataliputra hear the call of the battle conches in a single sound of a kettle drum? This episode has disgusted me. As the official representative of Nalanda University, I have given you my cooperation and the most plausible explanation. Please put a stop to this. Pandit Dharmapada must be buried with full honour before dawn. And you must leave now and give your official report to the symposium of Pala kings or whoever it is you give your report to. Now I must depart. And so be it.'

I got up to make a dignified exit from this gruesome scene. Aditya Raj's voice cut through the air and the night trembled. 'Are you suggesting that he fainted in the sitting position? And before he bloodied himself, he thoughtfully covered the well?'

Though I kept on walking, I couldn't stop my steps from faltering. My brother's hot breath was on my neck, unnerving me. He put his hand on my shoulder and I stopped.

'This is proof that the death was unnatural. It's murder. The royal report will say so. The investigation to find the culprit cannot be stopped now.'

'Unnatural death yes, but murder, no.' I refused to relent.

He forced me to turn around to face him, but for some reason I avoided his eyes.

'Listen carefully; I'm sharing very classified information.' There was a dark and terrible silence before he said his next words. 'The Nalanda grandmasters are aligned in two rival groups. And they are fighting each other to death. Dharmapada belonged to one such group.' He gripped my shoulder as I kept shaking my head violently. He seemed to understand how much the reputation of my masters meant to me. 'You know it and I know it, there is something strange going on here.'

'Why are the kings so bent on besmirching my beloved university?' I exploded.

'You think this is some elaborate smear campaign?' my brother protested. 'No. We seek the truth. And if you give me your patience, tomorrow night, I shall show you something about this university you have not seen in four years of ordination.'

'Let me go.' I roughly shook my shoulder free of his hand.

'Tomorrow,' he said, as I walked away from him. 'Give me a chance to give you proof.'

I walked away feeling that I was hurtling towards a series of disastrous incidents that would change my life and my view of the world, life, existence and the universe forever.

I walked with the premonition that this day was probably the last day of my innocence.

9. *Suka the Stupid Dreamer*

Maybe it was the weight of the revelations so close at hand that made my feet drag and made me purposely miss my appointment with my brother. I avoided him for the next few days, floating through the university routine and whiling away my time at novices' cells.

It was on one such idle afternoon that my already heavy heart and leaden feet became harder still.

Preordained new entrants were housed in a separate monastery till the end of the monsoon retreat. This was probably done to protect them from older monks and nurture them for future austerities.

Still, some older youths would find their way to the entrant cells. Minor heckling of the juniors was not only customary, it gave us momentary reprieve from the dryness of monastic life.

Word had it that a new entrant was either extraordinarily stupid or an enlightened arhat in disguise. Admission to Nalanda was difficult to the point of being prohibitive, yet aspirants waiting by the outside walls were treated well because it was common belief that a great being might well be rubbing shoulders with the rejects.

Suka, the new entrant, had spent seven years selling jaggery from a stall by the Southern Gate before catching the attention of the Abbot. As soon as he entered Nalanda, he became the focus of amused attention. The acolytes, older monks, even the masters were confused about whether his ramblings were the delirium of happiness or insanity or the prophecies of a clairvoyant.

With Rahula and some other friends I went to see Suka and ended up as confused as the rest.

Suka, a Chinese native of Hiuen Tsang's land, claimed to have seen Nalanda in his meditations with a clarity that made us wonder whether Nalanda existed in two dimensions. One in his and one in ours. While he mapped out some of the inner precincts with great detail, there were other divinations that had us rolling on the floor in mirth, uncaring of how dirty our sanghatis became.

His claim that some hallways were opened by secret sounds was correct because I performed my service in one such department, the Seals Department. It was opened by a very sophisticated acoustic device designed by the Astronomy Laboratories. Sound vibrations produced by pronouncing the opening sounds brought changes in the magnetic field, breaking the circuit that kept the door locked. I too, like the rest, had been amazed when I first saw it.

But this information, though classified like a lot of other information about the inner precincts where the ordained monks worked, could still be easily accessed by an outsider.

But when he said that there were similar entrance tests for an Inner Nalanda that was separated from the Outer Nalanda by an invisible unseen wall, we started laughing. He said that he had seen it during his meditation.

He described the Inner Nalanda with great flair. People flew here. Telepathy used primitively in Outer Nalanda was honed to a fine art in Inner Nalanda. Masters appeared magically in the midst of their students by teleportation. Visions were implanted collectively by teachers in the minds of students through telepathy. In the Akash Library, all conceivable knowledge in the universe was made available by meditators who dictated, translated and copied it into great forbidden books. Here is when we started laughing harder. But Suka continued, heedless.

Its inner walls echoed with hitherto unknown incantations, he declared. Secret conclave meetings were held in a stadium constructed at the core of Nalanda. Here is when tears started flowing and uncontrollable laughter made our bellies ache. And we ordained the monk as Suka the Stupid Dreamer and promised that the name would stick for life. A secret order of monks, Suka did not stop from telling us, decided the future incarnations of mahasiddhas in the inner stadium.

But even as I laughed with the rest, a thought crept in to my mind, like an interloper in the night. I knew that in Nalanda, meditation was used for much more than self-realisation. Consciousness tools honed mastery over the arts, science, music, even metallurgy. Could it be that it was also used for magic? *Was the treachery of sorcery tainting my precious Nalanda?* Could it be that the more I learnt, the less I knew?

'If you can see all of Nalanda's sorcery, then you must see its murders as well,' Asita the Great said. He was lounging on a pallet in a neighbouring cell, eating grapes raided from the monastery kitchens.

'Sorcery and murder always go hand in hand,' Rahula laughed with much glee.

I stared at Rahula. I was suddenly unable to laugh anymore.

Suka was not listening. Neither was he looking at us. He glazed across our heads with unseeing eyes.

'Dakinis live inside Inner Nalanda.'

The narrow cell crammed with monks bearing down on Suka erupted with even more mirth. Everyone spoke at once. Between lewd innuendo and obscenities, three questions stuck like leeches in my consciousness.

What really is a dakini? How are dakinis different from witches? Would you die if you fornicated with one?

As usual, the topic of women animated us like no other subject.

In the melee I heard Asita's grave voice educating the rest of the illiterates.

'We know that Tara is a female deity. Only highly accomplished practitioners who have received the Great Initiation are allowed to use other secret female divinities as their yidam, or ishta, their most personal object of worship. There are several masters in Nalanda, but only a few of them have advanced to this level. There is a divinity like Tara who is supposed to be a secret, such that you can neither utter her name nor see her statues or images anywhere. Yet, she is also considered the queen of dakinis.

Some dakinis are human females who through their enlightenment have become embodiments of She Whose Name Cannot Be Uttered. Their practices have made them more powerful than men can ever be. Thankfully, they have the capacity to bestow this enlightenment upon us. Some people say that all the grandmasters received their enlightenment from these women. Some other people call them witches. Not me.'

Everyone was suddenly quiet. And then a voice observed, 'That's what Bilwa was probably trying to tell us!'

'And we chased him out of Nalanda,' I grimly retorted. I noticed that Asita had turned his face away and was staring at a wall.

'Bilwa was a fool,' Rahula spat, 'who thought he could make a fool of us. He got what he deserved.'

I had lost my taste for mirth and my interest in the newcomer. I decided to walk back alone. It would be dark soon and I had no midnight oil stashed away. It was only when I slept at night that one by one, the hinges of the closed doors in my mind seemed to open. Each door was labelled with a name, a voice, a word, a rumour.

Dakini.

Warring masters.

Great initiations.

Dharmapada.
Bilwa.
Suka. Asita. Rahula.

The next night, I dreamt that I followed Suka's voice through the bronze-casting smithy. His incantations were magic passwords that led me through the pottery workplace and just beyond it to the Alchemy laboratories. Mysteriously, I found myself walking through Nagarjuna's gold mint that led to the Sonapahar hills in its outskirts. So this is why Nalanda is so rich, I thought in the haze of my dream. We make gold out of mud.

I saw Nalanda as a labyrinth of light interspersed with a darkness so intense that it felt like the edges of death. And in that maze I stood, perplexed. Because I did not know where I belonged. In the darkness or the light. I was stuck in the eternal damnation of the undecided.

10. *Baisakh*

Early next morning, I decided that I would unburden my soul to my master when I paid my daily obeisance to him. I would tell him that I was unworthy of the heavy responsibility foisted on me. I had neither the native intelligence nor the diplomatic skills to negotiate a senior palace official, even if he was my brother.

At the risk of remonstrations I would confess about Dharmapada's exhumation. I would tell him that I had been forced to use his seal. I would even tell him all the unsavoury details about Nalanda and its rival master factions that my brother had poured into my ears. I would report the unnatural nature of Dharmapada's death. His death was dragging me into areas of darkness I did not know existed in Nalanda, I would say. I would tell him that the welfare and reputation of Nalanda was in danger and needed the intervention of higher intellects. I kept very little secrets from my master. I would tell him that my brother and the throne of Magadha believed that something sordid was going on at Nalanda. My master would know what to do. He was a higher being after all.

I trusted him completely. The doubts that periodically surfaced in my mind were always ephemeral, like passing clouds in the sky. But of late, I would say, these doubts had been more pernicious, like indelible stains on my garments. I would confess all.

But when I reached his apartments in the fourth stage of the

Tara Monastery, I observed to my sore disappointment that he was not alone. Rahula was sitting at his feet, and they were deep in conversation. This was not irregular because Rahula was in my master's service and he had to commit a few hours everyday as my master's scribe.

What did strike me as odd was the fact that they abruptly stopped talking as soon as they saw me at the doorway. It made the now familiar feeling of unease rise up like bile to gag my throat and shook the resolve I had so firmly made on my way up.

I paused for a minute, then took water from my kamandal to wash my master's feet, all the while wrestling with the demons in my mind. I wiped his feet and raised his khadau sandals to my forehead in my daily gesture of worship. As I was placing his sandals back on his feet, I decided to speak, Rahula or no Rahula.

'Master, I have something urgent to discuss with you.'

My master was still in conversation with Rahula, now discussing something innocuous, and studiously ignored me.

Shocked and rebuffed, I waited for his blessings, but none came.

Humiliated, I left the chamber. From the balcony, I saw my brother waiting patiently in the outer courtyard under a sacred asvatha tree. I took the back route to escape both my master and my brother.

I perambulated the Giant Buddha statue in ritual worship, all the while trying to collect thoughts that were moving in circles around my head. I decided to accost my master again during his evening ceremonial worship.

In the evening, when I reached the outer courtyards of the ceremony shrine, my brother was there again, waiting, leaning against the lion pillar at the pavilion entrance, glaring at me.

I walked away, avoiding him in the same way my master was avoiding me.

In my disturbed state of mind I had forgotten that the Baisakh performing arts festival was to be celebrated that evening. As I neared the vicinity of the main shrines, the milling crowds became visible. And so did the unfamiliar noise of worldly life, since this was the one time Nalanda opened its gates to outsiders.

As I walked, my brother fell in behind me, keeping a distance of a few steps.

A cavalcade of fluttering pennants arrogantly crossed our paths, signalling royal patrons and the significance of the event. The caparisoned elephants and elaborate parasols that dotted the distance indicated that important officiating panditas too had decided to grace the occasion. The horse carriages and elephants tethered nearby bespoke the presence of high nobility, perhaps even the Magadha royalty. Soon, the acrobats on stilts and the pole vaulters were visible, and when I reached the centre, the evening was at its zenith. Each master arrived with fanfare, their karmadanas heralding their arrivals with honorifics and eulogies.

Singers, dancers, artists and artisans were given the deferential and courteous treatment Nalanda was famous for. An evening of devotional music was special enough to create a frenzy that extended many villages beyond.

The swells and ebbs of the elaborate orchestra were reaching a full-throated crescendo when I reached the main shrine.

Monks were in raptures of impassioned devotion. Bells, gongs and conches competed with the cacophony of a hundred sentinel dwarapalas pushing back a throng of country bumpkins who as usual had become too excited on seeing the lissome danseuses. Vast contingents of competing troupes had emerged from the neighbouring villages and cities and the sound of bugles, trumpets and drums rent the air.

Elephant and bear owners tried to attract attention away from the danseuses with their antics. Local craftsmen had already set up stalls selling baubles and Buddha statuettes for private altars.

They showed their wares, hoping to catch the attention of Nalanda craftsmen and the art sanchalas and karmadana officers.

I spied my master leading the chant in one courtyard. Girls from the village, all flower bedecked and in their finery, stood in a row and waved the tray of lights and incense around the imposing sandstone figure of the deity Amitabha in a charming circular synchronicity. Kumaris or virgin girls were commonly present during such festivals. They were worshipped with clothes, fruits and ornaments as the living embodiment of the Goddess principle. I can proudly say that I never gave them a second look. Only this time 'that girl' was there, like a persistence of vision, standing to my master's right, at a distance too close for comfort. With her were the other three girls I had seen at the Slave Quarters. All of them looked exactly alike, but I had eyes only for 'that girl'.

This time, it was not her lips but her waist where my eyes involuntarily lighted, and I fell back against a pillar, cursing myself. A host of confounding emotions, of shame and fear and guilt and doubt, set upon me with such a force as to make me dizzy. She turned around just then to lance me with such a knowing look that it pierced my heart like a poisoned arrow. Time seemed to slow down, and stricken by so much power, I felt that I had died there and then.

I tried to steady myself but my mind was a riot of confusion. No wonder my friends called me Siddhartha the Doubter. Why, I thought, when women, not even female animals except cows, were allowed to enter our hallowed university, when most of our common and uncommon vows were about celibacy, when the only women we were allowed to see were goddesses in stone meant for worship, were so many Kumari dancers allowed during our ceremonial rituals?

A voice in my ear said, 'Buddha said the temptresses, the three daughters of the demon Mara, will accelerate the downfall of Buddhism.'

I lifted my head to identify from where the voice came. All around, men were elbowing each other for a better view of the dancers.

Then again that voice. 'These kumaris being worshipped tonight will be deflowered by the priests before the morning comes.'

Again I swung my eyes around. 'Pupils offer kumaris to their masters as gifts.'

Was the voice coming from inside my head or from the crowd or from that old grey-haired monk staring at me as if he could see my soul?

I did not know when the worship finished. But the next thing I saw was the crowd dispersing and that girl simpering before my master. I forced my leaden feet to walk towards them. He was full of mirth at some witty comment she had made. He was laughing with too much fondness, I thought. And when I reached them, he was still tittering just like the rest of the maidens around him. My entire body recoiled at the sight.

'Listening to you sing is a blessing, Gauri,' he was saying. So, her name was Gauri. I knew that knowing her name would be like an affliction now. It would worsen my condition, make it chronic, like an illness. But this time, even though I was standing next to her, she did not acknowledge my presence, as if I were invisible. I pulled myself up to my full height and put as much dignity as I could into summoning the one word that I really owned.

'Master,' I said.

My master turned his head away to titter some more at the bevy of maidens crowding around him. I had seen them all before at the slave quarters. The maidens who looked exactly like her were probably her sisters. And the older, fatter woman with them must obviously be their mother.

I remained, head bowed, waiting for acknowledgement from my master. The light of the flickering butter lamps cast shadows full of suggestion. Their hair, their anklets, and other parts of their anatomies burnt through my trepidation, alluring with every contour. Exotic flowers made available for only the most special ceremonies adorned their hair. And I could not bear to look at the kohled eyes of my master. Anyway he wore too much gold, too much to be appropriate for such an occasion. I had observed that though he was known for his opulence—eating exotic meats in banquets and sleeping on a huge caparisoned bed—I had never seen him eat or sleep.

And then 'she' said, 'We shall meet later, Aryadatta.'

No honorifics, just 'Aryadatta!'

My master turned to her and smiled at the glaring impertinence of her too familiar address. All the while I was invisible to him. My heart hardened. I turned heel and walked away. I knew her eyes were on my back. A stray thought nagged me, weakening my soul.

I should renounce my master.

I pushed it away with all the force I had.

My brother, a picture of calmness, waited for my word. He had witnessed my humiliation. I feared that in his calmness he would clearly see the weakened condition I was in.

'I cannot help you,' I spoke before he could open his mouth. 'Apply for permission at the Department of Royal Affairs.'

'You know that I'll never get permission for what I want.' This was the first time that I had noticed my brother adopt a pleading tone.

'For the last time, what is it that you want?' I demanded.

'I want to show you an important facet of Dharmapada's murder. Make your decision after you know the truth.'

'I will need to consult Pandit Aryadatta,' I replied.

'Your masters will never grant permission to uncover their own ugly truths. You have to do this alone, elder brother. Both our futures depend on it.'

I paused, overpowered by the need to be alone.

'Three days from now, on the night of the full moon,' I said, 'in the third watch of the night, wait for me by the amra grove.'

'So be it,' he said gravely, his eyes locking with my troubled own. And the very next instant, his gaze shifted behind me and he let out a colourful expletive.

'What is it?' I exclaimed, quite alarmed.

'Blasted woman!' He continued to swear, 'I forbade her to come here. She never listens!'

'Who?' I asked, whirling around to look at the object of his alarm.

He began to stride away from me towards the ceremonial dances still taking place at the community festival.

'Sometimes, I envy you, brother,' he spoke over his shoulder, 'You are emancipated from the fetters of marriage.' He was heading towards a perfumed pavilion called The Dance of the Mirthful Noblewoman.

'Are you not going to introduce me to her?' I asked his retreating back.

'What use does a monk have for such things?' his back seemed to reply.

'So be it,' I sighed and turned away.

When my brother was gone, and I was leaning against the pillar, trying to gather my strength, Gauri walked up to me and called my name. It was an act of so much intimacy that I couldn't bear to look at her.

'You are very quick to expel one of your own,' she said. It took me a while to realise that she was referring to Bilwa.

'I can have your tongue pulled out for disrespecting a monk,' I said before lifting my tired bowed head to look at her. I noticed that under all the ceremonial finery she was wearing, she was not really beautiful, not in the way most girls are beautiful. She was too lean, and her face too angular. Only she was maddeningly enigmatic. She smiled at me with an impertinence I was now getting used to. It was a smile that held the power of its own sweetness. It unerringly pierced my heart as it was aimed to do, and I could have easily wrung her neck for it.

'How then will you taste the nine elixirs I release in sixty-four different positions?' she said, reaching close to my ear and biting my earlobe.

And then she was gone. Pulling away with her the power of her immense attraction. Leaving me to practice my eight-fold breath for equilibrium.

After some time, I noticed that the sun had set a long time ago. The lights of the festival were going out, plunging Nalanda into darkness once again. I decided to approach my master in the morning.

11. *Tara Monastery*

When I reached Tara Monastery, my master was descending from his quarters with a following of four or five people who were hanging on his every word. Asita the Great was with him, and I saw familiar faces from the Royal Vihara and the Abbot's department.

The warmth of his greeting brought me back to life, immediately erasing all my previous turmoil. 'Siddhartha!' he called out, sounding pleased to see me.

'It has been a busy morning,' he said, addressing only me, 'and now I must go for my meditations. Come walk with me to the meditation caves.' His disarming smile brought me back from the brink of what was beginning to feel like an eternal precipice. I suddenly felt whole and worthy again.

It was only when I fell in step with him that I saw Aditya Raj walking behind Asita. Some primitive instinct prompted me to be circumspect and act with discretion.

'Your brother brings us news from Pataliputra.' My master kept me singled out in the group. We had reached the open courtyards and his pageboy desperately struggled with the parasol, trying to keep his master protected from the sun.

'Know, my son,' my master said, putting a heavy hand on my shoulder as he walked. It was the first time my master had ever touched me. I became alert for signs that he might be making.

'Know that today we have received notification from Pataliputra.

We must hold a council in answer to the letter posted at the Nalanda Gate. The council must be attended not only by all the important disputing Brahmin scholars of the land but also by the Hinayanist who wrote it. There will be beheadings and slavery for losers. Need I remind you that Hinayana Buddhism, our bitter lesser half, is ready to become the most effective instrument of destruction of Mahayana Buddhism?'

'But why has King Mahipala issued this order?' I asked, pretending my brother didn't exist. 'I thought he was our most ardent patron. And has the Abbot agreed?'

'No,' my master responded, also speaking as if Aditya Raj was not walking amongst us, his face dark as a thundercloud. 'The Abbot has politely declined. But that is only postponing the inevitable.'

Aditya Raj did a side step, so he too was walking by my master's side; now we were both on either side of him.

'Most Esteemed One,' Aditya Raj began, 'the death of Pandit Dharmapada has thrown Pataliputra into a terrible confusion.'

I couldn't help but look about me.

It was a beautiful day. The sky was a cohesive blue. The busy occupations of the pigeons and squirrels scurrying at our feet stilled my nerves.

We were crossing the Garden of Austerities. Here, a certain sect of monks only ate the fruits that fell from its trees. Ahead, an assembly of officers was busy sorting out notched sticks for the next monastery election. Every monk in Nalanda carried a stick with notches that marked his sun years, moon years, ordination years, and circles that calibrated his monastic education. According to the classification of chronological years, we would be called upon to vote for various offices and assemblies. Judging by the frenetic activity, it was obvious that an important assembly was in the offing.

'I know what your King wants,' my master said as we crossed

the assembly officer marking notched sticks with the monastery seal.

'It's not Dharmapada's murderer,' my master noted with some firmness. 'And he is not going to get what he wants.'

Even though my master was known for his quick temper, I had never seen him so abrupt and undiplomatic.

We walked in awkward silence. My master's steps were small and light.

'Esteemed One,' my brother picked up speed to keep up with my master's quickening pace.

'We have reason to believe that Dharmapada's involvement with a secret faction of Nalanda masters brought about his death. There is also reason to believe that the society of Nine Unknowns started by Ashoka, thought to be defunct, is still extant here in Nalanda, and may be connected to Dharmapada's death and the secret societies. We also know the code words of two societies. For the first, it is Kapalika, for the second, it's Nine. We also have information of their secret seals. We would like to submit to the Abbot an application that all cooperation regarding investigation in this regard may be given to us till Dharmapada's killers are brought to book.'

My master had stopped walking while Aditya Raj recited his incendiary speech in a respectful monotone. He abruptly turned and again put his hand on my shoulder. I tried very hard to focus on what signals my master may be giving.

'Nalanda is in danger, my most beloved student.'

I noted the open gaze of my master. His eyes did not seem clouded by fear or emotion. They seemed clear and expressionless. I might have been looking at the sky.

'Our ways may not continue for long. A lot of forces are arrayed against us, as if for battle. They have been gathering for many centuries now.' After a pause and some brisk paces, he said, 'You do know that over the centuries, Nalanda has been raided by the Huns.'

'Yes master,' I said. I looked around, seeking Asita, but the crowd had dwindled. Only the three of us remained, walking together. My master was playing riddles again, and like always, eventually a point would emerge. I enjoyed my brother's discomfiture, as he continued to shamefacedly walk with us, completely ignored.

'And now the Turaskas,' I said, 'the ones the yavanas call Turks, the Mussalman infidels, are also filtering down from the North. But master, Nalanda has always survived the raids. We have constructed over their destruction.'

'They are a great danger,' my master continued speaking as if I had not spoken. 'Not only to us and our lifestyle but to the entire land. They only understand the language of destruction. A potent negative force. But if you think they are our only threat, you are wrong.' *Was he hinting that like the Mussalmans, Pataliputra too was Nalanda's enemy? Was he relaying a message to me, about my brother? Or was it a message to him about me?*

'What other threat is there, master?' I increased my speed to keep up with him. It was discomfiting that he always seemed to be a couple of steps ahead.

'People think that Adi Shankaracharya, the great Vedic proponent, has defeated Buddhism in the famous debate. The ignorant feel that religion is a war and can be won or lost in a debate. Still, the rumours are true. Many dynasties that have funded Nalanda for centuries are turning away from Buddhism. Vedic Brahminism is creeping back; it never really did go away. The old rigid hierarchies that the Buddha opposed are raising their heads, not only outside Nalanda, but inside as well. There are many within our community who do not know that the million manuscripts in the Nalanda libraries are a tribute not to the power of the intellect but to the power of creation. The seeds of the New Science sweeping through the monasteries were born right here. My country Uddiyana is ruled by magic. This is not a myth. It is true. New Science magic rises quietly; like an invisible tidal wave, it is filling our chaityas and stupas and is ready to drown the very foundation on which Nalanda stands. But the mahasiddhas hold fast the key to its many mysteries. And we will never give up its secret books.'

At this point the dread I had been feeling all these days found the manifestation it was seeking. My bowels turned to water. And I knew why. Through me, my master was conveying a strong message to my brother, one that I was incapable of comprehending. Considering I was the centrepiece in this diplomatic exercise, my ignorance put me in great danger.

I looked about me. We were at the edge of the university. Fields and fields of cotton that was used to clothe Nalanda stretched before us. A wave of religious patriotism overwhelmed me. There was nothing for me except to do or die. So be it. So let it be written, so let it be done. My brother continued to walk with us, his face impassive, his fists clenched behind his back, betraying no emotion.

'But master,' I demurred. 'In the name of justice, Dharmapada's death deserves a fair trial. And these are but general things you speak of. I see no immediate danger. The Vedic way has always existed. I was born into it and so were you. Buddhist practices did not change our origins. We study Vedic scriptures here. Many of our royal patrons practise the Vedic ways. It seems to me the distinction is not only illusory but delusional. Moreover, Adi Shankaracharya's debate took place a few centuries ago. We survived it. We prevailed.'

At this point we crossed the entrance lane to the Sitavana Monastery, with the Dharmachakra prohibition seal emblazoned on it. In all my years at Nalanda, I had not known anyone who lived there. According to myths and legends, Nagarjuna's gold mint and the alchemical laboratories were located here. Its gates were heavily padlocked. Gold was a mysterious substance in Nalanda. It held in its depths secrets that I was yet to fathom.

The Seals office, where my service was designated, lay just beyond.

'My child, my child,' my master shook his head, 'When religion is practised by large numbers, it follows different laws. Mathematical laws, quantified and qualified by statecraft, numbers and the exigencies of politics. The days of the great Buddhist kings are over. King Ashoka and Harshavardhan are dead and gone. Today Nalanda hangs by a thin thread. King Mahipala is a devout Buddhist and, by Buddha's grace, he still rules Pataliputra and Magadha. But there are other dynasties—the Sena dynasty, the Chandra dynasty—that are rising all around him and these are staunch believers in Vedic Brahminism. The Senas are militant Vedic warriors. I have heard that Adishura, the Sena King, is importing southern Brahmins into his region because Buddhism has wiped out the brahminical culture there. Some Kulin Brahmins go about the countryside, impregnating the daughters of every household so that more Brahmins can be born. It is a pernicious, single-minded campaign. Our Buddhist liberalism cannot fight it.'

I was beginning to finally read between the lines. *Pataliputra is compromised, besieged by Nalanda's enemies. And Nalanda will not fraternise with the enemy.*

Here Aditya Raj, who had been silent for so long, interjected. 'If you are stating that Nalanda has enemies, you could not be more correct. Its opulent monasteries, gems, gold coins, religious freedom and knowledge will have to be surrendered, sooner or later.'

My master sighed. It was a long emanation from deep within. His robes fluttered in a stray wind. What a comforting feeling the presence of a master is, even when he is full of anxiety! The meditation caves loomed ahead, cut out of rock, lined in a row. While my master waited for the pageboy, also an acolyte and an acquaintance, to finish arranging the meditation seat and water for the cleansing ritual, he asked me, 'You must know about the latest religious campaign by Brahmin priests?' Then he answered his own rhetorical question: 'They are listing Gautam Buddha as one of the many incarnations of their God Vishnu.'

He did not speak in anger. He spoke as if he were accepting a nemesis. I hesitated.

'But Esteemed One,' Aditya Raj said. 'What can be so terrible about that? The deification of Lord Buddha as the incarnation of the greatest Vedic divinity should be a matter of pride.'

Here my master deliberately exchanged glances with me. Many moons later, when I would stand in the middle of a burning pavilion with fires blazing all around Nalanda, I would understand the meaning of that look.

'When wars are not won by force, O Worldly One,' he turned to address my brother for the first time, 'they are won by treachery. The germ of infection seems microscopic and harmless, but wreaks terrible destruction. By allowing Buddha to become a deity of another religion, we will pave the path for Buddhism to be subsumed and swallowed by the more omnipotent and omnipresent Vedic Brahminism.'

I was struck by the knowledge of his observation; how evil treachery looks when it is unveiled. My master's acolyte signalled that he had completed the meditation ritual preparations. My master stopped and turned to me. 'Do you still feel that these dangers are too general to be cause for worry? Know that Nalanda is being subjected to the same treachery. We too are suffering from the infection of subterfuge. Dharmapada's death is but a symptom of the disease within us.'

If that was meant to act like a threat, it worked, because Aditya Raj muttered an excuse and took my master's permission to leave. My master dismissed the acolytes who had collected around us. He then took me to a quiet corner of a rock-cut cave and whispered, 'My Siddhartha, knowing your sweet innocence, you are probably unaware of certain facts. What I'm about to say should be of immediate interest to you. Our spies say that

King Mahipala's brother, Vasantapala, is actively trying to usurp the Magadha throne.'

'Spies?' I expostulated. 'Nalanda has spies in the palace?'

'Siddhartha, Siddhartha,' my master shook his head in exasperation, but did not answer my question. 'Vasantapala is your brother's father-in-law. Did you know that he has convinced King Mahipala to make Aditya Raj the most powerful overlord of Pataliputra and the commander of all his armies?'

The news stunned me. I had never bothered to find out. All this while I had been content with the trivia my mother sent me in occasional letters—such as the news of my brother's marriage into a very important kingdom. I shook my head in a daze. My snivelling younger brother, who would cry when the palace barber nicked his toenails was now the commander of Magadha's armies. In the four years that I had been busy sharpening styluses in musty libraries, he had become the most powerful man in Pataliputra. I tried hard to divert my focus to the present moment.

I mechanically refolded my master's sanghati, the meditation garment, even though it had already been folded for his meditation. Each meditation cave had a little enclosure that could not be crossed. Attendants waited in the pavilion to ensure that the masters were not disturbed. Nalanda's meditation seats were fixed for life. A new master could not use another master's meditation chamber. He had to construct one for himself. He also had to create his own statue of a standing divinity unique to him, and keep it secret and undisclosed.

'I thought so,' my master responded to my stunned silence and the shock and dismay written all over my face. He was looking at me with great compassion.

'Then, you also probably do not know that Vasantapala has fomented a conspiracy with Adishura of the Sena dynasty to overthrow Magadha. Your brother is working for the king *and* his prospective usurper. Aditya Raj is a double-headed snake, my son. He mirrors all the goodness in you with an equal amount of darkness. It is probably at Vasantapala's and your brother's behest that this inquiry has been put under way. King Mahipala is terribly compromised by his own enemies, and those of Nalanda as well.'

'Only you can save Nalanda now,' my master said at the doorway to his cave, as I prepared to leave, satisfied with the meditation arrangements.

Somewhere a peacock shrieked in panic. 'You are our shield to his spear. A spear aimed at Nalanda's heart. This is a test, Siddhartha, and though our blessings and powers are with you, try not to fail.'

The vast firmament of bleached morning sky, the earth under me and the horizon beyond, were still, so still. And yet they seemed to be rotating around me.

'If you fail, Nalanda will be handed to the unworthy. And, Siddhartha,' he said before retreating deeper into the meditation cave. 'If doubting helps you find love, it is a good doubt. Because love conquers all.'

His laughter echoed with my footsteps as I walked away, without showing my back to my master.

'Dying at the hands of love is a worthy death,' he said as he dismissed me, his smiling face engulfed by the darkness of the meditation cave.

Now what could he mean by that?

12. *Ghostly Wind*

When I reached the amra grove, Aditya Raj was already there, waiting for me. The full moon was brighter than usual, as if she were determined to shed more light on our nefarious activities. In the distance, the gate bells struck to announce the ominous third watch of the night. And though it was autumn, a pleasant time of the year, the breeze was stiff and the trees bent their backs against it. Shivering, I looked up at the dark coagulated sky and wrapped my sanghati closer around me.

'A ghostly wind rides through the university tonight,' I said to no one in particular.

My brother seemed to be in no mood for conversation. I too was determined to keep my secrets close to me. I would disclose nothing.

'Where are we going?' I eventually asked after we had crossed the gardens outside the monasteries.

He pointed at the distance. 'To the observatories.'

I craned my neck to look up at the tallest building in the distance. Standing atop a hill, its topmost story touched the brooding sky. Clouds scudded to its peak as if gathering for a secret conference. I snorted. 'There's nothing you can show me there that I don't already know. I have studied there for four years.' I had spoken in bravado and immediately regretted my statement.

'We shall see.' My brother's replies were clipped tonight. Had he fought with his wife? I wanted to tease him but refrained from doing so.

After we had walked through a short span of scented kusha grass and crossed the Dragon Pool, he became more conversational. 'Can you see the pinnacle of the building?' he said, pointing in the direction of the fast-moving clouds.

'Yes, of course,' I said. 'Hiu-Tsang made those peaks famous in his travel book a few centuries ago.'

'Have you ever climbed the peak of that building?' he asked.

'No,' I said, my curiosity piqued. 'You cannot reach it. There are no stairs or ladders. Our lecture rooms end at least fifty feet below.'

'Exactly,' he said. 'Now I shall show you something that you have never seen before.'

It took us a while to cross the chaityas, hostels, libraries, lakes and parks. The narrow corridors, the winding alleys were familiar to me. But what took me by surprise was that they seemed familiar to my brother too. Rarely did the lay population cross the main pavilion and assembly halls. But Nalanda was a vast university city and it was possible for royal patrons to get access to the inner recesses of my beloved abode. Still, if it was my brother's intention to make me uneasy, he had succeeded.

Walking through the halls of the main assembly building, with footsteps that echoed in the stillness and legs that cast long shadows in the light of our torches, felt strange because these halls bustled with so much activity in the daytime. I knew my way around here, so I took over the tour. My wooden sandals clattered on the shadowy stone floor of the enormous main assembly hall. I had received my sandals only two moons ago. Before that I had walked barefoot.

'It is not only material grandeur of space and stone and architecture that you see here. For centuries scholars have come from throughout the world to partake and create the wealth of knowledge that can make even the Gods envious. Books have been revealed to us from the etheric libraries of the eternal firmament in many languages known to mankind—the Gupta script, Devnagari, Brahmi, Siddhaism and Avestan.'

I did not know why I was exhibiting Nalanda like a boy showing off his new toy. Maybe I was trying to talk him out of plundering my only home. Maybe I was trying to convince him of the wealth I had gained by forsaking my kingdom. Maybe he would then convince my mother of Nalanda's intellectual riches.

'In more ways than one, words are gods here. They walk here, they talk here, they breathe here,' I finished, looking at his face closely for any signs of admiration. There weren't any.

He said instead, 'Let me take you to another place, where the gods breathe.' My brother gently maneuvered me to the centre of the Assembly Hall.

'And huff and puff and sneeze. Brother, you are right about etheric libraries,' he smirked. 'In more ways than you can possibly conceive.'

An intricately designed circular motif of the ubiquitous Sarnath wheel and deer, made of wrought iron and stone, adorned the centre of the Main Assembly Hall. The Dharmachakra. In the centre of the wheel was another small replication of the same motif. Students and teachers walked over it several times a day. This was where the Chinese scholar had given her Dragon Body lecture.

The destinies of countries were moulded here.

Aditya Raj took out from his robes a heavy circular iron seal that held a wheel motif similar to the one on the floor. To my amazement he placed it on the centre of the motif and rotated it. What happened startled me—the entire design structure slid down and away like a well-oiled scrape, and in its place appeared a large hole, five feet in diameter.

'Who else has this seal?' I asked him sharply.

'The Abbot. Some masters, some students,' he shrugged. And I thought *I* was the chosen one. 'And King Mahipala,' he added.

'And King Mahipala gave it to you?' I was incredulous.

'I work as his emissary, elder brother.'

My brother's response was so pious I wanted to laugh. 'My father-in-law and he are very close allies. Or have become of late.'

'Of course,' I said, wondering what evil and slippery tricks my brother must employ to inveigle the trust of his patrons. Or was he like me? Did he have the same blind faith in his masters? The thought irritated me.

Aditya Raj began to climb down a ladder into the black gaping maw of the hole. 'Come.'

I stood frozen for a moment. A voice—or was it a rumour or a divination—played like a chant in my head. It was the voice of Suka the Stupid Dreamer.

'Only those who could hold the higher vibrations would eventually enter the inner chamber. Many in the outside world would not even hear of it. Some rare ones would gaze within and wonder at its mysteries. But for the rarest of the rare who entered the inner portals, reality as they once knew it would change for all eternity. And these, the rarest of the rare, then, would never look back again.'

My brother's voice was echoing from inside of what looked like a tunnel. 'We won't need a light here.' His voice sounded like the beating of brass tongs from inside. 'It's only a short distance.'

I climbed down the step down ladder and descended into the tunnel. We walked for a few feet, feeling our way in the darkness with our hands and feet.

The short tunnel opened into an inner courtyard full of dappled moonlight. It felt as if we had birthed into another world.

I looked around me in awe. I figured out that the area must be the centre of the old ruins, but it was surprisingly well maintained, which meant that it was not uninhabited and walled up as most of us presumed. We walked on and around it everyday and did not know it.

The ancient core of Nalanda was a living breathing organ, pulsating with activity in the dead of night. The acoustics of the buildings were so designed that no sound emanated into the outer world. Its walls were as high as our observatories. Looking up, I saw a stairway to the pinnacle of our observatory towers. Unlike what novices and foolish monks like me believed, it was not walled off or unreachable.

The air inside was fresh. And my brother, an outsider, was privy to this, while I, who walked the halls every day, was not. A sigh, trapped deep within me, finally let itself out.

Flameless torches, connected together with copper tubes, burnt around us, shedding continuous unflickering light. It made me recall the old Sthavira who had mentioned its principles during my first visit to the Ten Wisdom College.

Though encroaching creepers and the pernicious growth of pipul trees had weakened the walls, the courtyards were swept and clean. There was steady repose here and contemplative calm, although it was not wanting in the dynamic or even the demoniac. This was what I had started hating about Nalanda lately. This pervasive pretension that all was peaceful. When it wasn't.

I heard footsteps and the movement of people. Suddenly there were about a dozen dwarapalas everywhere. Some looked familiar, but most I did not recognise. Two of them came up to us and after looking at my brother's seal, handed us upper vestments. The robes were white silk spun in gold, immediately reminding me of rumours in the Baladitya College dining halls of special vestments worn by a secret Nalanda society. So, the rumours were true after all.

When I had taken my brother to Baladitya College, he had already known its secrets. The extent of my ignorance frightened me. I looked askance at my implacable brother and fear of him made me momentarily dizzy.

The dwarapalas, also dressed in white, offered us white hats that we wore. The dwarapalas then went their way. My brother lost no time in removing his white hat and after a while so did I.

'If anybody asks you who you are, say that you are a special invite by royal decree from the court of Mahipala,' his voice was suddenly controlled and anxious. As for me, the events of the past few days had left me beyond shock.

Though I cannot say that this secret place was crowded, it wasn't empty either. Every person we passed by seemed intensely busy and everyone avoided eye contact. Never in my life had I seen so much activity in the middle of the night. When the rest of Nalanda plunged into darkness, this was where the lamp burned.

I could distinguish the inhabitants by the different embroideries on their upper vestments. I could make out by design, the laity, Afghan traders, monks, royalty and masters. I wondered idly whether they were visiting or lived here. But I could not voice it because somehow my tongue had become incapable of speech.

'First, I shall take you to the upper stages.' Aditya Raj led me to a staircase winding up a narrow corridor that was also kept lit by flameless torches. What luxury! Fire was not allowed even to the senior most masters. And here it burnt unheeded.

The stairwell opened into a courtyard where a fire ceremony was in progress. The courtyard was full of scented smoke. Verses from books were being chanted aloud by monks in sparkling white robes and then consigned to the flames. Even as I idly wondered whether I had seen these monks at the Vaibhashika Monastery, I immediately understood what was going on. The sound, the smoke and the fragrance were embedding the knowledge of the books in the etheric template. I knew this because this is what Suka the Stupid Dreamer had told me while I had laughed at him. This knowledge could be accessed at any time and in any language by technicians trained to read etheric symbols. This was exactly what was happening in a neighbouring courtyard. Cloistered by many walls, this chamber smelled of burning cannabis and other strong aromas. Here transcribers sat in a trance, staring and listening to the smoke-filled chamber of light and shadows. Their slow and sometimes rapid pronouncements were immediately noted by translators and copiers. I scanned their silhouettes, searching for a familiar face but couldn't see any. I counted ten monks.

I watched stock still, completely spellbound. Scent and fire and therefore smoke, I had learnt in lectures, was the medium used to transcribe symbols in ether. But I had never seen it put to practice. I scanned some of the bound manuscripts that were arranged in bundles at corners. Mathematics, the science of herbs, linguistics, medicine, management of society and astronomy were some of the topics that I could read.

'Many forbidden books lie amongst these bundles. Books Mahipala is interested in. But your masters guard the catalogues zealously,' my brother said, but I wasn't listening. Water poured out of my eyes. From wonder or the burning incense in the courtyard, I do not know.

'Now can you see that I know more about your Nalanda than you learnt in your four years of ordination?'

Despite my undying faith, my abject surrender to Nalanda's every demand, as Aditya Raj led me down more darkened corridors, I could not help thinking that he was right. Torches burnt bright on wall niches, forcing us to walk through spaces of extreme dark or too much light.

We crossed a monk on his way down. I saw his clean unlined face clearly. It was Tarpa the Gentle, from the land of snows. He gave his service in the Translation Department. It felt strange to see him dressed in the mysterious Baladitya white robes. If he was here, surely so was Asita. He proffered a hurried greeting to my brother and studiously ignored me.

'How is the mahapandita, the Revered One?' my brother asked.

'He has stirred. I must rush to him forthwith,' Tarpa said and sped away.

'We shall come with you too,' my brother called out to him as he sped downstairs.

'I have someone from the city I want him to meet.' My brother could not tell that Tarpa and I knew each other, or so I thought.

I did not know whether my mind had any more capacity to hold on to the fantastic, but I obediently followed him after Tarpa. The courtyard opened out into an enclosure very similar to our meditation caves; only here there was a giant stone wall where bunkers were scooped out for meditators to either sit or lie down.

Unlike the meditation caves outside, the ambience here was more intense, more otherworldly. Scores of scribes and attendants, ghostly in their white robes, sat on either side of the wall, in some thirty nooks. Some were dishevelled and gaunt, some portly, some shaven, but all were in scanty white clothes, and they were all meditating. Either supine or cross-legged, they were immobile, deathly still. It seemed the attendants were meant to nurse the physical needs of meditators who had lost body consciousness. They were sponged, bathed and fed mashed fruit or gruel. Sometimes, nails and hair needed cutting. Temperatures were kept ambient with water, fans, parasols and blankets. On the other side of the walls, scribes wrote down what was dictated to them. Words came from lucid dreamers, or meditators speaking from altered states of consciousness. These words would later be copied and printed by copiers and printers working assiduously in adjoining chambers. The writing chambers housed at least fifty monks.

Taking in this spectacle, I did not realise I had stopped

breathing till Aditya Raj nudged me forward. Next to the giant wall, a narrow room led into a natural cave cut deep into a rock. Aditya Raj pulled out a torch from the wall and led the way. The tunnel wound about for a few feet and then lit on a niche where a master sat erect in meditation on a levelled seat at a height of about four handspans. His hair was matted but his face was clean. He looked oddly untouched by time—neither old nor tired. He sat with his eyes open, the eyeballs rolled back into their sockets. He did not stir even when the light of the torch fell on him. His attendant hurriedly appeared from the interiors of the cave like a bat from one of the nether worlds. The angle his emerging body made with the floor looked suspiciously like he had flown in. I had noticed this in some other monks too. It was not really flying but an awkward uncommon gait where the upper body moved in leaps rather than steps. The attendant's face was young and child like. I did not recognise him, making me presume that this area of Nalanda was a colony of some sort, whose inhabitants did not venture out.

And though I kept my back to Tarpa so he could not acknowledge me, I was determined to find him outside this strange place and force him to reveal what he knew.

'Any news?' Aditya Raj demanded with some authority. I took out the white hat and pulled the hood over my eyes. Tarpa, I am sure, understood that I did not want him to display any familiarity. 'What shall I tell the king?'

'I have bathed him.' Tarpa was at pains to explain to Aditya Raj. 'And fed him some bittergourd juice.'

'Any words today?'

'Not today, none.' Tarpa apologised with the gentility typical of the land of snows.

It was only after we came out and away, after we had crossed a tunnel and appeared in an open ground level courtyard, that Aditya Raj explained to me what I was burning to know.

'Pandit Yasha has been unable to come out of meditation for the last four years, but his tongue speaks. He seems stuck at a certain point in his journey where he experiences death again and again. His utterances give a graphic picture of the beyond. The words he recites are being compiled into *The Book of Death*. It will help the Pala Dynasty control its re-incarnations and hold on to previous memories in subsequent lives. It is a very important project. One that King Mahipala is nurturing with great care.'

If this is so, I thought, then surely plans for reincarnations were already being set in motion. Important masters must surely be involved. But I did not give my thoughts utterance. Instead, I said,

'I have never heard of it.'

Moving ahead, we came across intense activity—several monks were doubled over, carrying blocks for printing. I sucked in my breath as I passed one of them. It was Bilwa! He had been expelled from Nalanda only to be incorporated into its core! Had he recognised me? In a place like this did it even matter, I wondered. We climbed upwards towards stages that were quieter; the higher we climbed, the more deserted the area became. It seemed we were climbing into deathly stillness when grandmaster Siroha came rushing down at us with a parrot squawking on his shoulder. The parrot's screeching tore into the silence of the night, making me realise how quiet the innards of Nalanda were. Though it was teeming with activity, it was also as immobile as a samadhi. It was then that I realised that everyone here spoke in whispers. Siroha was followed by his usual retinue of monks. The way they kept pace with him, like soldiers following a general, was at least a familiar sight. Bhim the Burly rushed past us, blowing out Aditya Raj's torch.

The last monk I crossed was Asita the Great. So Asita was here too. But of course, I thought, entirely beyond shock or surprise. Asita, Tarpa, Bilwa were all here. As usual I had been the last to arrive.

We climbed the pinnacle and strangely descended again. This time into a large hall. My brother opened a huge iron gate in its northeast corner by pronouncing secret code sounds. We came out into what looked like a garden from all sides. The scent of hibiscus and jasmine wafted in the night air. The terrain did not seem enclosed or cloistered anymore. We were out in the open, exposed.

'The roofless temple,' my brother introduced, 'only there is no way in.' I responded by looking at him with interest when he added, 'not even for me.'

The garden was enclosed in intricate stone latticework that operated like a concentric wall. Some areas of the wall were padlocked and opened into chambers that we could peer into if we pressed our faces against the lattice. But we could not enter any of them. It reminded me of the laity wall outside the Assembly Halls where the public was allowed to press their ears and listen but not enter. It felt unnatural to be on the other side of the wall. Is knowledge linear? I wondered as I pressed my ear to the lattice, hoping for a sound to carry through the night air. None came.

All the silent padlocked chambers were marked with a seal that was unfamiliar to me even though I gave my service at the Seals Department.

Aditya Raj ushered me to the latticed wall and beckoned me to come closer. I did his bidding. He took out an eye piece from his sanghati with much pride. I looked at it, singularly unimpressed. Many such eye pieces were designed and manufactured in the Astronomy Laboratories.

'This has been made in Nalanda. Who gave it to you?' I asked.

'Mahipala himself,' my brother said a little too sombrely.

'The Abbot gifted it to him,' he added.

'The easier to help you spy with, my brother,' I replied, equally sombre. Then I started laughing, and the thick leaves of the audumbar tree shook with my laughter that was edged generously with sarcasm.

'You don't know how to use it, do you?'

I enjoyed seeing the flush creep across his face and would have heckled him some more if I hadn't been so curious about what was on the other side.

I pushed the instrument into the lattice cavity and after adjusting the focal length of its pieces, peered through it.

I looked into the lattice window of a small chamber well lit by the moon and spied a lone flameless lamp at its altar. The sight I saw so confounded my senses that a hush fell upon me. The chamber was like any other. It had stuccoed panels and a massive lion-headed beam overhead. The divinity here was a floor-to-ceiling sculpture of Mahakala, the great God of Time. Like most teaching chambers, this too had an altar.

But it was what was placed on the altar that stopped my breath.

Looking through the eye piece, I felt as though I were very close to what was before me. I stared at the machine in the middle of the hall and involuntarily breathed the name that was as deadly as its deed.

'The Brahmastra.'

'Aha! I knew it!' my brother exclaimed fiercely into my ear as I focussed on the winged and snouted iron animal. It was mounted on a wooden pavilion like a trapped marine fish. Though it was not very large, it looked every bit as ominous as it was meant to be.

'Is this part of your curriculum?' my brother's dripping sarcasm poured off me without effect.

Swinging the eye piece through that horrific room, dizzied by the magnitude of human action, I unwittingly started mumbling the texts.

'*So powerful that it could turn the earth into smoke and flames in an instant, with a great soaring sound... And on it sits Death.*'

'Louder!' my brother shrilled. 'Say it!' His eyes danced in his face and in the moonlight he looked like a man possessed.

Between him and the image through the eye piece, my voice iterated insanity in clear empirical terms.

'*The atomic energy fissions the ninety-nine elements, covering its path by the bombardment of neutrons without hindrance. Desirous of stalking the head, i.e., the chief part of the swift power, hidden in the mass of molecular adjustments of the elements, this atomic energy approaches it in the very act of fissioning it by the above-noted bombardment. Herein verily the scientist knows the similar hidden striking force of the rays of the sun working in the orbit of the moon.*' And then I whispered. 'Artha Veda.20.41.1–3.'

'I have heard,' my brother said, suddenly casual in the face of such a mind-shattering phenomenon, 'that the space between the atoms is called the chittakasha. It is a mental–physiological state, and it is on achieving this state, that fission is accomplished.'

'What you have heard are the fables of Ramayana and Mahabharata,' I said, spellbound by the vision that seemed to unfold through the eye of my device'. 'What you are seeing is the never seen before put to practical application.'

I found it amusing that he made no effort to look through the eye piece.

'Don't you want to take a look?' I asked.

The next moment, his hand clasped my mouth.

'Hark!' he cried. I froze.

'Voices,' he whispered eerily into my ear.

'So what?' I whispered back.

'From beyond the wall,' he replied.

This time he grabbed his eye piece and, pushing it against the lattice, peered into it.

Crushed behind the latticework I felt a wave of exhaustion course through me. I realised it was a tiredness that had started with my ill-fated visit to the Cockfoot Mountain.

Still I asked him what he saw.

My brother started laughing under his breath.

'What do you see?' My voice reminded me of the way I had been during my childhood, when we would play pranks. Only we were not children anymore, and this was not an infantile game we could stop playing anytime we wanted.

'It seems to be a clearing of some sort. A park or a garden. There are people in black robes. Eight or ten of them in a circle. They are quite far from us. I can't see their faces.'

'But all the robes this side of the wall are white,' I observed.

'So these are the famous Black Hats Pataliputra is talking about,' My brother calmly noted, his entire body concentrated on the extension from his eye.

'Wait, wait, wait,' he paused and the silence was unbearable. He spoke after an interminable pause.

'I see women,' he chuckled. My throat went dry. My knees began to wobble.

'They are very far in the distance. Standing in a circle and chanting something. Wait, wait, wait.'

He said and then he shouted so hard I had to clasp his mouth. 'They are rising off the ground.'

'The sky dancers. The dakinis.' I realised I was crouching against the wall.

He thrust the eye piece at me as if it were a poisonous snake.

'Why don't you take a look?' he said and so I did and handed it back to my brother in a moment.

'What did you see?' he demanded.

'The Chinese scholar,' I replied.

'What is so extraordinary about Chinese scholars!' he demanded.

But I could not answer. I was sinking to the floor because my face was bloodless and I couldn't feel my legs.

'Women in the heart of Nalanda,' I exhaled and collapsed in a heap on the stony floor.

My brother was now pointing to the seal above the padlocked chamber that had denied us entry.

'Look at that seal!' In the light and shadows, the seal shone with incriminating intent. 'Your master was trying to blame me for the destruction of Nalanda. When in reality, this is what is destroying Buddhism. And within that, beyond that,' he gesticulated wildly at what lay beyond the latticed wall and our reach, what we had just seen, 'is what killed Dharmapada. Because that is what your masters are hiding.' He was trying hard not to shout. In a frenzy I got up and started pacing up and down the stone path. My mind was a riot of militating thoughts.

'And how does that concern you?' I replied. 'I'm sure your king doesn't spend sleepless nights pondering the destruction of our religion.'

Aditya Raj turned and pointed at the world beyond the seal. An unreachable world full of deadly intent.

'Inside that is the real wealth of Nalanda,' he cried. 'We have been allowed access to the paltry baubles of the White Hats, while the Black Hats guard the real treasures. Black hats worn by women! We have a right to share that wealth. It is wrongful to deny us access.'

'And Dharmapada?' I was full of spite, goading him to disclose more, 'Does he have anything to do with this at all?'

'Dharmapada tried to access that wealth for us. And died trying.'

I was quiet, all my thoughts stilled with this information. Aditya Raj slowly sat down on the floor. I sat down beside him. My brother realised he had spoken too much.

'And that's all I can tell you,' he said.

'What is this wealth you talk about? Is it gold?' I asked after a long thoughtful pause.

'What is more precious than gold, Siddhartha?' he was fierce, my brother.

'What is more precious than gold?' It seemed I was mimicking him, but he knew how serious my question was.

'The power to create gold from nothing,' he said.

Suddenly terror struck my heart.

'Why are you really here, Aditya Raj? Who sent you?'

'I am not permitted to say,' he said, not meeting my gaze. 'But the truth will soon be revealed to you.'

'The truth?' I exclaimed. I was bitter.

'If this is the truth, then what is falsehood?'

'This. It is this, it is this that is falsehood,' my brother sighed. 'Every truth here leads to falsehood.'

For the first time my brother looked at me with affection he had never shown, not even in Vaishali.

'Come away brother, we are not meant to be seen beyond this section,' he said.

We turned and retraced our steps in silence. At the point of entry into the precincts of Secret Nalanda, two dwarapalas stopped us again.

I looked questioningly at Aditya Raj.

Aditya Raj stepped up to the dwarapala and cupped his hands. One of them was Bhim the Burly. He made me wonder about his master Siroha's importance in Secret Nalanda.

He took out a thurible from his robes and poured a white liquid on Aditya Raj's cupped hands.

'Repeat after me, the Brother's oath,' Bhim said, and Aditya Raj followed his intonations.

'Neither in word, thought nor action, will I disclose what I have seen, heard or known in this holiest of holy places, the Baladitya White, Innermost College of Secret Nalanda.'

I repeated the oath after my brother but hesitated while drinking the white liquid.

'Drink the rasa, Siddhartha. It is an elixir,' Bhim smiled, his robust face shining in good health, 'you cannot leave otherwise.'

Bhim the Burly was the only one in Secret Nalanda who did not feign lack of recognition and it was endearing. The liquid tasted of sandalwood and myrrh, scented like the sacraments offered in our temple ceremonies.

Our steps did not make much noise on the way back from Nalanda's secret place. I even knew what it was called now. Baladitya White, Innermost College of Secret Nalanda. We did not speak much either. All I remember are my brother's last words as we left the building, 'I know that the Black Hats are the Nine Unknowns. This I am sure of.'

'Oh really?' I retorted, 'I thought you would say the Kapalika.'

He did not reply. But when he looked askance at me, I was transported back in time. We were back in my father's court pavilion and my mother's railing against the Kapalikas echoed in my ears.

13. *The Law of Inversion*

When I returned to my cell in the early hours of the morning, I felt a foul mood coming up. Singularly alien to my physical constitution, it stayed with me for the next few days. I did not hear from my brother. Neither of us knew what to do next. Or so I believed. He had disappeared into the very lavish Royal Vihara, his world and mine cordoned off by the special luxuries and benefits accorded to him, like slaves and horse carriages. Benefits that my masters and the Mahasiddhas enjoyed as well, leaving me to be further alienated in this very special place reserved only for clowns and foolish monks.

I made a few enquiries with the Seals Officers, since they knew everything. It so happened that they did know of my brother's movements. I was told that he had rushed back to Pataliputra because his wife had given birth.

'His wife was with child?' I was aghast that in all these days Aditya Raj had mentioned nothing of it. I recalled how he had avoided introducing me to his wife during the Baisakh festival.

But what use would a monk have for such things, he had said, I remembered bitterly.

No instructions were forthcoming from the Diplomatic Enquiry either. As expected, not a single summon came to me in the next few days. Except one to vote for an increase in butter and honey rations for under-age novices.

My efforts to corner Bhim, Asita and Tarpa and confront

them about Secret Nalanda were in vain. Every attempt received a standard response.

'Remember the oath, Secret Nalanda brother.'

It was interesting how Dharmapada had disappeared from Nalanda's conscious memory. Neither monk nor master ever enquired about him, and there were no references or mentions in assemblies. The death of an existence comes only with the death of the memory of that existence. It seemed so with Dharmapada. He had drowned in a unanimous code of amnesia.

After much deliberation, and in spite of the risks involved, I was determined to investigate on my own. I decided to pay a visit to Rama, Rahula's cousin. Rama's father was a Nalanda temple priest, and brother to Rahula's father, a pandita in Vikramshila University. During the last monsoon retreat, we had all become very close. We had spent much time together when our lectures stopped because of the rains. I would often tease Rama and Rahula that good looks ran in their family, and all the sculptures of Buddha were made in their likenesses. Rahula became jealous of my closeness with Rama, and Rama and I drifted apart. I hadn't seen him for an entire year.

Wending my way through the broad opulent lanes of the temple priest colony, I found Rama's family mansion just behind the artisan's guild. His father told me that Rama was at the guild treasury, preparing for the Nine Day Goddess Festival. I retraced my steps and found him sitting at the entrance of a storehouse, making inventories on a fat ledger. The storehouse was crammed from the ceiling to floor with bolts of red Goddess cloth.

And though he greeted me cautiously, I knew he would be less tight-lipped than all the Nalanda monks because he was not tied by codes of silence. And I was in luck.

He knew Gauri and her family. They were four sisters who came regularly for Kumari worship and devotional music at the temples. Yes, the fat lady was their mother. The mother was a high priestess at the Wisdom Temple of the Headless Goddess located a day's mule ride from Nalanda. The mother was primarily of moolanivasi descent, but her lineage had been mixed by many generations in the Pataliputra courtesan boudoirs. It came as a surprise to me that high priestesses traced their lineage to courtesanry, and I said so. Rama said this was common knowledge in the inner circles.

Is it true then, I asked, that the temple kumaris we see every day during deity worship are prostitutes?

Rama stopped writing on his fat, well-thumbed ledger of yellowing parchment cloth and looked at me from under raised eyebrows.

'You mean you didn't know?' he taunted.

His taunt put to rest the torment of many unslept nights.

'But what of the vows of celibacy?' I despaired. 'The common and uncommon oaths, the ordinations, the Vinaya rules? The Buddhist samaya code?'

'Hinayanist rules. Applicable only to acolytes, novices and unsworn monks,' he said, and after treating me to an implacable stare, he added, 'like you.' Bilwa's sad bloodied figure came to mind and I pushed away his prophetic words.

'It makes sense now,' I said after an interminable silence during which he had got back to poring into his ledger and I to staring at the uncountable shades of red around me.

'Why did Dharmapada have the washerman pimp Vishnu whipped?' When Rama did not reply, I answered the question anyway.

'It was not because Vishnu the washerman was giving the university a bad name. It was because he was breaking the code of silence.'

'It's the code of silence that ensures that Nalanda is still functioning, brother,' he replied, cutting the ledger string with his teeth. 'Without it, Nalanda would be razed to the ground.'

Rama was refreshingly open about what he knew. He corroborated the suspicion that Dharmapada belonged to a secret society specific to Baladitya White by disclosing its name. They were called Vidyadharas and had a penchant for young girls. He knew because Dharmapada would frequently come to his temple asking after the kumaris. Kumaris like Gauri openly talked about their association with Vidyadharas. Vidyadharas were known in Baladitya White as an elite core of the most powerful sorcerers and alchemists in the world. Their code word was Kapalika. He furnished after some searching a Vidyadhara seal he had forged for someone he knew. I did not ask who that someone was. Neither did he say. The seal was embossed with the figure of a flying man with a short broad magic sword, the Vajra, or thunderbolt. He said I could keep the seal. I looked at his clean handsome face and told him I was deeply grateful.

'All about us, the Turks strengthen their battlements around Nalanda. To revive Brahminism, enemy kings offer a gold coin for every Buddhist monk's head, and you remain wrapped in strange reveries. What's wrong with you, brother?' Rama jibed. Refusing to pay heed to the apocalyptic scenario he so vividly painted, I insisted he divulge whatever else he knew.

'Almost every monastery has a secret conclave of initiates enrolled in the Baladitya White College,' Rama explained, finally caving under my dogged insistence. But mostly they were of the high sciences. The Winds and Channels conclave manipulated various known and unknown energies. Vimana mastered flying aircrafts. Cosmology and Medicine conclaves were quiet but very active. It was the Vidyadharas who were endangering the secret conclaves with their explosive instability. They were so uncontrolled that it was feared that this conclave would throw Nalanda's fulcrum off its axis.

'Are they also called the Black Hats?' I asked. Rama ruminated for a while, and then shook his head, his topknot swinging from side to side. Rama was a Brahmin priest. Since he was not an ordained monk, he could, from a young age, wear his hair to any lustre and length. Amongst Nalanda's hierarchy the lustrous topknot was only allowed to the mahapanditas, acharyas and arhats.

'No,' he said, 'I have never heard of the Black Hats.'

I was taken aback by this. What was it then that existed in the pulsating core of Nalanda?

'Have you heard of the Nine Unknowns?'

Rama looked blank as I watched him mentally frame his answer.

'Only that centuries ago, Emperor Ashoka created this secret conclave here to protect forbidden knowledge. Most people have never heard of the Nine Unknowns because they do not know that forbidden knowledge exists, so they don't know it needs to be protected. As far as I know, it's just a myth recounted by bored monks during idle monsoon retreats.'

Yet, I remembered with a riffle of excitement, Aditya Raj had claimed information of its secret seal. The code word for the Nine Unknowns is Nine, and Kapalika for the rival cult, I remembered him saying.

'What do you know about the Kapalikas?' was my final question. 'Are all Vidyadhara sorcerers Kapalikas?'

'All Vidyadhara sorcerers are Kapalikas. But not all Kapalikas are Vidyadharas.'

'That's profound. Would you care to expound, Mahapandita?' I taunted.

Rama laughed in that open carefree manner of his.

'I'm only telling you what I have learnt from my father,' he said, 'Kapalika is the pause between the breath of two great religions, Brahminism and Buddhism. And the Dakini holds that breath.'

'I said, expound, not confound!' I exclaimed, again feeling overpowered by a familiar exhaustion.

'I only repeat what I have heard from the elders,' Rama laughed.

'Now that you have the seal, I presume you are a Vidyadhara?'

'Did I not mention that only monks and acharyas can be members? I am just a poor temple priest.'

When I left Rama, I felt I knew everything and nothing at all.

In the inexplicable and interminable waiting, I was loathe to attend the quotidian routine of my studies. I shunned the monotony of a discipline that had been providing unceasing succour till just a few days ago. Days now seemed like years. I needed some way to put some order in the chaos that I had witnessed. Chaos that can only be described as insanity. Insanity that was sucking me into its core, and would surely turn me insane too, if I didn't put it in order, even though I failed at every attempt. I needed to speak to someone within the university.

The first person I thought of was Rahula, even though he was behaving strangely lately. He seemed to be avoiding me. Was he behaving strangely because I was behaving strangely? Every time I reached across to speak to him across our adjoining cell walls, my mind would become fuzzy and I would lose my train of thoughts.

Who wielded power over the Black Hats in the roofless temple? Dharmapada or my masters? Or Dakinis? Bilwa had said that Dakinis guarded the consciousness treasures. What was a consciousness treasure? Was it the forbidden knowledge of the Nine Unknowns? If so, who were they? Was the presence of women at Nalanda's core a sign of the deep rot within Nalanda? Surely then, the knowledge guarded for centuries by humanity's guardians, Emperor Ashoka's Nine Unknowns, was in terrible danger.

The clues to these mysteries were buried in the manner of Dharmapada's death, for sure.

Every time a coherent thought flashed in my mind, it would vanish when I tried to write it down. Could it be that the rasa I had been given by the dwarapalas had psychedelic qualities? I noticed that every morning, I would wake up in the same foul mood. This was by far the most frightening consequence of recent events, this fear that your mind was not your own. I wondered whether it was similar with my brother and the Secret Nalanda members.

In the quiet of lecture classrooms, I attempted repeatedly to note down my thoughts on a slate with a chalk, but was simply unable to write. However, words on topics unassociated with Secret Nalanda flowed fluently.

Could it be that when one was guilty, the oath was more binding than one knew? Did the elixir work on heightened mental states? Like obsessive secrecy, for example, I rationalised. Maybe the oath was not binding in places where the truth was already revealed, my theory went, for whatever my altered consciousness was worth.

I started taking all my meals at Baladitya College and surreptitiously stalked its monks. But I did not see a scrap of the secret gold-embossed white robes in all my espionage. One day, a monastery karmadana came face to face as I was skulking around in the kitchens. He had a sheaf of printing material in his hands and his well-groomed moustache bristled with calm brevity.

'You are henceforth forbidden to set foot at the Baladitya monastery again.' At a distance, a cook looked up and went back to stirring oil in a huge wok on a blackened mud stove.

In my nervousness I knocked off some brass utensils and stammered incoherently.

'On whose orders?'

But the karmadana had left and all I could see was his pirouetting silk clad behind.

He accosted me again at the indigo mills. I had crept behind a mound of blue dye in the collecting shed and was trying to make notes on my sanghati with colour.

'You are henceforth forbidden to set foot at the indigo mills.' Again he had appeared from nowhere and left, swinging his silken behind.

As an experiment, I decided to go to the slave quarters with The Broken One. He was incapable of lying even if he wanted and would never betray an oath even if he tried, and that simplified things. Nature had made his mind that way. After much cajoling, he agreed to go with me to the slave quarters. Instinct told me I was on the right track. I was convinced that the slave quarters was no man's land where all Nalanda codes broke down. It was not a coincidence that Dharmapada died here.

The Broken One was the most childlike amongst all of us and we expended much energy in protecting him from rapacious monks. Since he was not ordained but adopted as an orphan by Nalanda, he was neither laity nor monk. His status was somewhere in between, like the slave quarters, neither here nor there.

He sat on a mound of potter's mud in the deserted village, looking at me quizzically. His curly hair was unshaven unlike ours, but he wore monochromatic robes like us. He listened with great attention, his bow lips pursed and his head cocked to one side.

From somewhere deep within the deserted village emanated the sound of anklets and haunting melodies of unknown origin. I held my partner's gaze, pretending I had not heard the village's feminine presence making itself felt.

'Nalanda is an amra fruit,' I declared, so relieved to finally sort my thoughts out. 'The tough outer layer is the monastic establishment, bound by rules and vows. The flesh of the fruit is Secret Nalanda, the Baladitya White. It's fluid here and the rules are not so hard. The flesh of the fruit is always the object of desire. Also known as Mahayana, it is what the world wants. The monastic establishment, the outer layer, simply gives the shape and form to the fruit, but it has no content. In fact, to eat the fruit, one peels off and discards the outer layer, also known as Hinayana. But it is the innermost core of this fruit, the part that is thrown away after consumption, that burrows deep in the underground. It carries the powerful essence of the fruit, its imprint. I am talking, Broken One, of Innermost Nalanda. The seed. The Black Hats. The black heart of Nalanda.'

'You mean the Nine Unknowns,' he said. My feet slipped on the soft potter's mud as I ran up the mound to shake his shoulders. Since my brother had first mentioned them, the Nine Unknowns had become my last waking thought at night and the first at daybreak.

'Did you just say Nine Unknowns?' I shook his shoulders till I heard his bones rattle. The Broken One could never look you in the eye. He always spoke to a distance away from your face.

'The unbroken lineage of the Nines started by King Ashoka has been living and breathing in Nalanda in secret for centuries. They are right here, ready to die protecting forbidden knowledge.' I held my breath. Was he telling me that Dharmapada was a Nine? Did he die protecting forbidden knowledge?

The more I stared at the Broken One, the more distant he became. Fidgeting with the hem of his robe, he avoided my searing gaze.

'Each is committed to protecting one of the nine books. On no account must any of the books be exposed to humanity because the inability to comprehend only misuses and limits what cannot be grasped.'

'How do you know all this?' I demanded.

'Because I'm a Black Hat,' he simply said.

'What did you just say?' I must have looked utterly foolish, but the Broken One couldn't have noticed because he was incapable of judging anyone.

'I'm chief calibrator for the Brahmastra,' he continued as simply as before. I stared at him open-mouthed before collecting my senses and bombarding him with questions.

'What do you know about the Vidyadharas?' Instinctively I was making the most of a unique opportunity.

'The sky-faring holder of the short broad sword. He has command of all the magic known to mankind. Many white hats are Vidyadharas. They can fly, create objects from thin air, hypnotise, and turn base metals to gold.'

'What separates the Vidyadhara sorcerers from the Nine Unknowns?'

'Forbidden knowledge of the Nine Unknowns must be protected primarily from the Vidyadharas. They have been stealing and misusing forbidden knowledge for too long. That is why it is only accessible to the Black Hats.'

'What is this forbidden knowledge?' I asked as Aditya Raj flashed before my eyes. Dharmapada had died trying to access that knowledge he had said. How many more would die before Mahipala got it, I wondered.

'I can't say,' said Broken One for the first time. There was silence. I plummeted into the depths of disappointment.

'But you can't lie!' I complained, bereft of my strategy.

'Yes, that is true,' the Broken One replied. 'But I can keep silent.'

'Why are women wearing Black Hats?' I demanded.

Again he was silent.

'Why must I always be the ignorant one?' I smashed a stone against a potter's wheel and involuntarily sent it spinning in the sultry silence.

'Why do you answer some questions but not others?' I asked accusingly. If I had hair, I would have torn it out in frustration.

'Because my oaths are different from yours,' he said. In my anger I sent a few more stones flying across the potter's wheel while he concentrated on a particular thread in his sanghati. After a pause, he said, 'Look behind you.' I turned to see Siroha, resplendent and perfumed, towering over me, a parrot perched on his shoulder. Behind him was the monastery karmadana smiling genially under his bristling moustache.

'The Abbot's cur,' Siroha the Unconquerable dropped a casual glance at the Broken One, 'and Aryadatta's cur.' He then turned to look at me.

'Confabulating. Who will save you from the severe consequences of breaking your oath?' he asked me.

My experiment had not worked. There was obviously no way the oath could be broken. I had to think fast.

'The oath doesn't apply to Black Hats,' I offered.

'He is right,' Siroha said without blinking. I exhaled at my unexpected fortune.

'I'm also in a mellow mood. So you just escaped a fate worse than death.' He turned to walk away and I spotted a short blunt sword blinking from under his robes.

'Sword and diadem are the signs of the Vidyadhara,' the Broken One whispered beside me. As we all walked out, the Broken One broke the eerie silence of the abandoned village with a monotonous litany.

'Hair lock, diadem, armband, pearl necklace, belt hammer and sword are the accoutrements of a Vidyadhara. A Kapalika wears a bone necklace, earrings, a hair jewel, skullbowl, ashes and a sacred thread, and bears a trident and sleeps on human skin. The Nine Unknown books are on the sciences of propaganda to control mass opinion, physiology, biological molecules, alchemy, communication, gravity, cosmogony, light and the evolution of societies.'

I dared not speak.

Ahead of us, the karmadana cheerfully turned around to say, 'You are henceforth forbidden from setting foot in the slave quarters again.' And then, as if to sear into my consciousness, many things happened at the same time. The parrot on Siroha the Unconquerable's shoulder flapped its wings and screeched, 'Law of inversion!'

As I remembered that this is what the parrot from Siroha's shoulder had said that fateful night, shattering the Secret Nalanda silence, I also remembered Dharmapada's mutilated member. At the same time, I heard the tinkling of anklets from the wooden posts of an abandoned hut and the Broken One continued to speak to me in his characteristic monotone.

'Yes, Nalanda brother, you should apply the law of inversion,' the Broken One said. The moment was over. Ahead, Siroha the Unconquerable was still within earshot.

'I must be relieved of my duties of patrolling these idiots.' He was admonishing the monastery karmadana. 'I can't see why Aryadatta's cur is being given so many pardons. I know so many who have been killed with the death code at their first offence.'

But I wasn't listening to Siroha. It was the Broken One who had my rapt attention.

'Why are women wearing black hats, apply the law of inversion,' were his last stacatto words as he left me. This time he looked me straight in the eye.

As the legend goes there was a time when Nalanda ruled with such benevolent compassion that everything around it bloomed and flourished. Now only poisonous flowers bloomed and shadows flourished. Try as I might, I could not bear the thought of facing my master. The more I confronted this imperative, the more abhorrent it became to me. I waited for summons. To my relief, they didn't come.

I could not shake off the feeling that I was a mute bystander at the shore of time, watching Lord Mahakala rise up to the full height of a tidal wave. I was frozen in the moment before it swooped down to devour my era.

I went about my day avoiding everyone I knew. I tried to make myself as inconspicuous as possible. This was when I accidentally stumbled upon another mysterious article in Rahula's cell.

Since I had been too distracted to maintain the strict university routine after my visit to Nalanda's forbidden place, I had started skipping meals at the dining hall. Prohibition from the Baladitya meals had also whetted my appetite for food. Hoping to borrow some of Rahula's rations of ground millet, I entered my neighbouring cell.

I found Asita the Great sprawled on Rahula's straw pallet. Strangely, I did not feel awkward seeing him outside Secret Nalanda anymore. I even grudgingly admired him for his restraint. Not once did he question me about why I was there that fated night or who my companion was. Yet, Bilwa's sad big eyes were an unspoken and bloody presence between us. And suddenly Asita's sprawled out complacency irritated me.

'Rahula has been appointed to the Herbarium for today's service,' Asita informed, and I did not like that he knew more about Rahula than I did.

'I could ask you why you are sleeping at this appointed hour for service, but I won't. Considering that you are a great prince, rules don't apply to privileged ones like you, only poor miserable monks like us,' I said, hoping that he would be impressed by my allusion that I too was a prince, though humble about my origins.

I did not care for his response. 'My greatness,' he said, 'O Noble Born, does not come from my birth, but from my personal achievements.'

'O but surely that's true,' I parried, dripping sarcasm. And then I saw in Rahula's pit, stuffed between his earthen water jug and the clepsydra, an unusual looking manuscript.

In a flash, before Asita could stop me, I had it in my hands. The manuscript was written on palm leaves, very different from the Nalanda style. It was named *The Action Seal* in the Pali canon. The name burnt through my shifting altering consciousness.

Maybe it made an impression because it had no previous known connotation or reference.

'We are not allowed to keep manuscripts in our cells.' My suspicion was sharp.

Before I knew it, the manuscript was back in his hands.

'This does not belong to Rahula. It belongs to me,' he said.

We stood face to face in direct confrontation. I realised that I had recognised the seal on the manuscript before Asita snatched it away from me. This manuscript was not embossed with the typical Sarnath symbol that was the motif of all Nalanda library seals or even the prohibited Dharmachakra seal of Secret Nalanda. This one had two deer flanking an inverted palm leaf. I had seen this seal before. Only a few days before. On the threshold of the Brahmastra chamber.

I broke into a cold sweat.

'I apologise,' I mumbled to Asita, 'I made a mistake.'

I stumbled out of the hostel. Although I had seen Asita cross me on that fateful night inside Secret Nalanda, this seal was an identification of the Innermost Nalanda, the Black Hats, maybe the Nine Unknowns. Or Kapalikas.

Though I could not be sure whether Rahula was part of them, evidently Asita was.

It was an hour after noon. My hunger forgotten, I ran to the Seals Department where my service was appointed. If I could find where the Inverted Palm Seal originated, I would know who controlled and administered the Black Hats. I cursed myself for not coming up with this idea as soon as I was out of Secret Nalanda. I had put my life in danger, risked the death code, blundering about looking for answers when it had been staring me in the face. All I needed to do was find who sanctioned the Inverted Palm Seal, where and, hopefully, why.

My mind was not focussed as I ran. I noticed my environment in fragments. An officer saw me and suspiciously hurried towards the Chancellor cells. I saw a shrine. An edifice. I saw an amorous stucco panel I had never noticed before. At a distance, readers on lecterns recited holy scriptures. An ordination ceremony was being conducted by a master in Kapalika bone ornaments. Obviously, I was not seeing right. Would my impaired vision lead to blindness? Keep following the Law, voices in my head said. Into the dreaded morrow. *The mind is conjuring charnel ground descriptions. Into the dreaded morrow. The dreaded morrow? The dreaded morrow*! I realised my cognition was now as fragmented as my surroundings. Is this what the Chinese scholar meant when she said, 'those who walk the path with arrogance will be destroyed'? *Had the Great Goddess awakened within my body? Did Dharmapada's awakened state cause him to self-destruct? Would I be the next one to be destroyed by Her?*

Or is this a form of mesmerism Nalanda used to control its inhabitants? Concocted in its inner precincts, handed out by dwarapalas who forced you to swallow its secrets. Was the rasa laced with the death code programmed for the destruction of those who broke the Secret Nalanda oath? Is that why Dharmapada died? Did the death code kill him because he broke the oath?

I stopped at a fountain and let the gurgling water run over me for ten breaths. The image of Dharmapada's lanky body swaying in the Dragon Body conference persisted, refusing to be washed away by the water gushing over my cold head. When I finally reached the Seals Department, the dharmapala officers and dwarapala guards were not on duty. The karmadana administrative officers too were probably at their midday meal. I pronounced the sound codes five times and the password opened the lock with a snap. Monks like me who performed regular service at the Seals Department were given the sound codes in strict confidence.

Inside were many chambers and cells where the Seals Officers sat. They said that the Seals Officers were more powerful than the grandmasters. Since correspondence and all business was transacted through seals, they had their finger on the pulse of Nalanda. The Seals Office has the power to give permission or deny it. Almost every aspect of our life has the stamp of a seal on it. The grains in the kitchens, appliances in workshops, scrolls, letters, applications, were all embossed by the stamp of approval of a seal that came through the Seals Department.

My service was to keep an inventory for the material required by the seal cutters. These were copper, wax, clay, stone and some semi-precious and precious stones.

Since I was familiar with the environs, I made straight for the Seals Library, just beyond the seal cutter workshops.

Even though I tried to cross the seal cutter tool floor quietly, in my nervousness I overturned a clay jar and copper chisels; drills and blades clattered across the hall. The noise startled me and I stubbed my toe on a whetstone. My heart thudding in my chest, I crouched behind an engraving machine, waiting for approaching footsteps. But there was no one around, so I moved on. I tried not to race like my thoughts, but it was difficult.

The last few days of solitary contemplation had brought out clear and certain facts for me.

The Black Hat sect probably comprised the Nine Unknown masters who were in most likelihood confined to the circular roofless temple. I was not sure whether the Nine Unknowns were Kapalika or Vidyadhara and whether my master and the Abbot or Dharmapada were part of them. However, I was reasonably certain that Mahipala was in conflict with the Nine Unknowns. My brother had already confessed that Dharmapada had been aiding Mahipala in procuring the forbidden knowledge of Black Hat Nalanda.

So are my masters the Black Hats and did they kill Dharmapada? Is there a conspiracy against the king as well? Is my brother in danger? Would I be asked to kill him? And if I was asked, would I do it? Would I kill my brother to obey my masters?

The answers lay behind the stone latticed wall embossed by the Inverted Palm Seal in Innermost Nalanda. But if the inverted palm was a Nalanda seal, then I would find its origin somewhere in the Seals Department.

I looked around at the Seals Department's labyrinth. There were thousands of seals operating in Nalanda. For easy facilitation the Seals offices were architecturally arranged in a way that resembled Nalanda's layout. Each office was a small cubicle big enough for an officer to sit on a low desk with small box-like stone chambers to keep his official letters, scrolls and applications. Each office was embossed by an imprint of the seal they issued.

What was important was that these offices faithfully replicated the geographical structure of Nalanda. If there was an office that was transacting the Inverted Palm Seal, it would be proof that the stamp of approval to operate the seal was coming from my masters. They were officially involved. I might even get to know how and why. If it was a royal seal, or one unlawfully appropriated by the Abbot, that too would show up.

Still, inspite of four years of voluntary service in the Seals Department, I got lost in its maze of offices.

The chamber of the Supreme Body that elected the Abbot was sealed and counter sealed. The Department of Interpreters had many sub-departments that took much time to inspect. I crossed the department that categorised all the followers of panditas. There were separate seals for the evaluations made by followers for their panditas. I crossed the departments of Gatekeepers, Deputies and Document Handlers. I went through all the farms. The dairy farms, sheep, goat and buffalo. I sifted through the much-used seals of viceroys, counsellors and ministers. The Ecclesiastical Council, the Assembly of Superintendents, the Masters of Acolytes.

I wasted a lot of time at the seals of the trading posts. Merchants transacted the sale of manuscripts here, original and translated, and there were at least a hundred different types of seals to go through.

Every monastery had an administrative office. Some instinct made me focus on their Administration Office seals. Here is where, after much sweat, toil and tears, my efforts bore fruit.

There, in front of me, in the administrative section of the Sitavana Monastery was clearly embossed the seal of the inverted palm leaf. Made of copper, wax and clay, a small number, around fifty seals, were locked away behind iron meshes. Looking at Nalanda's layout, I could see Sitavana architecturally linked to the roofless temple in the heart of Nalanda's secret core. But most of it led to uninhabitable moolanivasi forest land. It was difficult to tell who held sway here, the Abbot's Office or the Royal Vihara. It could well be that Sitavana was the battle line drawn between the two.

I became acutely conscious of my heart thudding in my chest. Outside the open window, I heard the sound of a moolanivasi water-carrier filling water in the office tank. I quietly made my way out of the deserted office chambers before he could hear my footsteps or see me.

The Sitavana Monastery, dedicated to the famed Mahasiddha Nagarjuna, was one of the most inaccessible monasteries in Nalanda. Many thought Sitavana's inaccessibility was because of decrepitude created by centuries of disuse. But monks spoke about the Rasayana Mercury laboratories within Sitavana and its mysterious masters in hushed whispers. It was common knowledge that besides the heavily padlocked main entrance from Nalanda, Sitavana could also be reached through a dense forest infested with poisonous snakes. But only the suicidal or insane would attempt to step into the forest, and I didn't know anyone who had. A river ran through this forest. They said that it was so dark that no light passed through it. Like Sitavana, there were other prohibited places within Nalanda that were sealed by the Dharmachakra. These were never known to have been trespassed. And I do not know of anyone who tried. Or wanted to. But now I knew that Sitavana was not only sealed with the Dharmachakra but also with the Inverted Palm Seal Issued by the Abbot. The Inverted Palm sequestered the Black Hats not only from the rest of Secret Nalanda but from Mahipala himself. Therefore, it was amply clear that Sitavana was the officially sanctioned Nine Unknown Black Hat territory.

I did not know anybody who desired to work or live in the Sitavana Monastery, even though it was common knowledge that Nagarjuna's gold mint was within its premises. I had dreamt about it only a few nights ago. It had convinced me that Sitavana led to the Sonapahar hills where whole mountains were made of gold. Looking at Nalanda's geographical simulacrum created by the Seals office labyrinth, I reconfirmed that Innermost Nalanda was a circular roofless temple sealed by the Inverted Palm. It could be accessed through Sitavana whose forest traversed the entire university like a spine, or through Secret Nalanda, where my brother's seal had been stopped short by the Inverted Palm Seal. I doubted that my brother was aware of the forest path to Sitavana. Maybe this was what he was hoping to find, and this was why he was in Nalanda. Dharmapada was just a pretext. If so, my brother's mission had just been accomplished.

I consigned the architectural layout to memory. The forest grew straight and narrow between two Nalanda boundary walls into the centre of Nalanda and ended at the circular roofless temple, like a heart seed at the point of a needle. All I needed to find was whether the heart seed was really as black as I expected it to be.

Sitavana existed in full public view of the main roads of Nalanda. But the forest path was the only way to enter it without a seal. Maybe Dharmapada died trying to find this way. Unless he was a Nine Unknown who died protecting forbidden knowledge. I wondered what the Nine Unknown protocol entailed for a Nine who was murdered or died. Burial in the samadhi shrines of the siddhas? Like Dharmapada? Because he was a Nine?

I had to get inside Sitavana. And fortunately for me, I was not scared of snakes. Or death. If that was what the masters had decided for me, so be it, I thought.

I made preparations for my journey. I finally stole Rahula's rations of ground millet. It would last me at least three days. I pawned my monk's sandals for a pair of sturdy Turkish leather at the traders' market. From the astronomy library, I rented, actually stole, a pirated acoustic device to decode sound codes and a copy of my brother's eye piece. I also took some marijuana for medicinal purposes and venom antidote from my monastery's apothecary, and I felt ready to face certain death.

I left at daybreak. Day seemed to turn into night as soon as I entered the forest. A forest that even the moolanivasis seemed to avoid—there were solitary, crude, abandoned mud hutments I crossed once in a rare while. The jungle was a forsaken place choking with the heavy aroma of decomposing greenery. I believe I escaped the snakes only because I stayed the course of the river. I crossed it bit by bit on makeshift rope vine bridges. The river was infested with crocodiles, but as long as I kept my balance, I was safe from them.

After a while, I ran out of luck. Around mid-day, I realised there were no more bridges to cross. I looked about me. I reasoned that if I ran across two hillocks, as the crow flies, I would soon reach the Nalanda boundary wall that was visible to me from a distance. From where I stood on the rotting river-crossing rope vine, the bleached Nalanda stones looked like an ethereal paradise. If the snakes didn't get me, I might live to tell the tale, I thought. For a moment, I contemplated the suicidal foolhardiness of my decision, and then with a deep breath I called out to the Buddha and made a run for it.

The terrain was stony and relatively dry. My Turkish leather provided a good grip on the loamy soil and I ran with a steady speed. I mentally thanked the punishing physical regimen our monastery karmadanas subjected us to. Running up the hillock, I saw a broken moolanivasi stone shrine at its peak, a few furloughs away. If I could cross the shrine and the succeeding hillock, I would reach the Nalanda stones. It didn't look far. If I kept my pace steady, I would reach it before my breath ran out.

As I ran, I kept my gaze fixed on the Nalanda stones, but I could hear slow hisses erupting behind me. I turned momentarily to see the entire hillock come slithering to life. I had awakened hundreds of supine serpents. I picked up speed even as I lost hope for my life. As the earth trembled under my panic-driven feet, I roused to life more and more snakes. They slithered and lashed in great speed after me. They were countless, enormous and lightning fast. I was certain they would overtake me by the time I reached the hilltop shrine. I was not going to make it.

My pace flagged as the hissing around me grew louder, filling me with a surreal sense of surrender to my impending death. Sweat streamed into my eyes as I looked up one last time towards the hilltop shrine and this time I saw a woman standing on its stone platform. Completely naked, she had an infant suckling at her breast. With one hand nestling the infant and the other waving a kettledrum, she stamped her feet in an utterly wild, impetuous dance.

Thunderstruck, I almost stopped to stare at her as I believe did all the snakes chasing me. Her eyes were black as the cosmos.

As I kept running, I became dimly conscious of reading her lips.

She was moving them to say, 'Go!'

And then the wind carried her next words to me like an ancient voice from the sky.

'Follow the law of inversion.' I clearly heard these words.

I crossed the second hillock with ease and before I even noticed it, I had reached the Nalanda rampart. I could see her at a distance, still dancing on the stone platform to a wild tune on the kettledrum I could no longer hear, thousands of snakes at her feet, hoods raised, waving their boneless bodies to her rhythm.

I had left at daybreak and had traversed the forest for half a day by the time I reached the Nalanda wall. Following the boundary wall, it was late afternoon when I found the wooden gate leading to Sitavana. Sitavana was walled and surrounded by a crocodile-infested moat. From the gate where I stood, the interior gate could be reached by a creaky and rotten wooden drawbridge.

Here I was presented with the next problem. Sitavana was guarded by a dwarapala round the water clock. From my perch on an unused overhead watch tower, I discerned one master and two monks who comprised the important traffic the gates of Sitavana received. By appearance all three of them looked like moolanivasi native inhabitants of the forest. For the first time, in an institution as rank-conscious as Nalanda, I saw moolanivasis receive entry into a monastery, and at one as legendary as Sitavana. I again thanked the mischievous cell mates with whose help I had learnt the method to decipher the sound codes of a gate. The acoustic device placed at the gate, the eye piece I had borrowed from Aditya Raj, and the risk of losing body and limb revealed to me the sounds necessary.

It was late afternoon when I walked into the mysteries of Sitavana.

Still alive.

I would finally know the truth behind Dharmapada's death. I would open forever what the inverted seal of decadent Buddhism concealed. I was more determined than ever.

14. *Sitavana*

No sooner had I stepped into Sitavana than I realised I had been bitten by two snakes, poisonous no less. But I had travelled prepared with antidotes to snake venom, stolen from my monastery herbarium. Other than a slight giddiness I was fine, and very grateful for the physical health that I had been blessed with.

Snakes made eminent sense at Sitavana. Sitavana's presiding deity, the grandmaster Mahasiddha Nagarjuna's name meant that he was the conqueror of Nagas, or snakes. Snakes are commonly found in the most prohibited areas of Nalanda. Moolanivasi natives of our forest land are also called Naga. According to some folklores, Nagarjuna got his name because he had received alchemy knowledge from the moolanivasi Nagas. Turning base metal into gold was just one of the secrets he had known.

Nagarjuna, a Brahmin Mahasiddha Nalanda grandmaster from the South, was so prolific and lived for so long that future historians would study his works and wonder whether they were written by one person or more. He was the creator of both the logical theory of Dependent Origination and the gold mints.

Even in my time, we were not sure whether he was alive or not. Many masters said they received instructions from him. A few months ago, an entire college supposedly attended his lecture.

Now that I had the sound codes, I confidently walked up

and entered the interior gates of Sitavana without making eye contact with the dwarapala sentinel.

To the east, my eyes followed the ubiquitous Nalanda boundary wall till I saw the iconic installation of the Dark One as a speck in the distance. I immediately recognised it as the Ten Wisdom College. Dense foliage spanned the distance between me and the speck, but the verdure was garden variety and surely not snake infested, I could tell. A small one-hinge gate opened into the Ten Wisdom College. I knew gates like that. One could get out but not in through such gates. The gate brought me a wave of relief, I would not have to brave snakes and crocodiles on the way to my monastery.

I decided to bring my attention back to the strange powdery light and the overpowering scent of the Sitavana Monastery. The deathly quiet of an enigmatic afternoon was taking me out of my haze and heightening my sensory awareness to a fine point. I became conscious that I stood on ground that was meant for a chosen few. It was also dangerous ground, much more dangerous than the forest I had crossed. The back of my neck prickled with anticipation. I felt the presence of mahasiddhas watching me, detached, without curiosity.

A cursory glance and I recognised the latticework of another perambulating wall. I had reached the roofless temple.

The Nine Unknowns were close now, so close, I thought. The most forbidden Black Hats. The heart of the secret.

Pigeon wings flapped against the ear, and the satin sound of a bat in flight brought my attention to broken temple doors and the still trapped air of its pavilion in ruin.

Inside, I expected to find a deity statue or some other iconographical representation. Instead, there was an inscription mounted in copper on a standard issue iron Ashokan pillar. I read it with mounting curiosity. The Oath of the Nine Unknowns, it said. Surprised that an inscription so exclusive was written in the Pali canon, and not Sanskrit, I read it aloud.

My father is Wisdom.
My mother is Voidness.
My country is the country of Dharma.
I am of no caste.
And no creed.
I am sustained by perplexity.
I am here to destroy anger, sloth and lust.

My eyes were riveted by the inscription. My nose prickled with a sudden smell of sandalwood in the air. The plaintive song of a cuckoo heightened the heavy silence of Sitavana. Legend was replete with many Sitavana siddhas. I remembered hearing of a Sitavana siddha so evolved that eating his flesh made people immortal. Idle courtyard chatter came to me in a rush. I recalled another whose funeral pyre supposedly burnt for four days. It left behind a crystal of magical powers. I stood there trying to remember the siddha's name.

An infant mewled behind me. Stricken, I turned like a whiplash to face the sound.

And there she was again, in all her glory, so close I could have touched her. Still as naked as the moment she was born. Her streaming hair like a swarm of black bees covered much of her and her naked infant. Her only adornment was a nose ring on a petulant nose. It looked like the customary nose ring courtesans wear after they are first deflowered, or a noble woman wears during her wedding.

I gazed at her, knowing that this was my first visitation of a human Dakini. She did not look like a fearsome, flesh-eating witch, yet I feared for the infant she nursed. I did not know what to do. Would she kill me if I thanked her for saving my life?

'It was wonderful how you moved with the snakes,' I started by way of polite conversation.

'I did not move with the snakes. They moved with me,' her voice stung my ear with the vibrating buzz of a bee.

Blood was leaving my veins, making me suddenly light-headed again. I dared not move or breathe lest the conversational mood break and she question my presence. Rooted to the spot, I tentatively enquired.

'Who are you?'

'I'm sometimes called the powerful outlaw.' She was looking amused now, conversational even. The baby smacked at her breast.

'Where have you come from?' I ventured a little more.

'From the Pure Lands,' she said. 'Pure of men,' she added as an afterthought.

For a moment I thought maybe I had swallowed my tongue. Even though I was reeling under her devastating magnetism, I was determined to avail myself of as much information as I could.

'Can I enter?' I gestured at the roofless temple.

'No,' she slowly shook her head, all the while rocking her baby. 'Why do you think I'm here? I'm the guardian of this gate.'

Very slowly, I removed my eye piece from my sanghati.

'Can I see from far?' I gently pleaded. When she did not object, I removed the lantana branches and focussed my eye piece to look inside the roofless temple.

There was nothing to see. Except a carpet of fine gravelly sand and a four-faced brass lamp in the middle of the circular temple, there was nothing to see. But when I looked closely, the air around the four flames shifted and when I looked even more closely, it seemed that each flame had splintered into four more flames. I was looking at a hologram. The soot and flames formed a strange runic alphabet and moved around the lamp in a perfect circle. It spontaneously picked up speed with the rising pace of my thoughts.

'The Twilight Language,' I whispered. Sandhya bhasha, the secret code of the high sciences, I remembered. For a long time I watched the circulating symbols, entranced by their unfathomable depths.

'Was Dharmapada a Nine?' I enquired without turning around.

The runic alphabet meandered with the same circularity of my thought.

'No,' she said. Somehow I was unable to locate the direction of her voice.

'My master Aryadatta?'

'No.'

'The Abbot?'

'No.'

'Will an Action Seal give me entry into the roofless temple?' I asked, still peering at the swaying unintelligible alphabets.

'Must all the buffoons come to me?' she sighed.

Startled, I looked at her. I made one last effort to see if there was a Black Hat perched somewhere in her swarming hair. I didn't see any.

'There is only one way to the roofless temple from here.' She pointed at a mountain-sized, honeycomb-like structure protruding at some distance from the circulating roofless temple wall.

'If you are unable to make it through,' she warned, 'you can exit from the Dark One's gate,' she said, pointing at the Ten Wisdom College.

I followed the direction of her finger and when I turned back to look at her, she was gone. Staggering back, my eyes frantically searched for her. I saw her next standing at the crocodile moat, gloriously naked and completely free. And again she was gone. Like a mark rubbed out of a painting.

I was left standing in front of a forest of banyan trees rustling in unknown winds and the sweet smell of burning camphor around me.

The honeycomb, though carved out of a mountain, looked like a giant beehive attached to the wall lining the roofless temple's circumference. It had several storeys crammed with caves scooped out of rock and opened into a small entrance with a sandy hall with books and parchments concealed behind transparent crystal glass.

Further in, a wondrous sculpture of Kuber, the Vedic God of Wealth, greeted me. This was an obvious indication that I was close to the Gold Mint. I was right, for on my right, a new corridor opened with an inscription indicating the alchemy laboratories of Rasayana. Next to it was another corridor leading to the heavily padlocked gates of the Gold Mint, just as I had dreamt.

The entrances to both Rasayana and the Gold Mint were emblazoned with prohibitory inscriptions and the Dharmachakra seal.

I tried my best to peer into the Rasayana labs with my eye piece. Its outside hall was large, dark and completely bare but many inscriptions and plaques had been mounted behind transparent crystal panels. Try as I might, I could not read the inscriptions clearly. They looked like methodologies for Mercury alchemists. All I could capture were a few sentences.

'Then the white moon dew is extracted,' I read a copper plaque closest to me. There was another one directly below it.

'Blackening, then whitening, then reddening by fire.'

'Bound Mercury gives flight.'

'The five elements laboratory: space, water, air, fire, earth.'

'Liberation by taste,' was from another inscription written in the almost unrecognisable Brahmi script.

Though they all sounded like chemical procedures, it was curious that the hall was devoid of any laboratory apparatus. Were these mystical symbols of the Twilight Language, I wondered. Still looking through my eye piece, I saw the entrails of animals dangling from a clothesline. Next to it were shreds of human skin left to dry. I knew it was human skin by the hair on its pores.

Somewhere from the far recesses of my consciousness surfaced a memory of monks huddling together in a cell on cold winter nights gossiping to forget the chill biting into their bones.

The three goals of alchemy, they whispered.

Immortality, youth and gold.

My logician mind struggled to rationalise the scene before my eyes with frantic theorising. The three goals of alchemy—immortality, youth and gold—were corporeal in nature, was my first premise. The human skin hanging on the clothesline, like a sanghati drying in the sun, was a corporeal means to this end. This was the second premise. The means and the end to the means were both corporeal in nature, was the third premise. Therefore, with my logical conclusion I tried to hold back my sobs, the non-corporeal nature of Buddhist compassion, karuna, and non-violence was untrue in this paradigm.

Where was Buddhist karuna in all this, Siddhartha the Doubter lamented. Where was the Buddhist mindfulness of *bodhichitta*?

What was this? A test of my resilience or another indifferent presentation of Nalanda's magical show business?

I was poring over an inscription in another narrow room with many exits when I heard a voice from behind.

'That inscription is on the control of the force of laghima or antigravity. It is the aspect of our psychological make-up that makes us levitate.'

I turned around to face Bhim the Burly's smiling face. I did not want to see him here, neither did I care for his good cheer.

'Welcome to the Honeycomb,' he beamed.

'I have taken levitation classes,' I retorted. His presence here was as unnatural as mine. He probably shared my disorienting alteration of consciousness as well. Maybe we were both undergoing the Dragon Body metamorphosis the Chinese scholar spoke about. I decided not to be intimidated by his overbearing goodnaturedness.

'Levitation is not difficult at all,' I said. 'All it needs is a few basic sound codes and some expertise in meditation. But this...,'

I gestured at the Rasayana labs, remembering the human skin I had seen through my eye piece.

'I am surprised that King Ashoka, known for his boundless compassion, could allow such sorcery. And to think that Nalanda panditas have kept their real activities secret for so many centuries.'

'Do not be so quick to judge, Nalanda brother,' Bhim said with uncharacteristic belligerence.

Not wanting to start a war in this unholy place, I hastened to change the topic.

'What is the law of inversion?' I casually asked.

'The law of inversion flips illusion to reveal its opposite as reality,' Bhim smilingly offered, his anger gone like a passing cloud.

Stupefied, I stared at Bhim, unable to come up with a suitable response.

From the corner of my eye I spotted movement. Turning a corner of the hall, by the Rasayana courtyard, I saw moolanivasi acolytes with laboratory implements, endlessly stirring mercury vats and sifting through ores. They did not look up as I walked to them. It made me wonder whether we were all in a dream.

'That's mercury,' I said, standing very close to where they sat with their instruments. Most of the implements and material substances were unfamiliar to me; this unfamiliarity filled me with foreboding. At last I pointed to a stone urn, a connection to the familiar world I knew.

'And that is sulphur,' I said.

They did not respond. Except one moolanivasi with a shaven head tattooed with blue ink, who looked at me in a piercing moment of uncharacteristic temerity. I could not identify his mood for he seemed devoid of any emotion. For some reason I found it more eerie and frightening than my situation.

Benumbed, the only real sensation that I became aware of was the smell of Bhim's sweat and the heat of an invisible sun on my head.

'You are in the mercury labs,' Bhim said. 'They are making mercury pills. For levitation. Very popular in the alchemy trade market.'

'And that is cinnabar,' he continued, pointing to a reddish ore that an acolyte monk was patiently grinding in the granite mills.

'Also found in menstrual blood,' Bhim quietly added.

My breath stuck in my throat. I gasped.

'A source of exceptional power. Just like semen, the male seed.'

'Bhim!' I exclaimed. 'What impropriety is this!'

Before Bhim could reply, I was overwhelmed with giddiness. My body trembled. A buzz had started deep within my right ear.

'Come away, Nalanda brother. Do not look too long, lest it blinds you,' he said. I shook my head. The numerous claustrophobic cave walls seemed to be elongating into the distance, the overly unctuous ministrations of my companion echoed off every wall that seemed to be closing in on me.

'Since I'm on guardian duty today, let me take you inside.' Bhim's voice came to me as if from afar, like a whisper. And though we stood at one spot, facing each other, it seemed as if the entire building was spinning around us.

'But the forest woman told me she was the guardian.' I was feeling weak as a kitten, willing to be led wherever he took me.

'No women are allowed here, Secret Nalanda brother,' Bhim said with a short mirthful laugh. 'Unless they are tools for the practice. All tools, Action Seals and female properties are catalogued and registered before entry.'

By now a mental haze had settled in and I was feeling distinctly befuddled. Also, the fragrance of sandalwood in the air was overpowering me. Were the toxins of the snake venom also having a psychedelic effect, I wondered. Bhim looked concerned at my plight.

'All this is too much for you. It is best you leave now. Before leaving, please recite the sound code and leave through the west gate,' he said, pointing at the way that led back into the forest of snakes. But that was behind us. Before us was an open gate that led into a long corridor with black entrances on each side like dark impassive faces.

I was sure that this was the direction to the Black Hat territory, the roofless temple. If nothing else, I wanted to reach it to spite Mahipala and my brother and also see the part of Nalanda that killed Dharmapada.

'I beseech you, Nalanda brother,' I said to Bhim, 'let me enter.'

Bhim stared at me expressionlessly for a long time. Then following some hidden protocol, he seemed to make up his mind.

'Repeat after me,' he finally said loudly, probably to shake me out of my stupor. I folded my hands and stood next to him, facing the tunnel-like corridor and repeated.

'I fold my hands and praise the Dharma kings, translators and panditas who have kept the flame alive for centuries.' I repeated the words three times.

'You may now take the forgiveness walk,' he instructed.

'Why forgiveness?' I muttered.

'For all the transgressions made here. It's protocol.'

'You can choose to enter any of the gates,' Bhim said, 'while I will recite to you the litany of this world you have entered.'

I looked hard at the dense black entrances I passed. Over the top of each door were symbols in a language I did not know. Keeping step with me, our bodies casting no shadows anywhere, I could hear Bhim's soft breath as he walked alongside me like my shadow.

The corridor suddenly seemed endless. Without turning towards me, with every step he recited in a practised monotone.

'Never look for the Nine Unknowns.' One step.

'The death code will always find a broken oath.' Another step.

'The rasa changes everyone who leaves to enter again.'

He would stop and start walking again with punctuated rhythm. It was a strange military step. But then, maybe not.

'Wait for forbidden knowledge to find you. Do not try to find it.'

'Forgive or go insane.'

'The essence of the Baladitya White etheric libraries are hidden in the Nine Books.'

'The Nine Unknowns are the dharma protectors of the Nine Books.'

'The death code protects the Nine Unknowns.'

'The death code protects the Nine Books.'

'The death code protects the Nine Unknown library.'

'Don't try to find it.'

'The books are everywhere. They are before you and around you, but you will never see them.'

As he spoke the last words, we reached the end of the corridor. Ahead lay a small gate that opened into the thick dark forest. I could smell and hear the river close by. Knowledge is like water, I thought. It needs to flow. I stopped because I had made my choice of entrance. The corridor behind me stretched back into an inverted infinity.

'You stand at the entrance of the Kapalika,' Bhim said.

There was a moment's silence when my fate collected itself for my next step.

'Forgive the transgressions, made with ruthless compassion for the good of all sentient beings.'

'Forgive those not worthy. Do it with ruthless compassion for the good of all sentient beings.'

'Forgive disrespect. Do it with ruthless compassion for the good of all sentient beings.'

'Forgive ambition and lack of compassion. Do it with ruthless compassion for the good of all sentient beings.'

'Knowledge has its price.'

'Consequences will always be wreaked. For the wheel of karma must turn.'

I was losing patience with Bhim's practised litany. It sounded a lot like the prayers we said in the Nalanda dining halls for the animal's afterlife before eating its meat. His eyes closed, repeating by rote, his hands folded, Bhim was a picture of fervent earnestness. Just when the stifling ritual had risen like bile to gag my throat, my companion's disconcerting monotone stopped. And with that Bhim the Burly was gone.

I started walking. With every step I walked further into the decrepitude of my time. Crossing the gate, I saw the white sandy shore of the quietly flowing river. Immediately to my right, a narrow doorway led to a series of interconnected caves, each opening out to the sandy beach.

I could have walked straight ahead, but I turned right to the interconnected caves. As if by some premonition, my legs became leaden and I had to drag my feet forward. Later, I have often wondered whether I would have still taken the walk through the chamber of cannibalistic horrors had I known what it contained. I still do not have an answer to that.

At the centre of each cave was a chopping block for human sacrifice and next to it a fire pit. The white sandy floor around the chopping block was black with warm blood gone cold. A sickly sweet smell of unidentifiable origin pervaded me, like a miasma. Each cave had murals depicting what went on there in great detail. Mounted copper plaques and inscriptions by unknown authors removed whatever doubts were left in the imagination. There were eight interconnected caves and I staggered through them all. A close look at Dharmapada's intestines had made me vomit, but what I was seeing here left me incapable of any reaction.

Unnaturally gory depictions of young royal princesses burnt

alive after widowhood immediately brought in me a flash of fear for my mother. I learnt from the plaques and inscriptions that since most high-caste women were married to men much older than them, almost all were widowed in their prime and were ideal material for the Kapalika's magical practices. The fire of a burning woman gave the same blessings as the sun of immortality, said the inscription. It granted longevity to those who felt her heat. Her flesh granted superhuman strength to the Kapalika and the black seed of her lotus, her vulva, procured after burning had rare medicinal properties.

The murals depicted hundreds of men in Kapalika accoutrements eating by fire pits, the mahamamsa, the great meat. Her meat.

Other than long treatises on the necessary incantation for rituals, the plaques also gave detailed instructions on the procurement of high-born royal women. If the woman was older, she should be burnt, while a younger woman should be decapitated. One mural showed in excruciating detail a princess being brought into the midst of expectant Kapalikas. She was unceremoniously dragged out of her palanquin to a large chopping block.

Social inversion rituals of murdering your parents, burglary, sleeping with your mother, sister and daughter were described in visual detail as prescriptions for overcoming the five great obstacles. Without flinching I saw it all, read it all.

One cave was dedicated to the Dakini's heart essence. A girl with five requisite qualities—being nubile, a virgin, demure, low-caste and tender-aged—is laid on the chopping block with her back arched, exposing the heart. Strict injunctions and incantations follow the special technique of stabbing her with the Vidyadharas' *phurba*, the magical dagger useful for protecting treasure. If done correctly, the woman's soul became a guardian deity useful for guarding treasure and quelling enemies. Barren women were preferred because their bodies had not been defiled by childbirth.

The sacrifice of infants and the use of their skulls were also lauded for Kapalika practice, but they were not as highly rated as women.

All the murals had the dreadlocked Kapalikas conducting ritual cannibalism, showing either sacramental cannibalistic feasts or decapitation sacrifices.

A horrific realisation came to me, like a punch in the gut. Even though it was referred to as human sacrifice, all the humans sacrificed were women. I marvelled at human stupidity. No one had yet discovered why most hauntings were usually of women or young children. Mostly women. It was because it was the woman who was always sacrificed, rarely boys or men. This is what poor Bilwa had been trying to tell us. Women were killed for alchemical substances, ritual cannibalism or to turn into dharma-protecting demonesses with their heart blood.

A woman was burned so the viewer could absorb the light of her flames. She was eaten so the divine feminine could be ingested. Her most private part was made into pills of high medicinal value. Even her soul was entrapped in the service of the executioner because, as the plaque said, all the principles of alchemy and cosmogony manifest in the female body. It reminded me of the Chinese scholar's public declaration—'Every atom of the female body is an embodiment of the Great Goddess.' Nalanda consumed her in private places and denied her in public places.

I staggered out of the caves onto the sandy riverine shore. High above me was a broken rocky roof and a little light filtered through it. The river ran through the Honeycomb floor like a bloodied open vein in a diseased body. Its white powdery shores were expansive, unlike the cramped niches I had left behind. More beehive caves protruded like jagged edges out of the mountain. I walked up to the riverbank. Bleached sand slid off my Turkish leather shoes like the pulverised bones of women begging for mercy. The river gently lapped at my feet. The water had darkened in the dim light, or was it by the blood of unlived lives...

My eyes looked up to the opposite bank and my ears picked up the drumbeats of nagaras. It was a sound I had been dimly conscious of because it had been following me from the beginning with its peculiar melancholic melody. The opposite bank was lined with trees and three cremation pyres burnt at equal distances from each other. Behind a chopping block I could see the Sonapahar or gold mountain in sharp relief. Idly I recalled that meditation on impermanence, in front of cremation pyres, had been introduced in Nalanda before my time. But the practice, I had heard, was discontinued because it had begun to arouse necrophilia in monks. Obviously, I thought, looking at the cremation pyres, Nalanda malpractices are never discontinued, just simply removed from sight.

There was no way to cross the river, neither did I want to. I kept walking along my side of the river. Beyond the cremation pyres, at least a hundred Kapalikas came into view. Some dreadlocked, some conspicuously wearing the secret Kapalika's triple hair knot. Body smeared with ashes from the cremation pyres, they poured the hellish contents of their skull bowls into their upturned mouths. They danced awkwardly, gracelessly, around a Kapalika who blew his five-tone signature conch. Others wearing all the Kapalika accoutrements, their foreheads anointed with red vermilion marks, danced to the beat of the nagaras. They sang in the highest key and their chanting filled me with a dread that made my knees buckle. In their centre was a mound of neatly arranged skulls belonging to children.

As I walked along, naked moolanivasi women tied to trees came into view. Some doe-eyed girls could not have been more than seven years of age. Some dressed in bridal attire cowered in a huddle like sheep for slaughter. The ones naked waist up were dark-skinned and short. They wore necklaces of seashells and hibiscus flowers. Coral beads surrounded their small soft wrists. Some children were tied with them. I recognised the moolanivasi boy from the slave quarters. His dhoti in rags, his face streaked with blood and mud and tears; he lay slumped, tied to a tree. So this was where the inhabitants of the slave quarters had disappeared.

I tried to catch their attention, but they could not see me, making me wonder whether I was invisible. Or maybe their fear had made everything else invisible. The Kapalikas could not see me because lust had made everything else invisible to them. They probably expected me to be another nefarious visitor, here to attend some cannibalistic feast.

The soft keening of women reached my ears. Suddenly suffocating for air, I started running. I don't know when I became conscious of the elaborate white, silken, pleated lower garments with headdresses to match. In perfect simulation of dancers from Tushita heaven, I saw beautiful lissome young men dancing before me. Their beauty was ethereal. I followed them in a trance. Pearls and moonstones were strung around their necks. They beat the double-handed drum nagaras strapped to their waists. Some carried parasols. With faces beautifully decorated with sandalwood paste, they too did not notice me, or pretended not to. Enchanted by an expensive, intricately embroidered shawl swaying before me, I followed them. I was drawn again and again to their feet, decorated with intricate designs in sandalwood paste.

I do not know how long I followed them.

After some time I found myself alone, walking down a forest path lined with white flowers that opened into another small sandy river shore. Up ahead at a distance, I could see the trees on the other side of the white shore. By the side of the stagnant, petrified river was a funeral pyre. It was clearly another ritual cremation ground. On top of the funeral pyre was an unburnt corpse of a woman dressed in red bridal attire with long flowing hair streaming across the face. She did not look long dead or perhaps she was still alive. Crows and vultures circled the horizon. A low hum, sounding like the deep lament of human voices, started from a distance and moved towards me in a rising crescendo.

Two men appeared and stood facing each other, one on each end of the pyre. They wore grandmaster robes. One wore white, the other black. The one wearing white had his back towards me, but the shoulder stoop and the long elongated neck seemed oddly familiar. The realisation that the other, in black robes, was my master Aryadatta stunned me senseless. He was holding a skull cap bowl aloft in his hand. The kapala.

Even though he was far away, he was within earshot. Or maybe the wind carried his voice over the low humming of disembodied voices. It was making me so dizzy I thought I would faint.

Larger than life itself, my master turned his red flaming eyes towards me and commanded.

'Turn around and run, Siddhartha. Run! Follow the Law! You are not ready yet!'

Maybe it was my Nalanda training to never question my master that made me turn around in a lightning flash. I ran so hard and fast through the Dark One's one-way hinge gate that when I became conscious of my surroundings, bells were tolling for my monastery monks to retire for the night.

For many nights after that I would wonder whether my obedience to my master had ruined my life or saved it.

15. *Sakya, The Monk Who Never Sleeps*

'I believe congratulations are in order,' I said to my brother. 'What use does a monk have for such things?' Aditya Raj muttered.

'The monk is still the baby's uncle,' I replied. When he did not answer, I spoke again.

'Explain to me again why we are here. And why I should help you?' I asked.

We were staring at the Inverted Palm Seal again, emblazoned with all its quiet arrogance on the stone lattice separating us from its world. This was our second sojourn together inside Baladitya White, organised after much coaxing, cajoling and threatening by him.

We had tried using my master's seal to gain access through the gates of the roofless temple, but the White Hat dwarapalas had refused. Only the Inverted Palm Seal was permitted, they said.

I wrapped my sanghati closer around me. The air in the most secret places of Nalanda felt rarefied and cold. After Sitavana, I felt a mild fever burning under my skin all the time.

'Because answers to Dharmapada's death lie across this beautiful wall. And we need to find a way in,' my brother said without taking his eyes off the embossed seal on the eaves, as if staring at it hard enough would make it crumble and fall.

'For the last time, Dharmapada's death was an accident. The matter is closed. I do not want to discuss it anymore. Neither do my masters.' I was amazed at how calmly I said these words. Subterfuge becomes so easy when it is a necessity. I had thought of confiding the Sitavana events to my brother but finally decided to hold my silence a little longer.

'Dharmapada's mutilated organ was not an accident,' came my brother's sarcastic rejoinder.

'A venereal disease contracted by whoring with the temple prostitutes,' I returned somewhat bitterly my practised response.

'I shall prepare the official investigation report and submit it to the Royal Vihara with the Abbot's Seal in a fortnight,' I said. 'My masters are busy with the Buddhist Council that has been forced on them. And now if you'll excuse me, I too have better things to do.'

But I made no move to leave, and my brother smiled because he knew I was caught in his trap.

'There is another way we can get to the roofless temple,' he said finally, turning to me. I looked at him in consternation. I had learnt from the forest Dakini that the only way to the roofless temple was through the Honeycomb. From where we were sitting, we were immediately west of Sitavana, the Rasayana labs and the Honeycomb. If we kept walking east of the circulating wall, we would be finally obstructed by the Honeycomb. It stuck to the entrance of the roofless temple like a hornet's nest. There was another university entrance to Sitavana, only for Inverted Palm Seal holders and not Aditya Raj. The part of Secret Nalanda my brother had access to still denied him more than it permitted.

'Come with me,' he said and in one rushed movement, he started walking north purposefully along the concentric borders of the stone latticed wall.

We soon lost sight of the greenery pushing through the lattice as we entered a darkened covered space moving along the stone lattice.

'Where are you taking me now?' I complained to Aditya Raj. The shadows of empty corridors stretched before us.

'To the Inverted Palm library, where the most precious manuscripts are kept,' he said, staring at the upper stages of the observatories, wrapped in clouds.

'There is another library here?' I felt a shiver of excitement. I had still not recovered from the wonder of the etheric library. Hearing of another one sounded like a feast for a glutton. It was not just that books were a welcome respite from my recent tortures. They could provide clues to recent events, some logical explanation for Nalanda's mind-bending activities. I remembered Asita's manuscript with the Inverted Palm Seal. So this is where it must have come from, I thought.

'Up there in the pinnacle. That is where the secret books are kept, away even from the eyes of Nalanda's best students and masters.'

'Are these physical books, or is it an etheric library?' I enquired.

'The contents of the etheric library are transcribed and maintained here in physical manuscripts,' my brother informed, 'but there are other books too, written by masters and mahasiddhas.'

I feigned a disinterested expression but could not suppress the excited spring in my step. When we reached the uppermost stage of the pinnacle, it opened out into several mezzanine halls and courtyards. There were no sound codes or dwarapalas in this part of Innermost Nalanda. The architecture and inside environments were also shorn of the intricate carvings unique to the Nalanda style of art. They were typical of the opulent luxury of Nalanda's material life, something I had begun to hate with every breath.

We reached its inner chambers. What I found very interesting about Innermost Nalanda was that nobody seemed to be interested in the identity of the other. Every one was preoccupied and unconcerned. The light too was different here, a strange inky blue.

The sanctum sanctorum of the most secret library was guarded by thick stone walls. We walked in without inhibition. Still, even though I crossed its threshold without permission or intermission, I knew I had stepped into a chamber reserved for very few.

Inside, palm leaf manuscripts wrapped and tied in silk were stacked from floor to ceiling. Just like Asita's manuscript, they were different from the Nalanda style of printing books. The pigments and paper were unique to Uddiyana, my master's homeland. Stone chambers designed to hold the palm leaf manuscripts and cabinets for scrolls lined all the walls. There was only one low-lying librarian desk with an ink pot holding a sharpened peacock feather stylus unknown to the Nalanda style.

My eyes were drawn to manuscripts wrapped in red silk, tantalisingly visible but locked away behind thin, wire-meshed panels.

The lone librarian sat cross-legged behind a low writing desk listing a bundle of new arrivals of scrolls wrapped in gold-embroidered yellow silk. He was none other than the Nalanda gatekeeper Sakya, the Monk Who Never Sleeps. The man who had given me permission to cross the first portal sat before me guarding the last portal. This time I did not hide my face. I looked at him openly and he returned my gaze unflinchingly. My brother showed him the king's seal and Sakya took out the keys to neighbouring anterooms. I could not help looking at Sakya with a great deal of curiosity. So, I thought, he works one watch at night and another at daytime. Does he ever sleep? Maybe he doesn't need to.

My brother moved me to a small anteroom lit by a single flameless torch. Every wall here was lined from floor to ceiling with manuscripts. My fingers trembled as I scanned them. I recognised the Book of Time that was also available in the outer Nalanda libraries, Ratnanidhi and Ratnasagar. I saw some books on Sun Science and Conquering Space. All available. I opened a manuscript tantalisingly called New Science and, looking over my shoulder to see that no one was watching, quickly scanned the pages. My eyes fell on a book on cosmogony that was so curiously titled that I could not read the script. I opened the pages to realise that it was written in ancient codified Sanskrit. My imagination fired, I thought of secreting it away in my sanghati. But I desisted. There would be time for that, I thought.

This was the moment Aditya Raj chose to step between me and the books to brandish a scroll before my nose. I read the two words written on the scroll. Action Seal. I remembered this was the manuscript Asita had snatched from me. Chasing the Inverted Palm Seal embossed on this manuscript had led me to witness the genocide inside the Honeycomb. But it didn't take me long to piece together the logical premises of the situation. Something I would have deduced had I paid a little more attention. I looked at my brother's face. I locked my eyes with his in combat. He spoke before me.

'Find this book.' My brother's command held urgency, even though he avoided my stare. 'Quickly. Then we must go. The night is almost done.'

I did not hurry. I continued to squarely face my brother.

'So that is why you are here. Your King, a petty thief, has sent you to steal magic from my masters.' My face must have crumpled in disgust for I spat on the badly swept library floor. 'And you need me to find it for you in the Inverted Palm libraries because illiterate that you are, you can't read. And no one here is willing to give it to you.'

He peered over his shoulder at the voices emanating from the adjoining corridor.

'I'll explain later.' His whispers were fierce, but not just in anxiety. There was something else. Terror. I could smell it like a faint stench.

As I confronted my brother without any intention of backing off, I saw the desperation in his eyes. As I looked into his face,

I understood why he was in Nalanda. Why Mahipala had sent him, and why my masters were avoiding him. He had not been sent to find out who killed Dharmapada. He had been sent for this book. There was probably a handsome award waiting for him when he handed the manuscript to the king. Mahipala depended on my brother to acquire the book. My masters depended on me to prevent him. With that thought a lifelong training of master-disciple integrity kicked in.

'Never,' I said. 'You will have to kill me first.'

'Don't make me,' he said grabbing my arm in a vice-like grip. I was acutely aware that the only one who could break this dangerous standoff was me. I decided to buy time, delay the inevitable. After a suitable show of aggression, I said, 'Only on one condition.'

'What?' he said, relieved that his ploy had worked.

'I will read the book before handing it over to you.'

'Done!' He was sighing in happiness. 'Now let us hurry. If we are discovered here, both of us will be consigned to the Nalanda dungeons. I don't know about you, but the faster I get away from here the better. Nalanda is more frightening than all the ghouls of Vaishali.'

But try as I might I could not find the book. It was possible that Asita had the only copy. Even as Sakya watched me from under his eyelashes and my brother grew more and more desperate, I finally had to tell my brother that the book did not exist in this library.

'The book you are looking for is only accessible to the Black Hats,' Sakya gently reproached, 'you will need the Inverted Palm Seal to get a copy of the book.' Fifty such seals tantalisingly visible behind wire meshes in the Seals Department appeared in my mind's eye.

'But Secret Nalanda regulations say,' my brother argued with ill-controlled frustration, 'that if an ordained disciple of a Black Hat requests the book, he may acquire it.'

'Only for the books in the White Hats section,' Sakya explained with infinite patience. 'The Black Hats books require a different seal.'

There was an uncomfortable silence that I was determined not to disturb. I was amazed at the brazen and elaborate nature of secrecy in Nalanda's forbidden place. An intricately woven system of regulations kept a pact of confidentiality operational amongst at least a thousand most powerful people associated with Nalanda.

'But Siddhartha is Aryadatta's pupil. Grandmaster Aryadatta is a Black Hat.'

'But Siddhartha is not a Black Hat. Not yet,' he said without even looking in my direction. 'He has not received the Great Initiation. So he will be declined. Just like Dharmapada was declined on your behalf the last time.' I looked askance at my brother. So he had already tried to acquire the book once before, my expression said. He was flushing to the roots of his city-styled hair.

'You cannot stop me, Nalanda man!' My brother was losing his sly calm, looking apoplectic with rage.

'We are committee members of the royal investigation!'

'My apologies on behalf of Nalanda,' Sakya said. And as a peace offering, he handed to my brother a book that he picked out of many manuscripts lying on the floor.

'This is *The Book on the Twilight Language*. As the name suggests, it is similar to what you are looking for. Take it. It may be of interest to you.'

My brother looked at the manuscript with complete indifference. Without hesitation, I bound the manuscript securely under my sanghati and turned to my brother to leave. Hesitantly, he moved towards the exit and we retraced our footsteps.

Outside, we could not yet hear the rise and fall of the early morning chants. Another day in Nalanda was yet to begin.

I walked up to him and peering at his crestfallen face I demanded, 'What is the Great Initiation?'

'The end of me,' he said in bitter sarcasm. I waited for him to come up with the truth. And finally he did. 'The Great Initiation confers the power of the Nine Unknowns on the initiated. Some Magadha Kings have received this in the past. Mahipala has been requesting this initiation from the Abbot for many years, but it has been constantly denied to him. Dharmapada tried giving Mahipala the initiation to the best of his knowledge and ability but failed because an important aspect was missing. That missing aspect is explained in *The Action Seal*.'

'Does the Great Initiation involve burning and eating women?'

He looked at me quizzically. 'No,' he said.

'Beheading them?'

'No, calm down, elder brother.'

'Do not look at me as if you have not seen it!' I was so loud I could feel the phlegm rise in my throat.

'So you know about the Honeycomb?' He smiled in sarcasm. 'You are finally catching up. No, I have no interest in such depravities. I was born and raised in Vaishali. And you know we were taught to respect all women.'

I stared at him in great awe.

'And so, you expect me to believe Mahipala believes the powers of the Nines can be transferred to him through a book!' I said. My vitriolic comment went unheeded because he continued without interruption.

'Yes, but it can. The Great Initiation transference follows certain scientific laws that can be put down in a mathematical formula. As a student of Logic, you should know that. The formula is clearly enunciated in the book. It is full of aspects that are beyond your comprehension.' I would have kicked him for his arrogance had he not yawned, opening his mouth to display the dark stinking microcosm of his mouth, full of secrets he would not speak of.

'Now I shall sleep. But we shall meet again. There are too many unsolved mysteries. You agree that the murder investigation is not over. Tomorrow we shall speak to more of Pandit Dharmapada's students. Especially the one who renounced him.'

An image of Bilwa's enormous eyes swam before me. I could have told Aditya Raj about the trial, and how I saw him inside Nalanda's secret place after he was stoned and expelled, but I didn't. Tomorrow, I postponed.

He left uninterrupted, only to come back and brandish a finger in my face. 'The missing aspect mentioned only in *The Action Seal* killed Dharmapada. Even though I do not know what the book contains, this much I know.'

'You mean it's another seal like the Inverted Palm Seal?' I blurted out, confused. My brother smirked with a glint in his eye.

'How little the Nalanda monks know,' he smiled. 'How ignorant they all are.'

What fresh hell is this, I rued.

O Buddha, I prayed, *how could you allow Nalanda to nurse such a cruel viper at her breast? Are you going to stand by and watch the systematic shredding of her compassionate heart?* What perversions fill the sutras and shastras? What heinous and deadly manuscripts poison her libraries? Here in the very place where the Buddha had walked a millennia ago. Has time corrupted the goodness of Buddhist mindfulness to such an unimaginable extent? Where is the purity of knowledge I have sought and worshipped ever since I was a child? For four years I have slept the sleep of ignorance. While I have slept, Nalanda has awoken. But when I was awake, Nalanda slept. *What a strange journey have you set me on, O my master. Give me reprieve, Buddha. Give me deliverance.*

Deliverance from masters I could not face anymore. I was too scared of what they would say and what they would want. I was too scared to find out which side they were on, the good or the evil. We were always taught to take the leap of faith. How does one take that leap of faith when there is no reason for faith?

My master was a Kapalika. Quite easily proven. Just as my mother had warned.

This is where faith had brought me.

16. *Kapalika*

I got up from the dark shade of the Bodhi tree and walked back to the monastery, taking care to step in the shadow of trees so as not to be visible to the accidental eye. I crossed the Abbot's white palace where the lamps still burned. I was suddenly overwhelmed by the need for sunlight. Only the very privileged were accorded the right to burn lamps after dusk. I did not want to go back to my dark oppressive room. And since I was not as privileged as so many in Nalanda, I would wait for the Sun God to throw down his largesse. I longed for the freedom and simplicity of the common folk. I remembered the pangs of envy I sometimes felt when I saw the goatherds and cowherds leaving the Nalanda gates to bask in the glory of sunshine while we concentrated on our studies in dark chaityas.

I made up my mind that I would meditate at a quiet spot till morning because I was in too much of tumult for sleep. I would beg the karmadana of rosters to compensate my lack of attendance with extra hours of service later. I decided I would follow the goatherds out for the morning pasture and spend the day in the company of innocence. I would surround myself with the bleating of goats and bathe in blessed sunshine. I would listen to the simple folk strains on the cowherd's flute, so unaffected by the pretentious sophistry of the university arts. It would be a severe act of rebellion against the oppressive discipline and ritualism of Nalanda. They would miss me in the lecture halls and the thought gave me perverse pleasure.

Regarding the death investigation, pragmatism demanded I report to my master, or at least visit him. But even at the risk of death, I could not face him. I would wait for his summons. For I knew with certainty that they would not come. Therefore, simply put, I was doomed.

In this emotionally charged state I walked to the point where the Buddha had taken his steps. Blossoming lotuses had been lovingly designed on the spots where the Buddha's feet had fallen. The pink stone flowers looked pearly white in the moonlight, as if blanching in fear. My breast roiled. *Why was it,* I thought, *that my brother who was a worldly man felt no rebellion towards his masters, while I, a monk, who should be more capable of spiritual surrender to my master, was behaving like a skittish kitten at the prospect of taking a swim? Were his intentions purer than mine?*

Skepticism was a fungus that ate into the soul.

Yes, my masters had written down that doubt, not skepticism, is a mindful practice for the process of introspection. We called this contemplation the Yoga of Doubt. Which of the two was I? The doubter or the skeptic?

I stood in front of the 80-foot-high statue of the Giant Buddha and looked into his expansive face, searching for strength in his magnificently magnified serenity. Let me not fail whatever challenge you have laid before me, I prayed. Show me the way, I whispered, craning my neck to behold his benign smile. The balcony above his head, from where thousands of milk pots were poured for his ritual bath every day, was empty.

But his smile wasn't. It was full of the compassion that I so desperately needed.

It was when I was gazing at the Buddha's smiling face that I saw the intruder of my prayers.

This was the time when most of Nalanda slept.

There he was, on the Giant Buddha's left, in the clearing meant for daily recitals, dancing at a dizzy pace to some hidden music. For the second time in the space of two days, I broke into a cold sweat. Somehow he looked naked in spite of the streams of necklaces he wore. Bone ornaments in his hair, arms, ears, and waist made sounds when he moved. A loin cloth barely covered his essentials. The only distinguishing feature that proved he was a monk was his shaven head. But ashes covered his face and body and the contours of his genitals were on display in such an unbecoming fashion that it made me flush to the crown of my head. He looked like a ghost under the light of the moon, dancing like some bloodless forest spirit.

For a moment I did believe he was a ghost, but when I walked hesitatingly up to him, it was clear he was made of flesh and bones. It was evident that he was a monk who had conducted some secret rite, very similar to the Kapalikas I had recently witnessed at Sitavana.

When I reached him, he saw me, yet he did not see me. His eyes kept rolling back into their sockets and he seemed unable to stop the whirling motions of his body.

'Nalanda brother,' I said softly so as not to disturb the unearthly spaces he obviously inhabited. 'Which monastery do you belong to?'

His body jerked into standing position and his eyes returned to their sockets. I realised that his were blue, like some of the yavana students who came from the west of the Saraswati river. And then I recognised him. It was Bhim the Burly.

If someone had asked me about Bhim a few moons ago, I would have said he was from the Sarvastivadin Monastery and studied Aryabhatta's mathematics with me. I would have said he was a quiet student who mingled only with his fellow students from the far west. He gave his master's service by translating Brahmagupta's works. And once I had played a game of kabaddi with him. But this was not the Bhim I once knew. The Bhim before me was beyond recognition.

He saw me, but I do not think he recognised me either, even though he broke into an ecstatic laugh.

'Do you know,' he grabbed my shoulders in a vice that felt amazingly gentle. His touch was cool, but not cold, like the touch of soft silk against a fevered body.

'Do you know?' he said dreamily, 'I get my Action Seal tonight!' Then his laughter pealed like all the bells of Nalanda. His voice was thin and heavily accented. He spoke in Pali so broken I could barely understand what he was saying. But understand I did.

'Tonight I find my real master,' he said, eyes shining as if all the light of the stars were trapped in them. His whitened face was so close to mine I could see sweat in the creases of his forehead. 'Do you know who gives me the Action Seal tonight? Him!' He gestured with his eyes to the Giant Buddha, as if he were a secret accomplice. Then he threw his arms in the air in a gesture of ecstatic abandon. 'Tonight the real master comes to me!'

And with strange incomprehensible incantations he started whirling in his dizzy dance again, kicking up a cloud of dust that swirled around him. I realised that I could not help him in any way, and wended my way back to my monastery.

Maybe I would sleep after all. Tiredness overpowered every limb of my body. I gave in to defeat. Defeat of all my efforts of comprehension. The goatherds would have to wait for another day.

17. *Dangerous Privileges*

When I awoke, several bells had already tolled and the Sun God had made a considerable journey across the sky. I felt an uncharacteristic surge of resentment for the bells that ruled our lives. I got up to wash my mouth and face and brush my teeth with the bitter juices of the neem brush sticks. I had missed my early morning community bath at the pond. I washed my hands and feet at the monastery well. I could not drag myself to the monastery kitchen where, thanks to my bribes, the cook must have surely reserved yesterday's milk cakes or some delicacy for me. I ate a few stale berries in my cell and went right back to sleep.

I awoke at noon and stared bleary-eyed in wonder at the items that lay around me. Somewhere inside my throbbing head entered the realisation that I beheld the greatest honour of my academic life!

In a corner of the cell, on the low desk where I did my studies, lay neatly folded pink silken robes of the privileged monks on special duty! My own lay monk's robes were rough homespun cotton so coarse that my pampered skin had chafed when I had first worn them.

Next to the robes was a silver kamandal water bowl so much more beautiful to the eye than my wooden one. And wonder of wonders, beside the rich embroidered shawl of a fully ordained monk on special duty were laid the most intricately designed sandals, the likes of which I had seen only on the feet of the most honoured. Rank among Nalanda monks was most evident in the elegance of their footwear and the fanciness of their hairstyles, and I stared in dumb amazement at what could only be deemed as a great benefit bestowed on me.

But that was not all. Proof of the greatest encomium were the lamps that had been installed in the walls of my cell even as I had slept like a dead toad. I would have light at night? Oh, Lord Buddha, what would Rahula and the rest of my friends say? They would die of envy. This was most unprecedented for a student of my standing, however accomplished I may be in my studies. And then a chilling realisation doused my exhilaration, leaving me dumb with misery. Under my silken robes lay the Inverted Palm Seal.

Were my masters punishing me? I thought, sinking into a terrible gloom. *You are not ready*, his red flaming eyes had chided. Follow the Law. I wallowed in self-pity for a while and then I did what any self-respecting monk in my position would do. I went back to sleep. Whispers of cremation grounds grew louder and riverine forests spread their roots in my sinking consciousness. It took a long while for oblivion to drown out the soft keening of women.

I awoke to a rude shaking of my shoulders and my brother's indignant voice.

'What?'

'You sleep when all of Nalanda runs about in frenzy?' He was shouting. I tried to prise open my eyes glued by the secretions of too much slumber. I was still trying to rearrange my coordinates of time and space when my brother's words firmly shook me awake.

'Hurry up and get ready. There has been another murder.'

'What? What? What?' I stuttered, feeling like the village idiot all over again.

'Yes, my most learned one. What, what and what. The corpse was lying in no other place than the main tank of Nalanda. Not in an unused well in the slave quarters. The body was found by the ceremonial pundits who went down there for the ritual annual cleaning.'

'The main tank has been defiled?' My hands flew to my mouth. I felt my eyes widening in their sockets. 'The main tank whose waters are used for the shrines and the masters?'

'Yes, the very same. Now please, hurry up. The entire university is in an uproar.'

'And justifiably so,' I said, hurriedly getting dressed. I looked at the silken robes but decided not to wear them till I had finally spoken to my master. 'The defilement of the main tank is considered to be a very serious crime. The waters of the tank are more sacred than the water of the Ganga here.'

My brother was pacing up and down like a carnival bear, wringing his hands in great anxiety. 'This has gone too far. Much too far,' he muttered.

I asked him the question I was horrified to ask but had to. I was thankful that there was nobody in the neighbouring cells.

'Who died, Aditya Raj?' I asked, hoping he would not reply.

'An alien student. A yavana called Bhim,' he said. And my heart sank, for I had instinctively known. What cruel jest were the Buddhas playing on me that I must have one last encounter with the victim before he died?

'Did he drown?' I asked in a very small voice.

'No,' my bother answered, lost in thought. 'He burned to death. Charred beyond recognition.'

I mentally calculated that the main tank was not very far from the Giant Buddha statue. Maybe a fraction of a yojana. I wondered whether I should tell my brother that I had met him last night. No, caution warned me. This information would only embroil me in further controversy.

'Should we go and see the body?' I reluctantly asked.

'There is no need for that,' he dismissed me. I would have felt insulted if relief had not overwhelmed me. But I could not help asking the question that came out from the far recesses of my mind.

'What position was the corpse in when it was found?'

My brother subjected me to a long hard stare.

'Sitting,' he said.

I wilted under this information.

'The corpse has been taken by the Nalanda undertakers for burial,' he added.

'Burial?' I said, incredulous.

'Yes, isn't that strange? And like Pandit Dharmapada's, this burial will also take place in the Nalanda samadhis.'

'And what is the reason for that? Only siddhas are buried in the Nalanda samadhi shrines!'

'The Abbot says that a cremation will attract too much attention. This way the secrecy of the burial rituals will keep the outraged students at bay. This conferring of honour is also a diplomatic ploy to appease the alien students.' He smashed his hand into his fist. 'I am in agreement there. But I cannot help thinking that the masters have colluded to distract attention from the council that King Mahipala ordered.'

My laughter was full of derision and without mirth. 'Oh yes. The masters killed a foreign student and defiled their own tank, which is held so sacred that only the most privileged monks are allowed to clean it, and whose cleaning ceremonies are conducted with more propriety than the Buddha's birthday. Yes, of course, they are risking hell and a rebirth in the lower realms just so that they don't have to conduct the council.'

'Brother,' Aditya Raj said, 'you are simple. You do not understand the political ramifications of this council.' My chest swelled in indignation. To stem the tide of my anger, which he knew from our boyhood days to be legendary, he changed the topic.

'Do you know the strangest aspect of the yavana's death?' he continued, sitting down on the rough plank that served as my bed. He must be used to silken cushions but what matter?

'I will when you tell me.' In extreme anxiety I involuntarily returned to our boyhood patterns of banter.

'Only the left side of his body was burnt.'

'What?' I said, bells tolling inside my head.

'Only the left side of his body was burnt beyond redemption. Well, his head had shrunk to the size of a mango, and his torso had turned to ashes. But his right hand and right leg was unscathed, completely intact. It was as if the right side was somehow protected and separated from his burning left side. Almost as if his right side watched his left side burn to death. The burns were clean and uniform. And there was no smell of spirit or ether on him. I have personally checked the corpse, though the Raj Vaidya will inspect too. And this time, permission has been granted to inspect the corpse.'

'Could it be an instance of self combustion? I have heard of such cases. Self-immolation is a common theme in many pantheons.'

'Those are myths,' my brother waved aside my speculation, 'and there is only one complication with your theory.' When I did not ask, he answered on his own.

'His male organ was found in the same condition as Dharmapada's. Bloodied. Execrable.'

18. *An Interview with Siroha*

The site of poor Bhim's death was milling with fellow yavana students. Taking a detour, we crossed the theatres in the temple shrine where preparations for a traditional play were in progress. Actors wearing rice powder masks and bells on their fingers and toes were unmindful of our deep quandaries.

I had been unable to prevent myself from slipping into the ornate sandals before we left my cell. I had cursed my treacherous vanity for this weakness and knew that this temporary lack of mindfulness came not from anxiety as I would have liked to believe but a desire to impress my brother. In the dark corners of my mind lurked many monsters. They disappeared when light was shed on them, but I did not have time to deal with my own demons. I needed to prepare in the same corners of my mind a questionnaire for the dead student's master, whom I knew to be Siroha the Unconquerable.

I had to remember that Siroha was a deeply revered pandita in Nalanda. I nostalgically recalled attending some of his instructions on the exposition of quadratic equations. I recalled how uncharacteristically quiet he had been at the Chinese scholar's conference. But I had to face reality, follow the law of inversion. The last time we had met was at the slave quarters and before that at Baladitya White. He had called me Aryadatta's cur and we had not discussed quadratic equations.

As we made our long way to Siroha's residence, I could tell that Nalanda's famed regulation was in complete suspension. The University looked like the aftermath of some calamity. So much so that a passing monk asked us whether the Huns had invaded again. The emptiness of lecture chaityas was strangely disconcerting, like a biorhythm gone awry. Masters walked determinedly to and fro in unattended Assembly Halls, their faces stern and determined. Clots of students in the gardens and corridors spoke in hushed whispers or raised their voices in ill-contained perplexity. The maroon robes of the menial merging with the red of the acolytes, the blue of the laity and the yellow of the monks bespoke a day of confusion. It was most alarming that we could hear challengers beating the drums at a distance, by the Nalanda walls.

A few masters were addressing a large congregation of angry yavanas in the Assembly Hall. Instinctively, both Aditya Raj and I took a detour. Despite his stoic demeanor during the dissection of Pandit Dharmapada's body, I could tell that the sight of Bhim's corpse had deeply disturbed my brother. I was glad that the corpse had already been taken for burial and I would not have to lay eyes upon it. The picture raised in my mind by Aditya Raj's words was horrible enough. From a distance, a faint refrain was audible; we could not tell whether it came from within the gates or without.

'*Down with the Nalanda skull men*!' It finally reached our ears in a staccato rhythm.

'Deaths in Nalanda are becoming increasingly mysterious,' my brother said, deep in introspection. I was in no mood to disagree.

'Yes, indeed,' I agreed.

'I have seen many corpses in battle,' my brother continued in the same vein. I knew better than to interrupt him. 'But never have I seen anything so horrifying, so godless.'

I did not change the pace of my gait. My face remained impassive. Even the birds were irritable today, scolding from the trees. A roll of thunder and a clap of lightning beyond the observatories signalled the threat of rain, or perhaps the displeasure of the gods.

My mind kept returning to a hushed whisper I had heard in passing. A secret order of acharyas was establishing an order of reincarnation for future times. The shadow of sorcery and magic loomed larger on my precious Nalanda.

'I do not understand,' my brother was saying, for once not choosing his words carefully, 'his body seemed to have been burnt by a great degree of heat. He was near a large tank of water, yet it seems he did not get time to douse the fire. A fire so intense that it burnt even his ribs to ashes.' I shut my mind to the image of what that might be like.

'Yet,' and here he looked at me in complete defeat, 'his loincloth, and the right side of his body were unburnt.'

It was clear to me that poor Bhim had died immediately after I left him. Who knew, maybe the killer had been there already, in the shadow of a tree, watching us. Maybe, I thought, shuddering, if I had stayed with him, and not gone back to slothful sleep, he would have still been alive. My sins were accumulating, I thought. Even my sandals were hurting me.

'Maybe the killer was modest-minded. That is why he covered Bhim's secret parts after he died,' I said, with little faith in my own theory.

'Surely that would be more a reflection of the murderer's cold-bloodedness than of his compassion,' my brother said, in some anger.

Siroha's house was adjoining my master's. Like my master, his garden and interiors were shorn of embellishments. This was a characteristic I have noticed in most of my Logician teachers. It was almost as if the stark cleanliness of their surroundings was an effort to simplify clutter and reduce space to the straight lines of pure mathematics.

The master was in his courtyard, attended to by the Head Barber and his entourage. His pet parrot never left his shoulder throughout our visit. We waited at a respectable distance as the barbers finished clipping his nails and decorated the single tuft on his head, a hairstyle allowed only to panditas. After the barbers had paid obeisance to him, and accepted his token dakshina tip of one cowrie, they arose and left in single file, beating the particular rhythm of the barber's gong, to announce their arrival in the next monastery or master's house.

When the pandita beckoned us to take our places, I was maliciously pleased to note that both my brother and I were accorded equal places of honour. An occurrence that my brother could have taken as an insult. But if he did, he did not show it.

Siroha was a long-faced taciturn teacher from the South of India who never gifted to Nalanda a truly mirthful smile. He wore a great prodigious beard and an air of indifference, even in the face of his own genius. His lineage was impeccable, and though he was a dark-featured Brahmin, it was said that his lineage went back to the foreign Saka kings who ruled centuries ago.

The fact was that most of the panditas were either Brahmins or yavanas, slant-eyed, dark-skinned or fair-skinned. The days of the Sangha when the poor, infirm, low-born and destitute were taken in were long past.

Siroha was the presiding mentor for all the western foreign students in Nalanda and I knew from his wards that he had a deep empathy for their foreign culture. But today, sitting immaculately on his cushion, the singular tuft of hair on his head resplendent and well-oiled, he showed no signs of mourning a ward who had died in the most tragic way possible.

After we had paid our respects—I washed his feet and my brother bowed low—we sat down to discuss the death. A cursory glance around us showed that the courtyard to receive audiences was fairly large. And he had his own kitchen and herbarium. He had all the trappings of a mahapandita.

Words of commiseration were exchanged and before my brother could turn the direction of the investigation, I asked the acharya the question I had prepared. 'Revered master, could you shed some light of knowledge on the culture of the foreign yavana people? Something that could be relevant to our investigation?'

If he felt surprise at my unusual question, he did not exhibit any sign of it.

My brother frowned at the apparent irrelevance of my query and barely held his peace. And so Siroha embarked on the telling of a strange and confusing legend taught and given much import in the lands of Yesu in the West.

Adam, we learnt, was the first man talked about in Yesu's Holy Book. Adam was much like the Vedic Manu but of different and irrational attitude. He and the first woman Eve, created from a rib of Adam's body, lived in a fruit garden called Eden. God, apparently they had only one in their pantheon, was a stern old man who set upon Eve and Adam strictures on not eating the forbidden fruit of the Tree of Knowledge which would cause their eyes to open, help in the understanding of good and evil to fall upon them, and make them like Him. He gave no explanations why, save that if they did so they would be killed. A serpent prompted Eve to partake of the fruit, and on Eve's encouragement Adam did the same. On eating the fruit, they became naked, (before this they had worn some vestigial leaves called figs native to their land) and God found them cowering in the bushes and immediately knew they had eaten the forbidden fruit. They were banished from the Garden of Eden but not killed. They were made to wear animal skins signifying their descent to the kingdom of beasts. Adam was cursed to till the soil. Eve was cursed to suffer the pain of childbirth, and the serpent was cursed to crawl on the dirt. *Dust thou art and to dust returnest,* God said unto them and forthwith, the fire emanating from the spinning sword at the base of the Tree of Knowledge protected the tree from further digressions. Adam and Eve then lived like normal householders of today and begat two sons. Cain, born of the intellect and the mind, killed Abel, born of the soul but weaker than his brother. The acharya also mentioned a second woman called Lilith who existed at the same time as Eve but was not given much credence by Adam.

By the time he finished his story, my brother was shifting about in his seat and the acharya did not ask me why I had asked him such a question, even though I had my answer ready. Seeing a breach in our conversation, I ventured to put my foot in further. 'Whatever little I understood of the yavanas, their God seemed to me like Brahma, the Vedic Father of Creation. If he is the Father, do they not have a Mother, a Goddess, a consort for their God?' This first question was purely out of curiosity.

'No, Siddhartha,' and here I was surprised to see the glint of an almost impish smile. 'While all our Gods have consorts, sometimes more than one, their God is not allowed such a luxury. But they do have a very strong overweening entity called the Devil, a negative force almost equal to the power of the positive force of God.'

'He sounds like Mara,' I said, 'and Eve sounds like Mara's temptress.'

Acharya Siroha nodded and Aditya Raj like all city people, slow on the uptake, looked about stupidly.

I used my rudimentary understanding of the Twilight Language and the law of inversion to understand the legend. The serpent was the Great Goddess Kundalini, coiled three and a half times at the base of the spine. The forbidden fruit was the knowledge of subtle human anatomy the Chinese scholar had tried to teach. The Tree of Knowledge was enlightenment. The spinning sword was a prohibitory seal denying access to knowledge. Nakedness was the symbol of truth. Any covering, like the fig, was the false mask of illusion. God was the male principle in direct opposition to the Great Goddess mother principle. I had to approach Siroha delicately.

'In my interactions with students from Western lands,' Siroha continued, 'I have learnt that in the battle to hunt down the Evil One, the Temple of Yesu has achieved remarkable success in the last thousand years. In this age of darkness, their Temple's light shines bright. Pagans, sects, priests of the old religions, and heretics have been burnt in living cremation pyres to strike down the Devil. Women especially have been effectively persecuted. Their influence has almost been burnt out of existence.'

'Why women?' Aditya Raj pondered.

The acharya used his palms to make a gesture of the obvious. 'The world knows them as Mara's temptresses,' he said. I knew he was lying. But I did not know what he was lying about. I was struck by the plight of the yavana women. It seemed similar to our women in the secret cremation grounds. His parrot squawked on his shoulder.

I broke out of my reverie and said, 'It is fortunate that Mara's temptresses blessed their prosecutors with the warmth of longevity even as they burnt to ashes.'

There was silence. I became intensely conscious of the parrot on Siroha's shoulder, its head cocked to one side, looking at me with its mosaic vision. Making a pyramid with his fingertips over his rounding belly, Siroha observed me with keen interest.

'Using the law of inversion,' I said, 'the reality revealed in this illusion would be thus...' And here I gave a long pause before resuming.

'The women are flaming Buddhas burnt to ashes, and the persecutors are Mara. Therefore, it is not the temple of light the yavanas live in, but the temple of darkness.'

Again silence prevailed like a prickling sensation. After a while the acharya broke it, as if he were doing us a favour.

'I concur,' he said. How quickly our grandmasters changed their stances, I thought. Using the law of inversion again, our most revered should be the most reviled, I thought.

But the acharya was speaking.

'In Goddess Tara's declaration,' he was saying, 'it is said: "To some extent we are all guilty of the degeneration of the Mother principle."'

For me this was a personal moment of stunned silence. The acharya continued to speak in a strained choking voice.

'We live in a time when the Mother is held pinned to the ground with nails through her heart.'

The moment passed. His voice was normal again.

'It is because of persecution that followers of the Mother principle flock to Nalanda. Followers of Socrates and Aristotle, Pythogoras and other masters from the neighbouring lands of Alexander the Mighty live and study here.'

'Who?' my brother asked. Clearly, he was struggling to follow the discussion.

'Sucrat, Aristu, Pythaguru and Sikander,' I enlightened my brother.

'In Mahayana Buddhism, they grow the discarded seeds of their ancient religions,' Siroha continued.

'Together we try and remember their forgotten learning. Aditya Raj must be aware that a strong Arab confederation seeks admission into the University of Nalanda. Of course, admission to them has been denied.'

'And justifiably so,' Aditya Raj fell for the bait. I could tell it was a bait because of the wry satisfied expression on the master's face. 'The treasures of Nalanda have crossed the boundaries of our lands for too long now.' Aditya Raj scowled.

'But,' I interjected, 'if you will pardon my bringing this very interesting treatise on the western Puranas back to the point. Can you tell us a little more about the nature of the dead student, and when you last saw him?' I was pleasantly surprised to note that the authoritarian voice was mine.

'The student was an obedient boy and of a quiet disposition. He was punctilious regarding his studies and never broke any of the university laws. He kept mostly to himself and had few friends,' Siroha said.

That was a very different boy from the one I met, half-naked and dancing in the moonlight, I thought.

'You, Siddhartha, are probably aware that he had applied to the university council for a change in tutorship?' Siroha continued evenly.

'Change of master from you to somebody else?' Aditya Raj asked in some disbelief. Changing masters was an infrequent phenomenon that was frowned upon by the university and caused much gossip. My master often used to say that changing your master was like changing your spouse. It benefited nobody. Change of tutorship haunted the two murders. In the last murder, Bilwa had asked for a change of tutorship and the master died. Here the master Siroha was alive, but his student had been murdered. Surely a change of tutorship invited great misfortune.

'Whom did he want to change to?' Aditya Raj continued.

Without a flicker in his eye the acharya said, 'Pandit Dharmapada.'

Our gasps were inevitable but inaudible. Why had Siroha given us this information? Was he a Black Hat? A Nine? Or a royal stooge? With nothing to lose I decided to take the plunge.

Looking at Pandit Siroha equably and with a confidence that surprised me I said, 'I see a pattern of logic in both the deaths.' I still desisted from calling them murders.

'Both involved a change in tutorship,' I said. 'In the first case, the tutor died. In the second, the student. Both instances are somehow connected to Dharmapada.' I did not know that I too was intimate with this connection, for the connection was doubt.

It was lack of faith in the master that haunted both cases, as it was now haunting me.

Even though there was very little in Siroha's face that was not covered by beard, not a muscle had twitched on any exposed part of his face.

'There is something else common to both the victims,' his voice vibrated with a deep resonance.

'Please expound, Mahapandita,' I said deferentially.

'They were both buried,' he said. Our eyes locked. It was an impudence on my part as a disciple that could have led to much censure. But that would have been in another time, another place, in a different Nalanda.

Before I could ask for the reason, he gave me the answer:

'Nalanda is bound by agreement to bury and not cremate a certain sect of alchemists. These alchemists believe that even a few intact atoms of their body have the capacity of regeneration even thousands of years later. This is possible only if the body is buried and not cremated. *Both Dharmapada and Bhim were two such alchemists.* They had obtained the Nalanda seal for burial. The Nalanda administration was duty bound to honour that agreement.'

My brother and I exchanged glances. Alchemy and Baladitya White were now clearly connected. Instinct said that Siroha was inviting me to question him about the secret societies. A primeval self-preservation impulse that this was a trap made me cautious. I had to tread carefully. I was on dangerous ground. I strongly suspected that Bhim, like Dharmapada, was loyal to Mahipala. But I would not let myself get drawn into a dialogue lest I divulge information I shouldn't reveal before Siroha. Or my brother.

'Mahapandita Siroha,' I changed the topic with great respect, 'what is an Action Seal?'

I detected a fleeting flicker in the acharya's facial expression. He recrossed his fingers over his stomach and took his time observing me. Without taking his eyes off my face, he said in a measured tone, 'Though there are many Action Seals, only the best can be used for the Great Initiation.'

For a moment it was so quiet that all I could hear was a magpie's call at a great distance, as my mind registered the importance of what he had said.

Again I sensed the invitation to draw me into a discussion on the warring masters, and again I desisted. *Is he associated with the Abbot, I idly wondered. Are my masters subtly giving me clues and guidance through him?* I banished these thoughts with a shake of my head.

I was very clear that my involvement with the murder investigation was no longer a diplomatic exercise in loyalty to my masters. The murder investigation now was my own search for truth.

What mysterious reality connected Bhim to Pandit Dharmapada and had caused both of them to plunge to such untimely and vulgar deaths? It struck me that both had died close to water bodies. Could there be a connection? Yet, one died by water and the other by fire.

'I found no Action Seals in the Seals Department,' I said as evenly as I could.

'Maybe you are looking in the wrong place,' Siroha said in the same equable tone. 'Your master's homeland is renowned for the best Action Seals.' This puzzled me. Siroha was hinting that Action Seals were not manufactured in Nalanda. Was it made of some unique alchemical material then, I wondered, like mercury, or the philosopher's stone, the *shaligram*? But a primeval fear of the unknown prevented me from probing further.

'Can you tell me what a real master is?' I moved on to my next question. At this point Siroha started laughing. It reminded me of Bhim's last peal of laughter.

'There are three thousand masters and grandmasters, acharyas, arhats, panditas and mahapanditas in Nalanda. Do we look unreal to you?'

'Thank you, Pandit Siroha.' I stood up and and bowed with all the reverence accorded to a mahapandita. 'I have no more questions.'

We were at the doorway, bowing out without showing our backs to the master when he proffered the discussion I had been denying him so far.

'The Action Seal lies in the centre of the conflict between warring masters. One has the Action Seal, and the other doesn't. You, I am sure, know what wars I refer to.'

'But what is the Action Seal?' I asked, 'where can I find it?'

'It's the imprint of the divine,' he replied, 'and you don't find it. It finds you.'

'Many thanks for your cooperation,' I said, concluding the discussion.

'If you get permission from your master for a transfer, I would gladly teach you all that you need to know.' He sat immobile on his seat, eyes never moving from my face. Not once. Fighting against his captivating gaze, I repeated, 'Many thanks. And apologies for taking up so much of your time.' I quickly bowed out, my brother trailing after me.

When we left the acharya's house, my brother ranted on about how my silly theological questions had completely subverted his investigation. We walked fast and furiously. He was so suspicious that he thought I had purposely tried to sabotage the case.

'Tell me,' I stopped and turned around to face him, 'did nothing he say ring a bell? Do you not see the path opening out in the forest?'

'No,' he shouted, 'I do not know what you are talking about.'

I shook my head at the thickness of city people and kept on walking.

'Where are we going now?' he asked, completely perplexed.

'To the library of Ratnanidhi,' I replied firmly.

'I'll wait for you outside,' he said.

'Good.'

I knew my way within Ratnanidhi, a vast library, where steps automatically slowed in reverence and where even the glow of torches shone in humble obeisance. I quickly found the manuscript I was looking for. It was the one on New Science that I had hurriedly scanned in the secret library under Sakya's watchful eye. As I leafed through a copy of the same text I had seen in the Innermost Library, I realised that my suspicions were founded. An entire section was missing in the same book I held in my hands. A section that had been intact in the manuscript in the Innermost Library. And though I had not caught much of it, a term titling the entire missing section had stayed in my head.

The missing section referred to the Action Seal.

In Sakya's library, I had noticed the Action Seal section explained in abstruse Sanskrit that I didn't have time to read. Reading it would have been useless because it was probably codified in the twilight language, the sandhya bhasha. With a flash of brilliance I realised that *The Book on the Twilight Language* was in my possession, and I could use it now to decode all the secret symbols of all our texts.

It was not just the Action Seal that was obviously not meant for public consumption but many others as well. A logical pattern had emerged. Esoteric subjects were available in texts in monastic and lay libraries such as Ratnanidhi, Ratnasagar and Ratnadadhi with essential sections missing. The same text was available in secret collections, but they were codified in the Twilight Language. The unabridged texts with the essential sections of our most seminal books were with the Black Hats and the Nine Unknowns.

Lives could be lost to guard these texts. But acquiring these precious texts did not suffice. Living, accomplished masters were probably required to decode the essential sections. These living masters may not be as easy to acquire as the texts. The Nine Unknowns had clearly created two polarised groups around the books. And it was only the Unknowns who were the guardians of the secret texts guarded by the Nine, the Keepers of the Unknown.

I located abridged versions of the *Book of Time, Book of Space,* the *New Science, Sun Science* and *Cosmogony.*

I unfastened the books from their hooks and after issuing them and strapping them around my waist, I paced out of the echoing halls of Ratnanidhi. My shadow walked before me, soulless in its elongation, full of doom.

The time to confront the great acharya of Nalanda, my most revered master Aryadatta, had come.

19. *Doubting Faith*

I could not meet him.

My master had bestowed upon me the highest honours of the university and then turned his face away from me. If this was an elaborate plan to break my spirit, the plan was succeeding. *Help me, O my master, for I stand on the brink of madness.* I could not stave off the force of doubt and suspicion creeping into my body and weakening my faith and reason any more. I felt it would soon become a deluge and sweep me away.

The great Aryadatta ignored me again and again, with each attempt to meet him. And the more he ignored me, the more I avoided my brother. I cannot describe the frenzy my master's apathy drove me to. In spiritual and academic life, and the two are not different at all, it is only the relationship between master and disciple that destroys darkness. A guru, the dispeller of the dark, alone is the light that illumines. His importance is akin to that of the umbilical cord that ties the mother to the child. The guru is the blood that courses through the cord that nourishes. The guru is the flame that lights all flames.

My master's cold indifference was like blood blocking up and depriving me of sustenance. His stony silence when I greeted him was the umbilical cord winding around my neck and throttling life out of me. Nalanda had become a dank airless womb where I was gasping out my last breath.

Some rationalising voice told me that this was a test of faith, a challenge of the spirit, not a modern torture designed only for me. Almost every disciple worthy of note has been put through similar tests and some of them are harrowing tales indeed. Each emerged from their tribulations stronger, full of faith and enlightenment. *Was I so weak, then, that I could not brave a few challenges my masters had designed to combust my mind*? I have known masters who put their students through terrible atrocities for decades and the students emerged from the self-destruction much improved. And here I was, driven to the point of insanity by a few cave murals. *Yet, yet, yet, O my thoughts, how fierce are your clutches.* I could not will myself to believe that the events of the past few days, moving at such breakneck speed, were without a deeper logical pattern.

It was imperative to find it. And do something about it. Or else the misfortune the collusion of masters would wreak on Nalanda inhabitants, nay Nalanda itself, would be unimaginable. *Could it be that premise by logical premise, by trying to find out what my masters wanted and who they were, I was divesting myself of self-centred identifications of the mind?* It was true that all the esoteric practitioners were Logicians. Was I walking down a path they had taken? And like them, was esoteric Buddhism my final destination too?

The images of Dharmapada's bones crunching under the Raj Vaidya's implements, the ecstatic whirling of Bhim's ashen body, Nalanda's secret core pulsating in the dead of night, human skin hanging on clothes lines, women beheaded on chopping blocks, heretic letters posted on Nalanda gates, my appointment as an aide to a murder investigation conducted by my own brother, were step by logical step to reach a point where there were no more steps left to take. The most logical step left would then be to leap away from logic. The leap of faith. Could it be that the law of inversion was proving that guidance comes when guidance is no longer sought? Could the dispelling light of darkness, the guru, be taking me back to the source of light? Darkness.

If this were true, then it was the most brilliant Logical Method ever designed by my masters.

Step by logical step, it annihilates the premise that the logical mind is built on till only mind-numbing mindfulness remains. Is that *shunyata*? I remembered a word Tarpa had once mentioned. He had heard of a similar process from his Japanese friends. They called this process a *koan*. I wondered whether their koans were as painful as what my masters were subjecting me to. Because mine were unbearable.

I was at a place where faith stood before a contradicting and ugly truth that barred its way. My master used to say where there is truth there is beauty. Therefore, either my faith was false and unable to see truth which is why there was truth but no beauty. Or, the truth was false; there was neither truth nor beauty.

Faith, truth and beauty grappled with each other in a death rattle.

All through my academic life, I had been constantly reminded of Nalanda's rules. Don't go here, don't go there. This place is forbidden, that pavilion is beyond bounds. My faith had survived the knowledge that these rules were necessary to inculcate discipline, but it was now evident that the basis of the knowledge it rested on was falsehood. Ugly falsehood. For these were rules derived to hide guilt. The Inverted Palm Seal proved it. The missing pages of manuscripts in our revered public libraries proved it. The Rasayana labs and chopping blocks of Sitavana proved it. Guilt could not be true or beautiful. Guilt could not, should not, inspire faith. Guilt cannot be Guru, the light that dispels darkness.

Darkness was not approaching Nalanda. It was already within it. The darkness of decadence. The Black Hats.

And what was the Action Seal? Throughout my hair-raising adventures in Sitavana I could not find it. It was the reason why my brother was here, and why my masters were willing to sacrifice me like a goat. Was my master deliberately avoiding me because he somehow knew that I had stumbled upon the key to the mysterious murders? Was he trying to break me into submission, punish me for finding it?

I was finding it increasingly difficult to fight off that treacherous question every disciple fears and abhors. Should I apply for a change in tutorship? Or should I simply leave Nalanda and its terrifying decadence and forbidden places? Should I just get up tomorrow and follow the sunlight? Walk out of the gates and back to my father's kingdom where the throne awaited me?

The more I tried to fight off the idea, the more debilitating it became.

My master used to say, if you decide not to think about a monkey, obviously you will think of nothing else. How right he was! I could not erase the image of his burning eyes and the sound of his voice rushing towards me like the wind. 'Run! You are not ready yet!' I could not erase the image of his right hand holding the skull cap of a human that had once been alive.

I could not escape the fact that my master was a Kapalika.

Disaster had struck all those who had tried to bring about a change in tutelage. Pandit Dharmapada's student Bilwa had wanted to give up his discipleship. Pandit Dharmapada had drowned to death. Bhim had wanted to change his tutelage; he too had died a terrible death. If I made a similar application, would the same fate befall me?

Was I destined to be the next to go?

Both Dharmapada and Bhim had been dizzy, disoriented, and in an altered state of consciousness before their deaths. Just like me. Filled with certainty that I was going to be the next victim, I became more gloomy and morose. But I did not speak of this to anyone.

Again and again I was driven to circumambulate the clearing of the Giant Buddha statue where poor Bhim had danced his dance of death. The rolling whites of his eyes shining in the moonlight haunted me. I felt his unearthly ghost watching me as I tried to solve the riddle of his murder.

My brother and I quarrelled a lot over the death investigation. According to him, my contention that the activities at the Honeycomb needed to be investigated was irrelevant. My insistence inflamed him beyond his limited patience. He said the Honeycomb was disputed territory and prohibited for many years now. I remembered Bhim and my master there, and held my tongue.

He was also extremely scornful of my theory that the key to the murders might lie in the mystery of the Action Seal.

While we debated in the Royal Vihara, I confessed to Aditya Raj the last words that I had heard Bhim utter moments before his death. But Aditya Raj did not consider the information relevant. Once, while his servant was plucking out calluses from his feet and I was biting into one of the juiciest mangoes in Pataliputra, a thought occurred to me.

'It's the death code,' I said, 'both Dharmapada and Bhim were members of Secret Baladitya White. They were killed for trespassing into forbidden knowledge.'

'Horse dung,' my brother scoffed, 'there's no such thing as the death code.'

'How do you mean?' I asked, quite surprised.

'It's just a clever ploy by the Baladitya White administration to ensure confidentiality. I've never heard of anyone dying because of the death code. No one knows who uses it, or how it is used.'

'That is proof of its efficiency,' I argued, 'not its lack of existence.'

But my brother did not allow me to educate him about the simple beauty of my logical thesis. He insisted that the answers lay somewhere else. Somewhere in the roofless temple hidden and sealed by the Inverted Palm. He felt that Pandit Siroha had his finger on the pulse of the mystery, but I did not ask the right questions because it might implicate my masters. He said that Bhim had discovered these secrets and was punished for it. I rubbished these theories.

I strongly suspected that Bhim's association with Dharmapada was a clear indicator that he too was connected to Mahipala and also Dharmapada's murderer. My brother replied that since Dharmapada's murderer was a Black Hat, I was proving his theory correct.

Find out which Kapalika sect Bhim belonged to, I commanded my brother. There are at least ten different types of extant Kapalika sects, I said, regurgitating information from the cave plaques. And find out which hat Siroha wears. Black or white. My experience in the last few days, I said bitterly, is the more ascetic the Logician, the more esoteric his private practice.

My brother's investigation showed that Bhim had no known enemies. Apparently he had been a devout worshipper of the Wisdom Goddess, the Headless One. And like so many other yavana students, he did extensive research on the alchemical effects of mercury on levitation. His colleague Vallabha from Baladitya White had said that last year Bhim had conducted some dangerous experiments in the five elements lab, and Siroha had temporarily banished him from Secret Nalanda. We could not identify what form of esoterism he practised, or which Kapalika sect he belonged to. Since Kapalika sects were generic in nature, they did not come under any school or doctrine sanctioned by the university. This made it difficult to identify how it was operated.

It turned out that like many other students, Bhim too was excited about the discoveries of the New Science and had to be repeatedly warned to stay within its strict parameters. Unsupervised formulae not yet codified in New Science texts were frowned upon by Secret Nalanda masters. Unscheduled visits to the Wisdom Goddess, the Headless One's shrine, were not permitted. Secret Nalanda was bound and counter bound by many hard regulations, and Bhim had broken a lot of them.

However, if I had looked into this matter more closely, especially Bhim's alliance to the Headless One, I may have prevented his death. But who can stop the wheels of Time from moving when they have been set in motion?

There was no witness besides me that night, and I had found no reason to believe that he would be burnt to cinders moments later.

The only suspicious link we found was his interest in Pandit Dharmapada. His closest aides were ignorant of his desire for a change in tutorship and doubted that the two had ever interacted with each other.

Finally, both Aditya Raj and I agreed that some mystery bound Pandit Dharmapada to Bhim, a mystery kept secret from all. Whatever it was, it had killed them both. There was a third factor. A factor that could be a man who had knowledge of this secret and the motive for murder.

Aditya Raj was adamant about his theory of poisoning because on the night of his death, Bhim had denied dinner, complaining of a bilious stomach. Pandit Dharmapada too had seemed ill before his death. But I demurred, saying that it did not make sense for the murderer to poison and then drown his victim, or to poison and then burn his victim.

We argued indefinitely over this and his allegations that my masters had to be involved in these crimes. Given the knowledge that I carried inside me, of the missing pages of the book, of life-altering memories at Sitavana that I had not disclosed to my brother and wanted desperately to discuss with Aryadatta, I was at a complete loss. I took to avoiding my brother by day and haunting the gardens of Nalanda by night.

My brother left in a few days to submit his report to King Mahipala in Pataliputra, and I of tired limb and hollow eyes, stalked the chaityas and stupas of Nalanda in a vain attempt to flee my obsessive thoughts. Little did I know that the noose around my neck was firmly in place.

20. *Kama Sutra*

The monotony of my misery was broken by an incident very vivid in my memory. A general assembly was called for all ten thousand residing students and was presided over by the three thousand acharyas. We met, ironically, in the gigantic Assembly Hall, the entrance to Secret Nalanda. I stood on top of the iron motif that opened into the hidden tunnel with a knowing albeit manic smile on my face.

When the Abbot and five other grandmasters entered the hall and took their places in the seating cushions on the teaching platform, we sat down in concentric circles around them according to rank and monastery. The Abbot's voice rang out across the hall and the multi-robed sea of monks listened in a classic pose of reverence. The Abbot was brandishing a pamphlet in his hands and even from far I could see controlled thunder flashing in his eyes. Some in white robes and some in gold and silk, worn only by the highest grandmasters, stood next to the Abbot. The Abbot was bedecked with gold earrings, necklaces, armbands, waist girdles and rings.

The monks' accessories were the bowl, the cup, the rosary, roasted barley and a knife.

'It has been brought to our knowledge,' the Abbot said, 'that many illustrated copies of this pamphlet have been distributed in secret among not only the lay monks but the senior monastics of this esteemed university. All the masters stand here to deride and condemn this most reprehensible activity. For those of you who are standing at the back and cannot see this vulgar piece of literature in my hands, know that I am alluding to copies of the *Kama Sutra*.

A wave of tittering riffled through the crowd—among the monks and even some masters—but the Abbot chose to ignore it.

'I had difficulty believing that students of the excellence and caliber of Nalanda were really resorting to this gross form of personal pleasure. It does not behoove students of your stature to distribute secret copies of the *Kama Sutra* and pore over them like unenlightened laity. Those who have indulged in this deplorable activity have broken the simplest and most fundamental vows of monkhood. They are wasting their time here. Scurrilous gossip and uncontrolled thoughts of carnal pleasure will only retard their growth and plunge them into the nether world of irredeemable ignorance. Is this why you sought admission here?' The Abbot's scathing words made me cringe in my corner though I had never set eyes on the *Kama Sutra*.

'To waste university money in carnal pursuits? To thwart the commandments of the Buddha? To eat our food, wear our clothes and turn your backs on the most honoured tenets of the sangha? Such students have nothing to offer this university, besides their faeces that fill our septic tanks.' The Abbot paused, because some of the masters were fidgeting and looking askance at him. For the usually unflappable, his tirade had gone too far. As if in immediate recognition of this fact, the Abbot took on a more conciliatory tone.

'The *Kama Sutra* was written as you know by Vatsyayana, a very rigorous student of the scriptures. He was a time-honoured celibate, and never once deviated from the purpose of his study, research and observation. This sutra is an important scripture that had been kept secret from the unenlightened eye of the general public because of their inability to understand the true nature of research. But unfortunately, this erudite manuscript has become a lewd illustration for the nightly activities of the gross and perverse. Nalanda tried to stop the circulation of this Sutra, but the lower forces of human nature are indeed difficult to combat. First, this scripture was secreted amongst the houses of the most important courtesans. Then it permeated down the royal brothels to the general public. Now it is being sold for a few cowries in the streets and bazaars of the village.

But it is a matter of great shame that the monks of Nalanda, on whose shoulders the future enlightenment of mankind rests, are unable to resist the most basic of temptations.'

To the left of me, across a section of tonsured acolytes, a ripple of activity made itself visible to my peripheral vision. It was like a pebble falling in the corner of a still lake. I did not see them as much as hear them. They were a batch of novices from a neighbouring monastery due for their full ordination the next monsoon. A clear voice amongst them rang across the hall.

'The vows of an ordained monk forbid him to speak, look or think of the opposite sex. So did not Vatsyayana break his vows when he was researching the *Kama Sutra*?'

A restless wave coursed through ten thousand monks, like a sea breeze teasing the ocean. All eyes from the teachers' platform turned in the direction from where the audacious question had appeared. The question held us in its thrall, powerful and lucid. Never before had an arhat, nay mahasiddha no less, been questioned by an unordained monk in a public gathering. Never. I was witnessing sacrilege.

The voice of rebellion was soft but sure. And when the masters turned away to ignore it and I thought it would die down, another voice emerged from behind the first one, stronger than the first.

'The Buddha forbade us to touch gold. How come that does not apply to you?'

'The Buddha said shave your head. Why do you then have a team of hairdressers?'

The ocean of monks turned to watch the Abbot's reaction. Five masters decided to control ten thousand men by staring them down. And surely for the first time in the history of Nalanda, it did not work.

Shouts of 'moral depravity', and 'the rot of decadence', 'down with the sky flower doctrine', 'sorcerers,' and 'black magicians' rose in a torrent, picking up a wave of protest from the monks. They had got up from their seats and were rushing about. There were dwarapalas everywhere, hundreds of them, circling the teaching platform. I remembered that the last time policing was required, it was for the Chinese scholar. The dwarapalas on duty were from the Sarvastivadin Monastery and Bhim was one of them. But now Bhim was dead.

The grandmasters stood stoic, unflinching as a volley of abuse was hurled at them.

'*Cannibals! Bloodsuckers*!' came the shouts from the western corridors. When a skirmish between the monks and the dwarapalas knocked a few monks unconscious, it resulted in a stampede.

A protective ring of dwarapalas appeared from nowhere and escorted the grim-faced grandmasters away.

Asita the Great was standing next to me, alone, atop a pillar to escape the rushing crowd.

'Mahipala's men are inciting the monks,' he said above the din of shouting.

'Outside, angry mobs have not stopped hurling stones at the Nalanda walls.' Rahula appeared, climbing a platform next to me to avoid the stampede.

'And now the rebellion has moved within. The monks are revolting,' I agreed over the shouting, shaking like a leaf as a mob crossed me.

And then, just like the torrential rain so typical of our land, it was over. The noise died down. The masters returned. The dwarapalas took their positions outside the Assembly Hall. The remaining group reassembled in an automated and trained response and the Abbot gently continued to chide us for our misdemeanours as if nothing had happened. At least half the monk population remained to again find direction in their lives. And in an instant the uproar had diminished. Just like a summer afternoon when the torrential rain suddenly stops.

That was the magnitude of Nalanda. Like the mythical Leviathan, it abided over all rocky seas, withstood all cyclones, all typhoons.

The few thousands of us who remained were quickly under the sway of the Abbot's rhetoric again. It was exceedingly embarrassing to hear the Abbot, who had hitherto only expounded on the highest principles of the sciences, speak to us so. The masters took turns to chide us first in angry, and then loving tones. The faces of the innocent and the guilty reddened in acute discomfort and we hung our heads in an effort to hide ourselves. A sea of young men stood in collective shame of their basic instincts.

Later, a fire sacrifice of expiation was conducted in the fire courtyard where copies of the *Kama Sutra* were burnt. Chastened students were dispersed very late in the day, each I am sure, carrying a firm conviction never to indulge in frivolous self-shaming again. The rebellion was forgotten.

As for me, clear of conscience and not besmirched by guilt, I enjoyed the luxury of a few laughs with my friends, who I knew to be pitiful victims of their unvanquished libido. But the instant my elbow nudged Rahula's ribs, an image of Gauri flashed across my mind and my knees went immediately weak with the fearful conclusion that I was not any different from my rightfully castigated friends.

This immediately sent me into a state of confusion and anxiety. I remembered what the Abbot had said, about how the *Kama Sutra* had been kept hidden from the general populace because they were too immature to comprehend the true nature of research. And again the bubbles surfaced, like beaten down monks rising from the Assembly Hall.

Like the *Kama Sutra,* Kapalika too thrived in the shadows of secrecy.

Secrets, again secrets. Secrets exist only to hide guilt. And then I thought, *am I looking for guilt because I myself am guilty*? Had my own inabilities afflicted me with the rot of doubt? Is this what happened to Pandit Dharmapada and Bhim? Would my doubting lead me to my death? But would not my blind surrender to faith destroy my intelligence and lead me to superstition? Either way, the prognoses for my ailments were not good.

It was with these thoughts and a flailing determination to keep both my rationality and my faith alive that I attended, after a long time, the evening worship conducted by my master at the Avalokiteshwar shrine. As if to test my new resolution, the Buddhas placed Gauri there, and I took in her presence with a sharp intake of breath. Usually, my brief and chance encounters with Gauri had been so electrifying that I noticed little else. But this time, standing in a shadowy niche of the shrine during the long ceremony, I had ample opportunity to observe her and the other women comprising the contingent of virgin girls who led the chants in Nalanda shrines. Gauri, oblivious to all else, was riveted by the crescendo of the chant, her eyes looking on adoringly at Avalokiteshwar, the embodiment of Buddha's compassion, an artist's tribute in stone. I could see that her companion, who on every occasion had been by her side, must be one of her sisters. I had found out that her name was Uma. They both had the same high forehead and the same proud stubborn jawline. She wore heavy jewellery unlike Gauri, and an elaborate nose ring glinted sharply as she turned to smile at her sister. My gut churned in cold precision. I had seen nose rings like that in Vaishali. Courtesans received them from their patrons after their first deflowerment. The richness of her other jewellery too contradicted the poverty of their household, which I had seen with my own eyes. Only kings and temple priests owned gems like that.

My eyes then went to her extremely fat mother who stood to my master's right, blowing into a conch. I recalled another memory of her from a harvest dance competition during Baisakh celebration, and was surprised that I had missed the immensity of her proportions. She was a middle-aged woman, very fair of complexion, and of many chins and several stomachs. She had about her an aura of extreme power and looked as if it were her and not my master who was presiding over the ceremony. The force of her personality seemed to dwarf my master, and he looked like a small subdued child beside her.

I quietly walked up to Rahula and stood next to him. Like me, he too was more an observer, while the others remained enraptured by the devotional trance, the whirling lights, the thick scent of incense and the rhythm the drums and music were creating. Something quite unique was happening here. As the suffusing smoke of burning camphor billowed into the dank airless hall, many devouts raised their arms in gestures of ecstatic surrender. Some with eyes closed had fallen into involuntary raptures and many had started prostrating and even fainting on the ground.

'Is the fat woman moving the crowd?' I muttered to Rahula, suddenly self-conscious that my coldly clinical tone sounded incongruous in the frenzy of devotion the ceremony had created.

I had seen the forest Dakini do something similar with snakes. Could this woman be doing it to people?

'Don't you know?' Rahula muttered back, equally coldly clinical.

'She is considered more powerful than your master.'

In shock I moved away from him. I returned awhile to hiss into his ears.

'What is it that you speak of?'

'I jest,' Rahula said, looking on at the pavilion idols. 'She is a high priestess of the Headless One's shrine after all. Bhim was only one in her long list of followers. Look at the power she exudes. And see how rich her clothes are. Many say she is high nobility of some inexplicable extraction.'

'Is this common knowledge?' I would not have been surprised to again be the last one privy to what appeared to be common knowledge.

'Nothing, my dear friend,' Rahula said with a laconic smirk, 'in Nalanda is common knowledge. Think, Siddhartha, every year, Nalanda conducts the Kumari Puja in reverential worship of virgin girls. Why should celibate monks steeped in uncommon vows feel the need to worship virgins? Is the answer common knowledge?'

'Come now,' I argued. The devotional chant over, the crowd was collecting around the prayer lamps, and with their palms they symbolically smeared the heat of the flames on their heads. There were quite a few laity here. Fruits and clothes were being distributed.

'The *Kama Sutra* incident is over. Don't linger on against the masters like another paid Mahipala stooge. Kumari Puja is an age-old custom of these lands. A time-honoured oblation to the Goddess. What could be wrong with that?'

Rahula dismissed me with a dry smile and moved forward to receive the flame. Almost as if he knew what I had seen in Sitavana.

'Let not the seeds of doubt sprout in your heart,' I said after him, like a pious thief warning others about the sin of stealing. 'It might destroy you.'

It was interesting to watch my master bend low to touch the mammoth lady's feet. Mischief danced in her heavily made up eyes and her mouth moved in a coquettish smile.

'Many call her a Dakini,' a whisper teased my ear. I turned to find its source and realised it was Rahula, irrepressible mischief glinting in his eyes. And then, he was gone.

Another feather touch, this time a brush against my shoulder, a touch too womanly, made my skin prickle. I turned again in anger to confront the perpetrator, and became like stone turning to water as I faced Gauri.

'You take your vows very seriously,' she said, a small sad smile playing on her lips, like a lone lotus bud floating in a pleasure pond.

'Should I not?' I said, calming my heart, pacing my breath that came rough and swift.

'Where does your chastity come from?' she asked. For me it was not a question. It was a leaf falling softly to the ground. Her eyelashes fluttered for a moment before she looked at me straight in the face. Her deep honest gaze was an arrow finding its mark. 'There is also chastity that lies beyond chastity. There, one does not have to try so hard.'

Her words brought my breast to boil. A treacherous fire coursed through my nether regions, shaming me. I tried to calm myself, flushing in the hellish inferno of her temptation.

'How can there be chastity beyond chastity?' I asked almost in a pleading tone.

And when she did not reply, I said, 'You are not a woman of letters, Gauri. You do not know that when two dissimilar quantities are brought together, they cancel each other out.'

I did not realise how much arrogance, how much condescension my words contained till she replied. Her reply dropped the bottom out of my argument and her wisdom left me speechless.

'Only when chastity comes from hatred for women does chastity become a dissimilar quantity,' she said, and then turned away from me.

'You are right. I am an unlettered village girl. I only understand the time when the cows come home.'

And giving me one last slanted look from under her veil, like a doe before bolting for cover, she disappeared.

At that moment she did not look like a girl, but like an ageless, eternal Goddess. That entire evening, I contemplated the teaching that lay in her simple words.

Had I been wrong all this while? Was I treating chastity as a negative concept? Chastity had always been to me a quantity qualified by don'ts. And then I thought, if abstinence from women was a positive value of chastity and hatred for women a negative value of chastity, they cancelled each other out. Love and abstinence gave a double aggregate of positive chastity values. Interestingly, a negative value of chastity added to hatred gave an equally powerful negative aggregate.

I thought that this would be a good topic for the debating pits. I did not realise that I had stumbled upon the biggest abiding secret of all time.

21. *The Bird that Won't Fly*

Over the next few days, Nalanda continued its way of being what it was, a giant ship in the galaxy. Only here and there, shadows of bad omens seemed to have befallen it. There were prophecies of doom and that the Evil Eye had been cast on Nalanda. Some prophetic texts surfaced, saying the end was nigh, and the Apocalypse was at hand. In various precincts, fire sacrifices and ritualistic oblations were conducted to appease the Evil Wind and the impending darkness progressing towards us.

Periodically, every time this refrain came up, a shiver would run through Nalanda. Briefly, even I came under its grip. My monastery's sandal-keeper was assiduous in his duties of keeping our sandals safe and arranged according to status and rank. He was also a close friend. Rahula and I always waited for him to come with us for the morning community baths at the ponds.

He warned me that he could see a perpetual shadow following me around. I sought out the Exorcism Committee for counsel. It was tradition—if darkness was perceived to bother or shadow a student, then the Exorcism Committee would conduct rituals to lift it.

On studying my darkness, the verdict they passed was 'disconnect with my master'.

Disconnect with the master signified a disconnect with the entire university, just as a thorn in the foot disturbed the entire body. The committee executed an order for an atonement ritual to nullify the disrespect my master was being subjected to by me.

I participated in the exorcism with full humility, almost relief.

Maybe because of it, or in spite of it, I made one last attempt to meet my master. I stood at the doorway of his sleeping quarters, my heart a thudding betrayal of my stoic demeanour. At least his servant, a lay monk, had allowed me into the portals of his inner quarters. This could be a portent of great good fortune or terrible disaster. I stood meekly by as my master was fussed upon by silent-footed attendants in an elaborate dressing ceremony.

He slipped into a bejewelled gown held up to him without looking at me who directly faced him, my head bowed. Gems were clapped to his ears and slipped onto his fingers. The tuft of honour on his head was massaged, oiled and combed till it became a thing of beauty. His robes were folded about him till all the creases fell exactly. He was obviously preparing for a council ceremony or a state guest. I could tell because his personal elephant, the ultimate honour bequeathed to only great grandmasters, stood outside, shifting from giant foot to giant foot, bedecked in all its glory, like an obese bride waiting for her groom. I watched him, feeling more and more ashamed of him with every passing moment.

My master's cosmetic beautification was becoming interminably long. I thought it would never end. Till at last, sandals inlaid with the intricate work of silver and gold leaf embroidery were placed at his feet. Then one unseen gesture from my master had the minions bowing away without showing their back to the master.

He approached me, jovial, perfumed, and evidently in a good mood. His cheeks were rouged, his hair reddened, his eyes kohled. 'So, Siddhartha,' his acknowledgement was full of convivial cheer, 'what brings you here?'

By this time I was fighting back tears. Exhausted and confounded by the vicissitudes of fate and the vagaries of Nalanda, I fell at his feet and sobbed noisily over his perfumed sandals.

'My master, why have you deserted me?' Days and nights of desolate reveries burst through the floodgates and I was unable to stem the tide. He waited for the wave to subside and gently lifted me by my shoulders. When he looked at me, his eyes were luminous from a deep and faithful light shining from within.

'A true master can never desert his disciple,' he said, his tone so gentle it wreaked fresh sobs of yearning within me, 'even when his disciple deserts him.'

His kindness washed over me like a cleansing flood and all my muscles released their tension. 'And you Siddhartha, you are my son. You are to me like my own Self.'

'But, master, I have never been apart from you for even a day. And yet, now you do not look at me, nor answer my questions, nor heed my presence.'

Molten steel freezing over my master's eyes panicked me and spurred me into a rush of words that came out unbeknownst to me. The purpose of my visit lay forgotten. I could not remember the carefully prepared logical treatise I had made regarding the death investigation. Dharmapada and Bhim were forgotten, furthest from my mind. It was as if my thoughts had been stuck with glue and my tongue gifted its own mind.

'I have never needed your guidance more than now. O my master, I am beset by too many questions.' And then I said the dreaded word. 'Help me, Venerable One, for I am assailed by doubt.'

I could sense my master's body stiffen. His mouth had become a grim line. I could not understand this. This was the same Aryadatta who provoked and encouraged our most scathing critiques during academic sessions. Doubt is the most important aspect of faith, he used to say. But now, the slightest whiff of doubt was drawing his scorn and condescension. His contempt goaded me on, making me more bereft, and I said things I shouldn't have.

'My master, relieve me of the responsibility of this investigation. I do not have the skills or the maturity for it. I am unable to go on without your guidance. It is a matter for stronger hearts and better minds. There are too many questions plaguing me.'

'Compose yourself, Siddhartha,' he said sternly, as if I were a child. And then he repeated the sentence twice more: 'Compose yourself. Compose yourself.'

As he said these words, a silence descended on me. My tears dried up and my breathing became normal. I suddenly felt as if I were in another place. My master's voice softened and reached me from a great distance.

'My son,' he said, 'it is the nature of the mind to doubt. And though it be an impurity, a klesha, it can be used by the mind to cleanse itself. Poison kills poison. And when your mind has cleansed itself, poison settles like sediment at the bottom. Then the mind, like distilled water purified of its sediment, reflects the clear nature of truth.'

'And what is the nature of truth?' I asked.

'Faith. Faith is the clear mind purified of doubt. Doubt is the turbulent, unclear mind.'

I didn't like the sound of the word. It sounded like a mousetrap to me. I implored him one last time, summoning up all our years of intellectual rigour.

'How can you say that? You, who is the master of Logic and Reason?'

'A truly knowledgeable man,' he said, picking up his walking stick, 'is a man who knows the limits of his knowledge.'

It was becoming clear to me that our interview was coming to an end. Not knowing whether I would get a chance to meet him again, I came up with my burning questions with some urgency.

'Why have the university honours been conferred on me? What have I done to deserve them? The silken robes, the Inverted Palm Seal, the lights, the ornate sandals?'

His smile was full of mystery, as if he had seen my future, and knew something I would never comprehend.

'These honours have been conferred on you, Siddhartha, because you have set yourself on an incredible journey even though you are not aware of it. It is a journey towards rebirth and much enlightenment.'

'Journey?' I was incredulous, 'By becoming an aide to some politically motivated murder investigation?'

'Yes,' my master's eyes sparkled with mischief, 'it is not by accident that you were chosen for this task that has put you in the eye of a storm of historical proportions. There are a hundred reasons why things happen. The average mind can comprehend only a few of them.'

'I don't understand,' I shook my head.

'You shall,' he fondly patted my cheek and moved out.

'Master,' I called out one last time. Like a snake rising out of a snake-charmer's hood, the question sprang out of me. 'Please allow me a change of tutelage.'

He turned like a whiplash seeking its target. 'What did you say?' he whispered.

'Please transfer my discipleship to Siroha.' It was too late now to withdraw.

'What depths of delusion are you descending to, Siddhartha?' he thundered. 'What calumny is this?'

He came up to me and brandished his staff in my face. I was rooted to the spot, transfixed in horror.

'Come on, out with it, you scandalmongering cur. Who put this idea in your head? Siroha? Why do you want a change of tutorship, you fool! Why?'

'He has the Action Seal!' I muttered. My master paused, petrified in fury. 'The Action Seal is the key to the murder mysteries,' I finished under my breath.

'You fool!' he raised his stick over his shoulder and with every blow he repeated this word, as if it were a punctuation at the end of a sutra.

'I gave you the Inverted Palm Seal!' My master weilded the stick with a strength far beyond a man of his age. I hunched my back so no bones would break.

'The highest honour!' All I could hear now was the whistle of his stick, sizzling the air.

'Why didn't you use it!' he raged.

'Is the Inverted Palm an Action Seal?' The question came from me like an inspired flash in the blur of beating.

'You fool!' his stick whistled.

'You fool!' his words rose like welts on my skin.

'I opened the cage for you. Why must you be the bird that won't fly!'

'You fool!' swished his cane, and I thought finally my bones would crack. Although I succumbed at first, after a while, as he rained down blows at me, I fended them off with my shoulders. Each blow created a bruise that I knew would take lifetimes to heal. Even though his staff came down at me without relent, surprisingly, I felt no pain. Humiliation must have so benumbed me. Even when he stopped, he couldn't stop muttering.

'What a fool you are, Siddhartha! What a fool!'

He got up to his full terrifying posture and screamed in a rage so fierce that his face was a mass of purple contusions.

'*Get out of my sight!*' he roared. 'And don't come near me.'

Shaken, shocked, I lifted myself and tried to leave with whatever dignity I could summon. I left my master's house feeling that I had never before sunk lower than this. But still, in spite of the daze, I was calm. A quiet white peace had fallen gently over me, like the gentle snow of distant lands. And my mind felt clear and light. I knew for sure now that the term Action Seal was the key to some great and terrible mystery. And by mentioning it, I had opened a trapdoor to some gory netherworld.

The secret texts of the New Science I had hurriedly read in Sakya's library flashed in my mind. And the truth behind some of its words revealed itself. I thought I knew now what the Action Seal meant.

I was certain now of renouncing my master. All I could do was brace myself against the beasts of hell that I knew would soon fall upon me.

22. *The Washing Ghats*

After I felt I had got over the shock of my encounter with my master, I decided that the most sensible course of action for me was to stay away from him, Siroha and the murder investigation. I would wait for my brother, put myself under the king's protection and take further orders from Pataliputra.

I presumed that I could not be in more trouble than I already was. There is a certain freedom in living as the doomed. What does a man certain of death have to fear? My bravado made me light-headed. I spent an inordinate amount of time trying to find out more about the New Science called Tantra that had captured the imagination of my beloved university. I became obsessed with its research and study.

'There are more whores in Nalanda's colleges than dogs in its village streets,' said the cook in my monastery kitchen. With this sentence beating in my heart like a ceremonial chant, I, recklessly, audaciously, thought of braving all of Nalanda's prohibited places once again, especially the inner halls of the Rasayana and Nagarjuna's gold mint in Sitavana Monastery. I made up my mind to enter the roofless temple as well. Even though I had had the Inverted Palm Seal in my possession, for the first time I toyed with the idea of using it. But the idea soon fizzled out like a firecracker during Buddha's Birthday.

I did not want to know anymore. My visit to the Honeycomb and Bhim's macabre death had killed all desire for truth.

My brother sent word through his pageboy that he would be arriving the next day. He informed me that the Nalanda grandmasters could no longer avoid the eventuality of the council. My elders had finally caved to kingly pressure and agreed to hold the council the next full moon, thus opening its doors to the harsh and growing oppositional forces of Brahminism, other schools of Buddhism, disgruntled Buddhist kings, and the politics of survival.

It is time, my brother informed, for Nalanda to come down from its giddy heavenly heights and answer to the masses. It is time for Nalanda to be accountable, was the royal decree. Kingly patience had worn thin. Hold the council, Mahipala had said to the Abbot, or I shall have your head on a platter.

Food in the Dining Hall was consumed in silence. Mahakala images adorned every kitchen in Nalanda. Care was taken to concentrate on the mastication process and the chosen incantation was recited inwardly even as the Dining Hall musicians chanted the various names of Buddha to create an atmosphere of contemplation. In some kitchens, sutras were declaimed from lecterns.

The Brahmagupta Dining Hall was the most well-lit and spacious of all and from where I sat, I could see a longitudinal row of shaven-headed acolytes sitting cross-legged, trying to eat their rich meal of beans, meat and rice without a show of relish. There were five different kinds of sweetmeats made of sugar and buffalo and cow milk. It was the night after the Parinirvana Uposatha, so the meal was special. Diligently we offered the food to the Buddha first. Since on this special occasion many meats were served, we fervently prayed for the reincarnation of the animals in better realms.

At the entrance of the Dining Hall stood a beautifully carved statue of the deity Annapurna, the Goddess of food, a special attraction of the Brahmagupta kitchen. Beside her was an entire mural of intricately calligraphed sutras in Arabic and Aramaic, languages alien to many Nalanda natives.

I looked askance at Rahula sitting next to me. He looked as if he had just roused himself from sleep. I took pleasure in breaking a cardinal law of the Dining Hall. Do not talk while eating. 'My friend,' I said, my mouth quite full, 'what ails you? Of late, you don't seem to be doing much, besides eating, sleeping and defecating.'

A suppressed titter coursed through our neighbours, but nobody dared reply. A reader was declaiming from his lectern.

'Vinaya is the achara of a bodhisattva,' his words wafted up to my ears. Virtue is the demeanour of the Enlightened, it meant. The law of inversion translated it into lies, vice and unenlightenment, I thought.

In the meanwhile, Rahula had let loose a good-natured laugh. 'A wise man can accomplish more while eating, sleeping and defecating than a normal person can,' he whispered his retort.

Some mischievous spirit inhabiting the Dining Hall made me reach out to his ear and whisper.

'Is it the Action Seal that has made you so wise, Rahula?'

I expected him to innocently enquire about the Action Seal, after which I had planned to engage him in a long banter. But, to my shock, he stopped eating and stared at me. When he saw the unwitting surprise in my face, he made an effort to swallow and continue eating. I grabbed his shoulder and became hoarse in my urgency.

'You know about the Action Seal.'

'Let go of my shoulder.' He shook himself free.

'Rahula,' I pleaded, 'talk to me.'

But Rahula had pried himself loose and left the Dining Hall, his uneaten meat languishing on the banana leaf plate.

I hounded him to the monastery, to the teaching chaityas and the play gardens. But each time, he warded me off, saying that he didn't know, or 'leave me alone', or 'I have never heard of the

Action Seal.' I even followed him to the washing ghats where our sanghatis dried in the afternoon sun.

'Are you Siroha's secret disciple?' I asked. 'Take me to him,' I said, following his receding back zigzagging across our dried ochre robes. 'I'm changing my master,' I shouted out when I could not overtake him, and panting, tried to catch my breath leaning against a large brass urn containing maroon dye. At a distance, I saw him snatch his loincloth from the clothesline and turning around to face me, he said, 'You are going to die, Siddhartha. And when you do, I don't want to die with you.'

I still made a step towards him, but when he said that he would complain to the authorities if I continued to harass him, I left him alone. I walked away from him thinking that I had not only lost my master but also my closest friend.

23. *Buffalo Farms*

After my encounter with Rahula, I suddenly turned my attention to the task I had procrastinated on for too long, the manuscript my brother and I had acquired from Sakya's library. *The Book on the Twilight Language.* I had completely forgotten about its relevance in the consciousness-altering encounter with my master. That and Rahula's antagonism had deeply traumatised me in ways I couldn't have ever imagined.

When I had told my brother to wait till I had finished reading the book, he had warned me that a scholar from Mahipala's court had heard about the text and had refused to translate it, calling it too depraved and an atrocity to all humanity.

The manuscript was wrapped in the finest silk. I fastened it securely under my sanghati. I carried the books I had issued from Ratnanidhi in a jute bag over my shoulder. The *Book of Time, Space and Cosmogony* had essential sections missing. Only the master copy in Sakya's library contained the secret sections. But by cross referencing the Twilight Language manual with the Ratnanidhi books, I was confident I could piece together the missing contents.

I wended my way to the Buffalo Farms. There, in a deserted place, away from the glare of intellectual showmanship, under the bird-soiled, untended statues of the great Logicians Dinnaga and Dharmakirti and the comforting smell of dung and bellowing buffaloes, I sat down to first use my contemplation practices to solve the murder mystery. Unfortunately, though, my introspection did not come up with a solution.

How could one possibly look for a clear and defined motive in a university of ten thousand people?

How did Bhim the Burly burn to death? Was he alcoholic? Did fat and his Kapalika accoutrements create a wick effect? Did he have weak bones? Were there imbalances in subatomic particles? Was there a nuclear reaction?

There were no answers today. Sitting in the corner-most feeding shed, behind the ample rear of a constantly relieving buffalo, I eventually turned my attention to the books.

I read with much trepidation. My body trembled as if with fever as I turned the palm leaves.

After that day, I spent many days at the Buffalo Farms. It took me a long time to make a list of references from the Ratnanidhi texts and decode them with *The Book on Twilight Language*.

By now I had picked up some knowledge of the subtle anatomy of the human body. What continued to amaze me was that texts like the Twilight Language were written by Buddhist Logicians! In a flash I saw a future world that would not believe that these texts were written by the same people.

Meanwhile, at the Buffalo Farms, time passed.

The buffaloes studied me as I studied the texts. Shadows lengthened. Days shortened. The dung pile increased. The buffaloes around me moved faster than me. I had stopped moving. Only the air shifted, to rustle the sound of palm leaves turning, and only my eyes fluttered, to follow the words dancing before me. When I finished decoding, my understanding of sandhya bhasha, the Twilight Language, was confirmed and complete. I carefully closed the books and let out a sigh so deep it made the buffaloes look up and take notice.

What I learnt was that the Twilight Language operated at three different levels. In the deepest twilight, language was not for communication but for direct transmission of knowledge. It could be seen and heard as the runic alphabet, symbols, seed syllables, melody and song. I had witnessed a runic alphabet demonstration in the roofless temple through my eye piece. The ordinary human mind could not grasp this, for it manifested at the most esoteric level. Here, language was perceived rather than conceptualised, it was a meditative state beyond the limitations of the fallible intellect.

The next level was the purest language of communication—Sanskrit. This language, I knew, was used in the high sciences, Logic and Mathematics.

The most common and crudest use of the Twilight Language, however, was neither of these two. In the common use, the medium was usually a baser language of local parlance, like Pali. It was a communication system for secret cults to pass on information and teachings. Through this code, clandestine meetings, locations and rituals could be relayed, away from the scrutiny of the moralising esoteric illiterate. Like me.

Bliss,
emptiness,
prajna,
wisdom
were key words for the female sexual partner.

A Vidyadhara literally meant wisdom holder. So by definition, he was the one who controlled a female sexual partner. There were no terms for the male sexual partner. I discovered this was because esoteric practice was catalogued and archived only for the benefit of the male adept. There were no written records or practices for the female adept.

'Gates of samsara,' 'lower door' were key words for the female sex organ.

Surya and cinnabar were synonymous with menstrual blood.

Lotus for vagina.

So was the downward triangle,
the eight petalled flower,
rivers,
caves,
receptacles,
mango leaves,
hibiscus
and the colour red.
Mercury or
moon and
the colour white was
sperm.
Linga,
skillful means,
method,
the upturned triangle,
the pyramid,
the mountain,
diamond,
jewel
guru
thunderbolt
all referred to the phallus.
The four doors,
The four joys,
Were the four points of the orgasm.
Sixty-four,
Was the female sexual adept who could release sixty-four elixirs in sixty-four different sexual positions.
Bodhichitta was the mixture of sperm and menstrual blood.
The jewel in the lotus,
Two feet,
union of space (female) and time (male),

hirayagarbha (the golden womb),
yoga,
sanctum sanctorum
the great seal were
symbols for sexual intercourse.
The tongue was a symbol for a cannibalistic feast.
The wheel for an orgy.
The skullbowl,
the scimitar and dagger for blood sacrifice.
Paradise was equivalent to
slaughter houses and
cemeteries.

The Twilight Language operated on the law of inversion, the cornerstone of the New Science.

Inversion revealed the true nature of reality as always the exact opposite of illusory appearance. The difference between appearance and reality is the difference between heaven and hell, my mother used to say.

As I read on, I learnt how, using the law of inversion, the negative, the cruel and the dark could be used to create an indomitable psychic body. This body was an adamantine diamond body made of subtle physiological energies. These were the same energies the Chinese scholar had tried to illumine, much to her detriment.

Enlightenment through the radical inversion of the opposite was now clear and evident. It was the pinnacle of all systems that most efficiently transformed sexuality into worldly and material power.

An exhaustive explanation of Action Seals opened up before me. I finally confirmed the nature of the Action Seal. It was not a seal made of clay or copper or gemstone. It was made of human flesh. The Action Seal was a clever subterfuge for the female sexual partner. How the forest Dakini must have laughed after I mentioned it to her. Why must I get all the buffoons, she had said.

'You fool!' said my master's whiplash.

I read about the four doors and the four types of Action Seals required to unlock the four doors. I read about their ages, the shape and categories of their breasts, vulva and pubic hair, their castes, demeanour, types of menstrual blood and five temperaments. There were exhaustive details on how to acquire the docile ones, control the ferocious ones, subdue the wild ones, pacify the frightened ones, and bribe the young and innocent. I read it again and again and again. In the fading light, with shaking hands, I took out a flint from my sanghati and read more. And more.

And I knew that it was not enough to be a woman eater. It was not enough to watch them burn and make pellets out of those charred body parts we could not eat. We needed to fuck them as well. Because superpowers were birthed in the female consciousness. And we could only appropriate it by stealing their sexual energy. And consciousness. That's how the powerful adamantine psychic body was created. By women. The great mahasiddhas we worshipped received their powers from the women they fucked. And no one knew who these women were.

In a world as inverted as this, we obviously needed a Twilight Language.

I recalled the last statement Gauri had made to me: *'I only understand the time the cows come home.'* Dust raised by cows returning home was called godhuli. The cows came home during dusk. She was hinting at the Twilight Language.

Under the benevolent gaze of two wide-horned, extremely well-fed buffaloes chewing cud, I wept. Copiously, bitterly, wiping my face with my sanghati, I wept for all of mankind. Mostly, I did not then understand why, I wept for Gauri.

I had always known that men and women participate in many rituals and practices unaware of their deeper significance.

Now I also knew that this New Science was an extreme denial of our humanity, the very cause, the very reason for liberation. Since the law of this science rested on the law of inversion, and the opposite also had an opposite, it followed that this New Science was the opposite of humanity. It was inhuman. It was the opposite of liberation. It was bondage. It was not freedom. It was depravity. How could depravity result in freedom? Depravity could only lead to dubious sorcery.

It became clear to me that a shift in consciousness from the mundane to the supramundane was defined as enlightenment, nirvana and moksha. The New Science had derived dubious methods to achieve this.

Is this really how the eighty-four mahasiddhas became enlightened? Through magic and sorcery? Even if great beings were created out of this, what use were such tortures?

So this was the knowledge that Mahipala, and surely there were other kings, hungered for?

Godhood and immortality through the murder and rape of half of humanity?

This was probably the surge of emotion that swept over me a day later as I sat listening to the chanting of the two hundred and twenty-seven rules of monastic conduct during the patimokka ceremony of the Uposatha under a compassionate sun in my monastery courtyard.

The Uposatha ceremony, conducted every month in all the monasteries, was extremely beneficial to monks and there was hardly anyone who disagreed with this. The Uposatha conductors were usually senior, genial, old bhikshus who took a benevolent stance at the vacillations of young acolytes and monks. The reading out of the patimokka always had a calming effect and meeting the lay people afterwards was a source of rejuvenation for us. The ritual confessions by monks were sometimes banal like oversleeping and sometimes serious like theft, but all transgressions were looked upon by the senior bhikshus with a benign eye.

Discipline was enforced by the Discipline Committee on issues raised by a unanimous group of monks. I have already mentioned such an occasion. Unless the digressions were really serious, such as disrespecting a master, or causing bodily harm to a peer, monks rarely tattled on their own and the Uposatha master seldom broached any strictness towards us. So the ambience was kindly and free of reproach.

In a crowd of around a hundred chanting monks, I sat on the floor squeezed between Asita and Tarpa, feeling exceedingly uncomfortable in their presence. Rahula sat in the corner-most area. Realising that Asita and Tarpa were less antagonistic than Rahula, I kept my peace and settled down. Both of them looked so content soaking in the sunshine and the twittering of birds, I could have strangled them with my sanghati.

A young monk was confessing to nightly emissions. And then, utterly surprised, utterly detached, I observed myself get up without any thought of the consequences. Interrupting the gentle reproaches of the senior bhikshu, I stood on my seat and blurted.

'Why is celibacy necessary?'

The lazy monotonous chanting stopped. All eyes turned to me in horror. Rahula was staring at me as if I were a disembodied ghoul. Never before in my entire monastic life have I been so indiscreet.

Asita and Tarpa grabbed my hands from either side and tried to pull me down to my hemp cushion. I refused to budge. I would not allow the senior bhikshu his dignity of silence.

'Answer me!' I used all my training in the discipline of speaking without heat. 'I demand that you answer me. *Why is abstinence necessary?*'

The senior got up from his feathered seat, his calm disposition gone. 'Because women are the spawn of hell,' he spat through his toothless gums.

He reached for his stick and started climbing down the stairs to the lower stages towards me, where we, the monks, sat. I waited, immobile, for him to reach me and beat me with his stick, the way my master had done a few days before.

But before he could reach me, nudging and pummelling, Tarpa and Asita pushed me out into the compound and did not stop till we had reached the adjoining deer park.

'Bring him to the refectory after you are done with him.'

I could still hear the cold stentorian voice of the senior and the ingratiating compliance of Asita and Tarpa.

'Yes master, we will,' they said, clamping my mouth and dragging me away.

24. *The Dessicated Pond*

'Unhand me, you blackguards!' my voice was muffled as I tried to peel away Tarpa's hand from my mouth unsuccessfully. The man from the land of snows was too strong for me. Finally, when I had stopped struggling, they let me go and I collapsed on a sawed-off tree trunk. The shade of overhanging Tala trees kept the park dark and scented with its sap. Swans glided serenely in a nearby pond in complete contrast to my mental state. Tarpa and Asita, quiet bemused expressions on their faces, waited for my breathing to become normal.

Finally they spoke, completing each other's sentences as if they were one person. They reminded me of how Rahula and I had once been.

'Before you do damage to yourself—'

'—And others—'

'—Before you get into trouble—'

'—And others—'

'It is better you know the truth.'

Bewildered, I looked up at their imposing figures. 'The truth? Now what Truth is this?'

'The truth about the new master you want to acquire.'

I gasped. 'How do you know about that?'

'You are not the most subtle man in Nalanda—'

'—Nor the most diplomatic—'

'—In fact, you may be a little bit of a thickhead—'

'—Walk with us.'

Their unsettling synchronicity had its desired effect on me. Obediently, I got up from the tree trunk and started walking with them.

As we walked out of the park and into the narrow lanes and bylanes of Nalanda, they continued to speak. As the day grew old, pageboys holding poles topped with flames appeared in the streets to light up the houses of panditas. I do not know who spoke when, but I remember what they said.

'Have you heard any stories of the Nalanda jail?' they asked me as we walked.

'No.'

'Of the judiciary?'

'No.'

'Have you seen the confinement rooms?'

'Yes.'

'Have you heard about unfair trials.'

'Maybe.'

'Rumours of extra-judicial executives?'

'No.'

'Try and keep it that way. Because they exist. In ways you wouldn't want to know."

The sun was beginning to set. Shadows lengthened. Stalls were shutting, karmadana officials were padlocking departments. Animals were wending their way back to the stables. The dust of dusk was rising to settle down again into night. It was twilight.

Gauri's godhuli.

After a silence that seemed as long as the gathering night, they continued. 'You need to cross the Honeycomb,' they said, 'and find your way back to your master. Or die. The choice is yours.'

'Neither am I crossing the Honeycomb,' I said, 'nor am I going back to my master. I have submitted my application for a change of tutelage to the Ecclesiastical Council.' This, the Buddha forgive me, was a lie. In my defence, I was in difficult times, in a desperate situation.

Asita stopped walking. He turned and brought his face close to mine, trying to hold my averted gaze. I detected pity in his voice.

'Then you will die,' he declared, 'just like the rest.'

I wasn't listening. But after a while, I looked back at their exasperated expressions and said, 'I hope you are here to tell me why? Because there is no good reason for a change of master to merit death. Unless my master wants me killed because I know his secrets, and might tattle to my brother and Mahipala. I have already seen my master brandishing a skullbowl at the Honeycomb. Bhim led me to him and then he died. I know that my master leads a Kapalika cult. Isn't that why he, the great Mahasiddha Aryadatta, sent you to me? To ensure my silence?'

'No, you fool!' Tarpa said. I sensed my temper rise to the brim. I did not want to be addressed by that word again. Perhaps Asita sensed my anger, for he said, 'You are the smartest one of us all. Think, Siddhartha, think!'

'I don't know where to start,' I sighed, my anger now like evaporated camphor at the altar of misery.

'Start with the Kapalika,' Asita prompted.

'What about them?' I replied.

'What do you know about them?'

'That they are scum and should be wiped out of existence?' I replied.

'Kapalika is the naked core of all world religions. Common to the Sufis and the Gnostics and the Buddhists and the Brahmins. Truth is, most Kapalikas don't understand the Kapalika doctrine,' Asita said, keeping equal pace with me. I noticed that he was never roused to anger, never lost his balance and never forgot his place. I looked askance at his swarthy face and wondered whether this was the mark of a mahasiddha or a cold-blooded murderer. Maybe both. Maybe there was not much difference between a mahasiddha and a cold-blooded murderer. If the murders had to be planned between the two of them, I thought, Asita would mastermind it and Tarpa in his bullish, unthinking, loyal way, would execute it.

I did not know what to make of what they were saying or what the intentions of this sojourn were. I kept my peace and my wits sharp, keeping them engaged in friendly chatter. We turned many shop corners and started moving towards Northern Nalanda where the craftsmen villages were. We crossed the Venerable Sthavira village where old monks and some senior administrators lived out their last days on earth. After we crossed the village of the Medicine Department, by the deserted pavilion of a dried-up lake, they sat me down for a serious talk.

'It is true that most Kapalikas cannot go beyond magic and miracle making. Instead of worshipping the supreme female principle, they exploit her in the basest possible way, in her life and even death and beyond. These men do not know the power of sexuality,' Asita said.

'They do not understand the laws that transmute abstinence to asexual compassion, to a final explosion of sexuality,' Tarpa finished for Asita.

I must have looked blank at this point because Asita sighed. Crossing his arms against his chest and leaning against the pavilion pillar, he said, 'The path is different for different temperaments. For the gross and unintelligent, celibacy is prescribed. For the slightly more refined, the path is concealed and revealed according to fluctuating and corresponding levels of comprehension because he is not yet ready to turn against the social order. You, Siddhartha, vacillate at this stage.'

'Forsooth, Nalanda brother,' I said bitterly, looking around at the dessicated pond, so much like me, 'I am an intermediate state being, vacillating between the various hells of women eaters and fornicators, decapitated heads and menstrual blood pellets.'

'The true Kapalika is the most heroic, the strongest and the bravest,' Tarpa too now joined Asita and they both sat down facing me, as I lay quite broken on the pavilion floor.

'You are evil,' I said, 'like my master and the Abbot.' They looked at me without moving, their faces devoid of emotion. Were they harbingers of light or darkness? I could not tell, but *Buddha*, I prayed, *I needed to know*.

'For such brave heroes, enlightenment now arises through the *radical inversion of the opposite*,' Asita said.

'The law of inversion again,' I whispered from the floor, my head between my knees. I was suddenly very tired, unable to look up.

'Look at us, Siddhartha,' Asita raised his voice.

'Why must they eat babies?' I said, 'what law makes this necessary?' I realised I was quite broken, my entire world view shattered to small irreconcilable pieces.

'Life pays for death. Youth pays for old age. Mortality pays for immortality,' Tarpa said, his impassive face glimmering in the dusk light.

'But this is the petty shamanism of the unintelligent,' Asita intervened.

'Women were the first shamans,' they both started together and Tarpa hesitated so Asita could continue. In the meantime, Tarpa took out a cannabis holder and started preparing a smoke.

'History tells us,' Asita continued, 'that women have always had an instinctive grasp of their own powers and were feared throughout the world as witches. You know how much the moolanivasi Dayani witches are abhorred in their villages.'

'It was Nagarjuna,' Tarpa took a puff before saying, 'who first discovered the female principle, right here in the Sitavana forest, living amongst the moolanivasi women.'

'And?' I asked, when he paused to take an inordinately long drag on the pipe.

'He taught the moolanivasi women all that he had learnt from ancient esoteric scriptures and Buddhist doctrines.' Tarpa was doing the talking now. Asita gazed dreamily into the distance as if at some imaginary Tushita heaven.

'All she needed to know was that her subtle physiology was different from a man's. And she need not imitate or subserve him.' Blue smoke from the cannabis hung like a cloud over us. I could feel its sickly sweet smell permeating into my being.

'And thus began her incredible journey from Dayani to Dakini, the supreme creative principle.'

Tarpa was blowing smoke rings above our heads now. Suddenly, everything was heavy and still. So much so that we could now smell the aroma of the distant sandalwood forest, and the incessant pecking of a lone woodpecker somewhere. I found myself concentrating on every word.

'More power to her means more power to man. Enlightenment is birthed from her vagina, her yoni, her bhaga. By definition "bhagawan" is a God birthed by a bhaga.'

'That is the foundational basis of New Science. And it spread like a private rash in the underbelly of all monastic establishments, Buddhist and Vedic. It was started right here in Nalanda,' Tarpa said. I laughed at his analogy, feeling giddy. The invasion of all my senses, the smell, the smoke, the talk had made me light-headed.

Tarpa had got up now, and was dusting his feet, getting ready to move on.

'The true Kapalika is not interested in burning women. That's cheap magic. He is interested in the Dakini principle in her highest form, *Shunyata*, the Void of eternal cosmic space accessible only in the ultimate flights of meditation. She is the cosmic Goddess principle. She manifests in a form that, for the sake of expedience, has been kept secret. Those few who know her are not permitted to utter her name.' I thought of the forest Dakini, what I wouldn't give for another glimpse of her. So this was what the Abbot and my master had attempted with the Chinese scholar, I thought.

They were trying to evangelise the New Science down the ranks of Nalanda, but it didn't go so well.

Asita too had got up to leave. We wore our sandals and started walking on the baked mud of the dry lakeshore. My sandals were the old wooden ones; I noticed I had not touched the ornate sandals again. It reminded me of my complete disconnect with my master.

As I kept pace with them, Asita again raised his voice, 'Now understand this carefully.'

'Please continue to expound, Nalanda brother. I have all the patience in the world,' I said.

Tarpa was impervious to my sarcasm. His expressionless face betrayed nothing. How he spoke in such chaste Pali was always a source of great wonder to me.

'Magic has become the gateway for power. And because kings are involved, this has led to corruption of unprecedented proportions. Rogue masters in the king's employment have brought Nalanda to the brink of destruction. The greed for sorcery has plunged teachers, lay students and kings into the horrors of the underworld.'

I suddenly realised we were standing before the gateway to Sitavana sealed with the Inverted Palm and the Dharmachakra. My impatience boiled over. I looked around me. Though the alleyway was easily approachable from all Nalanda thoroughfares, the Dharmachakra seal ensured that the road was always deserted. It was becoming clear to me that my companions and my master were intent that I should use the privileges bestowed on me. The Inverted Palm Seal.

'This is now beginning to sound like a very futile and elaborate scheme to turn me against my brother and our Dharma Protector, the king,' I said carefully.

Because I showed no sign of using the seal, Asita used his seal and the padlocked chains gave way with metallic sounds to reveal an unbeaten forest path away from the sight of the main gateway. Very soon the concentric stone walls of the roofless temple showed up to our left. My geographical memory of the place and the sound of the river made me surmise that the Honeycomb would be just a few yojanas away. How close the rotten core of Nalanda was to all of us. Like a fatal disease in the heart of our being. My entire body recoiled at the memory of the smell of human meat as I continued walking with my companions to the Honeycomb entrance, voluntarily yet against my will. Jackal eyes glittered in the shadows of the forest path, and their howls seemed to announce our arrival.

'All that stands between you and enlightenment is your refusal to face reality,' Tarpa reasoned, as we turned left from the Honeycomb entrance, instead of right at the Rasayana labs. Somehow I had never thought much of Tarpa's philosophical predilections, maybe because he always lost at the debating pits.

'You are wrong, Nalanda brother,' I said, 'facing reality is not the problem. Understanding it is.'

'What's to understand?' he shrugged. 'Use the law. The opposite is truth.'

'And its opposite?' I retorted. We had reached the river shore where many bones had washed up. Whether they were from unburnt cremations, decapitations or cannibalistic feasts, it was difficult to tell. Above us, vultures watched in anticipation. 'And the opposite of the opposite? And its opposite?' There must surely have been a maniacal gleam in my eyes, for I sounded like a madman, even to myself. 'Can't you see, Nalanda brother? The law of inversion doesn't stop the wheel from turning in a vicious cycle.'

'It does when you realise the truth,' Asita and Tarpa had boarded a makeshift jute raft to cross the river and I had no alternative but to join them. In the shadowy cavern, the river flowed dark, like the coagulated blood of murdered women. When we reached the opposite rivershore and alighted from our boats, my foot stepped across the skulls of many children, floating on the weeds by the shore. I looked up to see whether my companions saw what I saw. I could not make out anything from their expressions.

'Hurry,' Asita said, 'we must get back before it gets dark.'

A few feet beyond the sandy shore we came to a halt with a jolt.

Before us was a wall inlaid with skulls and bones glittering in the shadow. I shuddered at the sinister intent of what lay beyond.

'Whose vihara is this?' I had to ask.

'The people rise against us, Nalanda brother.' They were on either side of me as we looked up at the imposing pillars beyond the walls. High columns were adorned with the stone sculptures of mythical beasts. I recognised the gryphon hybrid of seven creatures. We had learnt about it from Bilwa, for this was a creature known in his islands. Rahula had often spoken about this wondrous sculpture, but I had never seen it.

In an open courtyard, some artisans were working on life-size statues of feminine divinities. I looked closely to see if I could recognise the divinity, but my memory failed me. The sound of chisel and rock, such a familiar comfort in Nalanda workshops, seemed diabolical here.

'They are making images of She Whose Name Cannot be Uttered,' Tarpa answered my unspoken question, 'so that her essence is erased. And she is reviled for all time to come.'

I could not make out the iconography of the deity, except her hair and breasts. The artisans had yet to give colour and shape to her form. She stood naked and unformed, under the chiselling knocks of the artisan's hammer, ready to be moulded to man's will. Many times I had seen Rahula at work in his college, but never had I been so revolted by the creation of an ambiguous identity. I could not understand the reason for my revulsion, till Asita, sweating slightly beside me, broke my reverie, as if he were following my train of thought.

'Women rule Nalanda because they can unlock every treasure chest that exists here. The Action Seals are keys to our future. They will either destroy Nalanda or save it.'

I moved my lips, but no words came out.

I was quiet for a long time, staring at the tableau before me. It was Asita who broke the silence: 'You are looking at the most private vihara of the one responsible for the deaths of Pandit Dharmapada and Bhim—Grandmaster Siroha.'

'But he is an austere pandita of the Sarvastivadin school. I interviewed him at his quarters,' I spluttered, objecting with much vehemence.

'The law of inversion, Siddhartha,' Tarpa said. 'You are looking at the private endowment given to Siroha by Mahipala, for his New Science practices and alchemical experiments. And there's nothing the Abbot can do about Mahapandita Siroha the Unconquerable's royal privileges.'

As we all stared at the gem-studded gryphons and mythical creatures gleaming in the twilight, there was a heavy quietness between us. For so long that it stiffened my bones.

Gradually, hiding behind the bushes, staring through the massive gates at the gigantic dwarapalas who guarded Siroha's vihara at the distance, I began to understand why certain students and masters were treated like royalty and had access to all the luxuries. They were all members of secret colleges that wielded immense power through magic rites, and maybe this was my master's intention when he conferred special privileges on me.

Riveted as I was to the shape of unformed female divinities, Asita was unable to keep his tryst with daylight. Night had fallen. The artisans packed their tools and left. Probably for some cannibalistic feast, I mused with bitterness.

Shadows from sooty flares shifted and made the statues in the courtyard seem alive, startling me. Every particle surrounding the place seemed to emit fear and subjugation. Even the trees stood in stupefied attention. It reflected the anguish I felt towards my master.

It was Tarpa the Gentle who spoke this time, full of the calm I knew him best for. Hands crossed against his chest, feet planted firmly on the ground, he stared across Siroha's looming steep courtyard stone steps, his jaw set in a grim line.

'Please understand that the battle between Aryadatta and Siroha is not for power, or even for the Action Seals. It is for the Dakini principle embodied in every woman in Nalanda, whether she be prostitute, virgin, high or low, beautiful or ugly. While the Abbot tries to acquire the Dakini principle by subjugating his male arrogance, by worshipping at the altar of the Mother principle, Mahipala and Siroha have been acquiring it by the systematic rape and plunder of women.'

'Woman gave birth to man. He would not exist without her. Yet, using the law of inversion, abusing her has its use. Much magic arises from the negative,' Asita added, taking his place beside me. They were both on either side of me again, scrutinising the ghastly, skeletal-looking dwarapalas standing immobile at the main doorways.

'More the abuse, more the use. More the lust for power, more the magic,' Tarpa observed, in agreement.

'I have been inside,' Asita whispered. 'There are banners and canopies made of human hide. Incense made of human fat. At night, the cries and groans of butchered women can be heard through the corridors and a revolting stench of blood spreads throughout the building.'

His words stayed in the air, like heat flashes.

From a distance, we could hear the sounds of revelry emanating from its bowels. I heard faint strains of music from within. A female choir, drums and cymbals reached our ears in snatches.

I could sense the dark, ill-lit chambers within. There were many such in Nalanda. Even the Abbot's White Palace and Aryadatta's inner chambers secreted a certain dark mystery that was difficult to fathom.

I sensed that the owner of the chambers before me was also an entity of similar stature.

'He has his own library,' Tarpa said staring at the pacing dwarapalas, their bones clanking as they walked, making us wonder whether they were starving humans or ghouls. 'His books are assigned the ultimate honour. Child ghosts. The Broken One is one such child the Abbot saved from the human sacrifice that would have made his spirit wander around Siroha's library forever to protect them.'

Again the uneasy contemplative silence. This time it was my curiosity that broke it.

'Who is the presiding deity of this place?' My voice sounded hoarse, even to me.

Tarpa laughed.

'Presiding deity? I have not seen any. His shrine is a small ghoulish chamber where nothing is visible. A virtual cabinet of horrors.'

'The laity offer their women here as prostitutes for petty powers.' Asita was equally grim beside me, his eye steady, his chin looking pugnacious in the dwindled light.

'I have seen what others have not. The demon shrine. Where the punished serve their sentences. The spirits of starved ghosts and sacrificed Dakinis abound here.'

'Who are his Action Seals?' I asked, suddenly unable to breathe. I did not want to know the answer.

'Any woman the Unconquerable can buy, steal, coerce, bribe or beat,' Tarpa iterated. 'Moolanivasis, low-caste brewers, prostitutes, dancers, washerwomen, slaves. Some are even Brahmin priestesses lured for a few pieces of gold.'

I did not reply. Of late, silence had become my chosen refuge.

'They are burnt, dismembered, powdered and used as ingredients for alchemy in the Rasayana labs,' Tarpa said.

'Some of the flying Dakinis you see in the roofless temple are not real women. They are the souls of murdered Action Seals,' Asita said.

At the mention of the roofless temple, I felt a prickle of discomfort. I did not want the Nine Unknowns used as bait to lay some elaborate web of deceit.

'There were no flying Dakinis at the roofless temple,' I protested. 'Only a few women in black, levitating.'

The hair at the back of my neck still rose in its pores as I remembered my brother's description of what he saw through his eye piece.

'Those are different,' Tarpa said. 'They are the sixty-four Dakinis who have taken refuge at the roofless temple. They are safe in the Abbot's Inverted Palm territory. And that is where the Great Initiation takes place.'

I remembered the most precious Inverted Palm Seal still lying amongst my robes of special duty. Yet, I could not believe my master was true. And even though I vowed never to use the seal, I couldn't help but be curious.

'Who are the Black Hats?' I asked.

'The Black Hats are the braves, the soldiers of the Nine Unknowns. They are the ones who are sworn to walk the razor's edge to protect forbidden knowledge,' Asita said.

'Two Black Hats stand beside you right now,' Tarpa added.

'What lies inside the roofless temple?' I asked, as casually as I could.

'The sixty-four Dakini principles embodied by the sixty-four human Dakinis, the Nine Unknowns, the dharma protectors of the Nine Unknowns called the Black Hats and the Nine Unknown books,' Tarpa said. 'It is the most beautiful and sacred heart of

Nalanda. And as Black Hats, we have vowed to protect it with our lives. Die for it if need be.'

In a flash I remembered the Inverted Palm Seal emblazoned on the gates of the Rasayana laboratories and the Gold Mint at Sitavana. Suspicion rose like a wave in my throat.

'You also protect Sitavana's Rasayana laboratories. Isn't that where the powdered Dakinis are kept?'

Tarpa's facial expressions did not change. Neither did his demeanour.

'The question you need to ask,' he said, 'is why Siroha wields all this power to wander untrammelled in the Abbot's Nalanda.'

'Let me answer that,' Asita said. I turned to him, very interested in his reply. Three white owls stared at me unblinkingly from a gnarled adumbra tree.

'Siroha took control of Sitavana a few years ago,' Asita explained. 'He has used its magic to establish himself as the leader of the Sitavana Kapalikas. They say that with the New Science principles, he has created a mystical diagram that gives its practitioner complete power over its geographical territory. Sitavana is a battleground, with much of its power vested, though precariously, with Siroha. And this is cause of grave concern not only to the Abbot and your master, but to all of Nalanda. Only the roofless temple's empowerment, the Great Initiation, eludes Siroha. The day he gets the Great Initiation, Nalanda will be lost to us.'

So, my brother was right, I thought. Sitavana was disputed territory.

'Is the Great Initiation codified in a text?' I asked, unable to meet Tarpa's eyes.

'Yes,' Tarpa replied. 'Sakya, the One Who Never Sleeps, guards it with his life.' I remembered my brother's frustration at not being able to acquire the book whose name was written in a scroll that he waved in my face. 'Action Seal,' it had said, but

I held my tongue. It probably contained the codified text of the Great Initiation, I thought.

The next moment, I found myself struggling against a wave of claustrophobia. This was because I somehow knew what Tarpa would say next.

'We hope you understand that this is why the masters are using you and your integrity and love for Nalanda to influence your brother into tipping the balance of power in our favour.'

I struggled to regain steadiness. Vertiginous, I had become a point of light hurtling through a wormhole. And now I floated in inky blue space.

'I presume that is a euphemism for beating me with a stick,' I said quietly.

'Nalanda brother, you misunderstand,' Tarpa the Gentle said. 'We do know you were handpicked for this mission. You were marked from the beginning as a chosen one, Siddhartha. Your integrity and faith in your master is legendary for us. Even now, as Mahipala schemes to appoint Siroha as the next Abbot of Nalanda in this council, our masters have not lost faith in you.'

This did not fill me with pride, only a vague unnameable dread. My master Aryadatta had often spoken about the trials and tribulations his own master had put him through. But my master had come out of his own terrible test of fire, good as burnished gold, and in his state of enlightenment, been raised to the stature of the highest mahapandita of our time. Was it now my time? Was I being primed? I did not want to know the answer to this question. If the answer was yes, I did not feel ready for it in any way. Not at all.

Glaring at Asita and Tarpa, I said, 'If this is supposed to make me reconsider renouncing my master, it won't.'

And I already knew what they would say next. 'Reconsider,' Tarpa said, 'your masters request you to reconsider.'

'Moreover,' Asita said, 'we repeat and reiterate. Siroha is

incapable of granting the Great Initiation. It has been codified in a manuscript and secreted in Sakya's library, far from the grubby reaches of your brother or King Mahipala. And the Great Initiation awaits you when you are ready.'

They must have read my questioning expression, for they both spoke together.

'Yes,' they said, 'we have received the Great Initiation.'

'But I don't want it,' I protested with all the vehemence I could muster. 'I did not come to Nalanda for magic.'

'Nalanda brother,' Asita exclaimed. 'It is not the magic of sorcery that is being offered to you in the Great Initiation, but the magic of enlightenment! The only difference between the king and the Abbot is that the king wants to use the enlightenment of the Great Initiation for magic. That is why he is not worthy of the Great Initiation!'

'And the reason behind the deaths?' I demanded. 'Why were Dharmapada and Bhim murdered?'

'They belonged to Siroha. In fact, both victims were his direct protégés,' Asita replied.

'Why would he kill his own protégés? Logically, the motive lies not within his own people but his adversaries, who as you say are the Abbot and my master?' I felt I was repeating myself. Must be the hallucinogenic effect of the last few days, I thought. Or an altered state of consciousness induced by the Great Goddess Kundalini. Either way, I was doomed. That was for sure.

Asita removed his shawl and wrapped it around my hunched shoulders. 'This is neither the time nor the place for a debate on Logic. We have told you what we know. We must return now before the next hour strikes. More will be revealed to you in time.'

We did not talk much during the long walk back. And though my head teemed with unvoiced thoughts, I held my tongue. They escorted me to my cell. I did not ask them about the Uposatha senior, knowing that they would take care of the matter.

'Do nothing for a few days,' Tarpa advised. 'Practise the austerities. Especially solitude. Eat sparingly. Only milk and nuts. Sleep as much as you can. Take rest.'

And with that, I was alone in my cell, staring at the intricate patterns that moss made on my ceiling, so low I could touch it. Inspite of all the resistance my intellect put up, I felt protected, taken care of, loved.

My last thoughts as I fell asleep were of my mother. The difference between appearance and reality is the difference between heaven and hell, she used to say. And I slid into the sweet dreamless sleep of the comforted. I wonder if I had reconsidered my decision to renounce my master that day, would the third murder not have occurred.

I will never know.

25. *The Sparkle*

Over the next few days, I sent word to my brother that I was ready to renounce my master. Since I didn't trust the Nalanda karmadana spies, I handed the scroll personally to the Royal Vihara message carriers. I picked up a reply a few days later. My brother said that a formal application for this would be submitted with a palace seal, and that I should wait.

The afternoon I received his reply, I sat down in front of the gold Giant Buddha statue to meditate. The enclosure around the statue was prohibited, so given my current state of mind, it became my natural choice as a meditation spot.

The difference in our sizes reminded me of my diminutive ant-like stature. As I looked up at His beautiful smile hot tears rolled down my cheeks, half in expiation and half in pity for my sorry condition. And the more He smiled, the more I wept, till my nose was stuffed and I had to wipe my face with my sanghati. There were a few people about. Two moolanivasi gardeners were clearing the dried leaves from the ground and some were weeding the flower beds. From afar, I could see a group of yavana students heading towards the clearing. They would cross me on the way to their monasteries. I did not want them to notice me, not only because I was obviously playing truant at a time devoted to studies in the lecture chaityas but also because I surely cut a sorry figure, red-nosed and weepy-eyed like a village girl.

To avoid the group, I walked up to the six-feet-high wrought-iron barricade that separated the public from the Buddha and prostrated on the ground in a gesture of devotion. As I lay on the ground, waiting for the group of students to pass, I noticed a concentrically running iron railing for the first time. It stood directly between the high iron barricade and the statue, and its gate was padlocked. The lock looked surprisingly well-oiled and used. This was curious because the high wrought-iron barricade in front of me where I lay prostrate was emblazoned with the Dharmachakra seal. I had never in four years seen or heard it being opened. The immediate precincts on which the Buddha stood were persona-non-grata for everybody, including the masters. Not even in our wildest dares had we ever attempted to cross the barricade, so deep-rooted was the fear of trespassing. The area between the barricade and the Giant Buddha was unkempt and unattended. Grass and wild flowers grew all around the Giant Buddha making it obvious that even the gardeners were not allowed into the hallowed ground. So what necessitated the camouflaged enclosure with the well-used padlock?

Was this also Inverted Palm territory? Did the king have access? If so, why had my brother never mentioned it?

I shifted my head ever so slightly to see whether the students had crossed me yet. They hadn't. It was when I was slowly inching my head back down that it caught my eye.

Glinting in the light of the afternoon, the sparkle of an unusual stone. When I turned my head, the light was gone. Obviously it shone only at a particular angle. My curiosity piqued, I waited for the clearing to become empty and the gardeners to move away. My body tingled in apprehension. Something unusual was happening again on the scene of a previous crime. I remembered that this was the exact same place where I had last seen Bhim dancing his dance of death. What other demonic acts must my poor Lord Buddha have witnessed, I wondered.

The stone lay in the grass some ten feet from the railing with the well-used lock. It mesmerized me. Shining like a mischievous glint in the eye, it dared me to come closer. Its scintillations held the promise of an untold story. I looked around me for a stick or twig long enough to reach it. When I found it, I stretched my hand out from the railing into the enclosure and in awkward sweeping motions, brushed the stone towards me.

It was not easy. But when I held the stone in my hands, I knew my efforts had not been in vain.

In my hands I held what I believed to be an important clue to the grisly tale unfolding in the shadows of the hallowed halls of Nalanda.

It was a nose ring. A female ornament. What business did a nose ring have inside the sanctum sanctorum of the most revered and celebrated statue of the Buddha in the monastic world? It was not caked in dirt, the sparkle of the stone was unsullied. The woman who owned this had lost it but recently. I examined the design. This was definitely temple or court jewellery, not the kind that ordinary village girls would wear. The curve and contours of its palmyra design was the result of exquisite workmanship. This was not just a nose ring. This was the hapless betrayal of some heinous secret.

As I sat on the grass, holding the nose ring in my fist, I noticed something else. The Giant Buddha's feet rose like two giant pillars from the ground. The distance between the hem of his robes and the ground was about five feet and a man of my stature could easily stoop and walk under it. Uneven grass grew all around the Buddha's feet, although I noticed that it was flattened under his stony hem. I would never have noticed it in all the overgrowth, if it had not been for a trick of afternoon light, the position in which I sat, the gap between two leaves from which my gaze pierced through and the grace of the Omniscient Buddha.

White light exploded between my eyebrows as I realised what this meant. My first reaction was to jump across the railing and rush forth to the statue. But I summoned all my will power and force of reasoning to calm myself down. There would be time, I thought. My brother would arrive during the full moon of Pausa. I would not do this alone. I would do this with kingly support, lest the discoveries further endanger me.

But before my brother came, I would seek out Gauri. She knew more than the obvious. That I was sure of.

In the alms-walk roster, I exchanged my name with the assigned walker, an acolyte from my adjacent monastery. I used my well-practiced subterfuge successfully one more time. My master urgently required the rare medicinal herb at exactly this time of the waxing moon and there was no time to lose.

Having assigned the acolyte my duties of the day, I left the university to beg for alms. Manipulating the roster was not easy as the Discipline Committee was harsh and focussed on deterring student absenteeism. It was rare to be at liberty, free from service and lessons. But by the end of the day, I had succeeded in my nefarious exercise.

I showed the committee seal to the western doorkeeper and took the road that led to Gauri's village.

The air outside Nalanda was a breath of freedom. I traversed the city square that I had left behind for admission into Nalanda. My thesis on the supremacy of the Buddhist doctrine, written just a year ago, was still pasted on the walls of the Rejects Colony. It amused me, since I could write a better thesis now refuting my own thesis.

I looked at the quotidian life around me and wondered whether this was where I should be seeking real knowledge. Cobblers, bird catchers, arrow makers, wine sellers, weavers—what treasures did their innocuous lives hold?

I turned left from the bronze makers' village towards the

Cockfoot mountain. Gauri and Uma were probably at home with the rest of their sisters and mother, cooking for their family meal. I was about to start my descent into the valley when I spied Uma coming out of her house and starting her ascent towards where I was.

This was even better! The Buddha was giving me an opportunity to follow her.

I hid behind some trees and waited for her to cross me. When she did, I followed her from a safe distance. She seemed to be retracing my footsteps and walking towards the university.

She entered from the Northern Gate and showed her seal for entry. I was not surprised. Many kumaris or village girls who regularly participated in temple celebrations were given the artisan seal. Ere long, I discovered that she had turned a corner that led to the forbidden Dharmachakra territory of the Sitavana Monastery. This gate opened from inside the university, unlike the east gate that opened into the inhospitable Sitavana forest. Asita and Tarpa had taken me through here just a few days ago.

With complete disregard for the Dharmachakra seal, she recited the sound codes that I had risked my life to decipher. I saw her entering the narrow forest path beside the deserted main gate. My stomach grumbling from the lack of food received neither through alms nor through the kitchens, I entered Sitavana behind her.

Hiding behind the Kuber shrine at the Honeycomb entrance, I saw Uma's shadow flitting through the Rasayana alchemy laboratories. It was not padlocked, as I had first seen when I had visited here. Uma had probably opened it, but still the iron gate would not open, though I could see her through the iron grills.

In a quick impulsive move, I stood outside the courtyard entrance and called out her name.

She turned at the sound of my voice and not looking altogether surprised, opened the iron gate.

'Siddhartha,' she said, pleasant in her demeanour. 'What are you doing here?' She was comely like her sister. Though shorter, she was slender and had a sweet smile.

'My master sent me to fetch some articles from Rasayana. I've left the seal in my cell.'

She smiled, but opened the door nevertheless. 'Why are you lying, Siddhartha? There is no seal for Rasayana. The door is always opened by the one who is inside.'

I frowned, I fumbled, I smiled like a sophisticated city man. 'Must have mistaken my master's instructions. You saved me punishment,' I said, entering the laboratories I had once spied on without being able to enter.

She did not look perturbed. She went about her business brooming a small brick kiln at a corner with practised alacrity. I looked suspiciously at the oven. It seemed unusually small in size. The kind used in the science labs, it was useless for either warmth or cooking.

'What are you looking for?' she asked.

'I'll know it when I see it,' I replied. The room was large, about the size of a lecture or convocation chaitya. But it was spare, except for the brick kiln and a series of vats and covered jars lined in a row in the sun streaming from a grilled window. The clothes line above the jars, where I had seen animal entrails and human skin a few nights before, was empty. It must have dried by now, must have been powdered and placed in the jars before me.

'What is in the jars?' I asked. I sniffed at the air. There was no overpowering smell in Rasayana. Except a hint of charcoal.

She did not reply. Conscientiously, she swept behind the brick kiln again and again. After a while, she said, 'I do not know, Siddhartha. My duty is to keep this place clean.'

I turned to face her fully. 'Is that all? Are you too important to be sacrificed like the others? So let me be specific. What type of Action Seal are you?'

She held my stare for a very long time. Her eyes were dark and fathomless. And then I saw a tear collect in the corner of her eye and roll down her cheek. My clenched fist was sweating. I took out the nose ring pricking me in my sweating palm and showed it to her. She was wearing one similar to the one I clutched.

'Is this the nose ring you lost?' I confronted her. 'I see you have already made a new one.'

She answered without looking at me. I was glad that she had finally stopped her systematic cleaning of the brick kiln. She stood with her back hunched away from me, looking small and so fragile.

'Where did you find it?' she asked in a muffled voice.

'At the feet of the Giant Buddha,' I replied, angry and threatening. She resumed cleaning the kiln as if I didn't exist. I kept staring at her waiting for a response and she eventually complied.

'You are not supposed to be here, Nalanda monk,' she said, cold now and indifferent.

'Who put this nose ring on you?' I demanded. The man who 'puts the nose ring' is the man who owns the woman, at least that was the common custom among courtesans. She silently renewed her obsessive cleaning, tears falling in unruly drops on the stone floor. Her back hunched even more, like a broken old sweeperess.

'It was Mahapandita Aryadatta!' I walked up to her with as much menace as I could muster. 'Admit it.'

In a fright she backed off against the wall and dropped her broom, but she refused to look at me.

'I stay alive because of my silence, Nalanda monk.' She finally looked up at me with eyes whose depths I could not reach. 'Do not make me say what I am not permitted to say.'

I held her gaze. I could not turn away. 'Why are you prostituting yourself?' I said. 'Are you that poor? That greedy for Nalanda cowries?'

'It's the only way to postpone death,' she was dry-eyed now, and spoke with the slow emphasis of the certain, 'even though there is no escaping it.'

'Lies!' I spat. 'Lies of Mara's temptress!'

I knew she was speaking the truth, but I wanted, the Buddha forgive me, to goad her into saying more.

She just stood there and looked at me, her eyes bright as stars. 'Would I stop being Mara's temptress if they sacrificed me? Would I then finally be redeemed? When my heart is plucked out and its essence entrapped to do your bidding? Then, when Mara's temptress becomes a Dharma Protector, will I be redeemed?' her voice rose in feverish excitement.

'Or when I become a hungry ghost protecting Nalanda's secret libraries!' She was lashing out at me, as if hoping to bring me to my senses, but I was not listening.

'Would I then be redeemed?' she shouted, her broom lying forgotten on the floor.

'Lies!' I threw the nose ring at her. It fell on the stone floor with a sigh. 'You do this for my masters' gold. For Nalanda cowries!'

'So you think your masters are that powerful?' Her eyes were dancing now, and there was something new. An arrogant tilt to her head.

I compulsively moved towards the jars overpowered by the nagging desire to know what was inside it.

'The women of Nalanda wield more magic than the men. Some of them don't even leave a corpse when they die. They go straight to the Pure Lands.'

'You were just talking about their rape and murder,' I mocked her. 'Make up your mind. Are you the victim or the vanquisher?'

Suddenly I was startled by a voice behind saying, 'Can we be anything except Dakini whores, Siddhartha?'

Gauri. I would recognise that voice anywhere. I turned to face her.

'There are as many Dakini whores in Nalanda as dogs in the streets, isn't that the gossip in your secret circles?' she said, looking pale and bloodless, like another Sitavana ghostly apparition.

'So they say,' I replied, and because she was standing inside the door, I asked, 'How did you enter?'

'She has her ways,' was Uma's quiet reply.

Something snapped inside me. Gesticulating wildly, I pointed to the jars. 'What's inside these?' I beseeched, very close to losing control.

'Bowls of excrement.' Gauri smiled. 'Waiting to be turned to nectar.'

In a flash she was holding my hand. 'Is that what you wanted to know? Is this interesting? Perhaps you are looking for something else?' Acutely conscious of her slim fingers around what I would like to believe were my manly wrists, I allowed myself to be led to the neighbouring chamber.

It held a small furnace and a long platform with unimaginable utensils and implements. All the implements seemed to be made of an ebony-like alloy. Through a small grilled window, I could see an enclosed cemetery outside with a pyre burning in a corner. Next to the cemetery was the quiet deserted river.

She uncovered the lid of a shallow terracotta dish containing a material burnt beyond recognition, of the strangest texture and smell. 'Perhaps you are interested in this?'

I could only see the eyes on Gauri's face. They were shining with a fierce wildness.

'Your Twilight Language calls it "black matter of the lotus".' That would roughly translate to the vagina of a burnt Dakini. 'Your' Twilight Language, she had said. How did she know what I knew, I thought in amazement.

'Are you a Dakini?' I whispered, unable to keep away the imploring tone in my voice.

'What do you think?' she asked.

'You are the epitomised exact opposite of Mara's temptress. Law of inversion,' I said looking deep into her eyes. They pulled me to the centre of its gravity and held me there.

'But let me show you Mara's temptresses.' Tears were rolling down her bloodless cheeks. She gestured wildly at the cemetery beyond the chamber window. 'There she lies, dead and decaying. Her corpses dismembered in cemetery rituals.'

'Who is responsible for this?' I cried, sensing tears fill up in my own eyes.

I realised that in truth the real question that was burning me up was: *'Was Siroha or the Abbot responsible for this?'*

But the question seemed to have taken the heat out of her body. She was cold now, limp and staring. I knew that she would not answer even on the pain of death. I shook my head in disbelief. My hands swept across the sickness and depravity around us and I said, 'Why is all this happening to us, monks ordained into the vows of purity and celibacy?'

My feet felt suddenly tired. I sat down on the floor, thankful for its empirical solidity. She sank down to the floor too. The floor at least was like any other floor, swept clean by Uma.

'Have you ever wondered why vows are only for men?' she was quiet now, conversational even.

'Not men,' I corrected her, 'monks.'

'Yes,' she said, 'but monks are men.'

'Not all monks are men,' I again corrected. 'We have nuns too.'

'The Buddha never wanted nuns in the Sangha,' she said pointedly.

And then she explained.

'Celibacy vows are only for men so they can understand and respect the Great Goddess. Women don't need it, for they are the embodiments of birth and creation. Sexuality is their substance.'

I, who knew nothing of this subject of women's sexuality, held my peace.

'The Buddha has said that the female body is better for enlightenment,' she said.

'Then why,' I enquired, suddenly full of compassion and an

awe-inspiring tenderness for the girl-woman sitting across me with her luxurious hair streaming down one shoulder, 'are there so few female siddhas?'

'It is the social order,' she made a small gesture with her hands, and I noticed that they were small and artfully tattooed. 'Social order can only function when the woman is kept in subjugation. It is more expedient for her to be simply used and discarded.' She indicated the implements around her to justify her point.

Uma came and sat next to us, making a third point in our triangle. 'Siddhas exist only in the world of men. They are appearances, not reality,' she added.

She was gentle, trying to take the toxicity out of the venomous content of her words, for she had just annihilated the validity of all great beings hagiographed by social order.

Dusk had again settled on Nalanda, carrying the weighty secrets of another day.

'The truly Enlightened do not need to be a leader amongst men,' Uma started singing. It was a soft enchanting melody that raised my spirits and took away the oppressive moroseness of the room. It lulled me into a peaceful calm that I did not remember ever experiencing before.

'The truly Enlightened do not cling to life, or gold, or immortality.' She chose an ethereal hypnotic tune that entranced even Gauri. And just when every muscle in my body had surrendered to relaxation, she broke my trance with a peal of laughter.

'The Nalanda mahasiddhas plan my heart blood sacrifice,' Uma said, as an unscheduled tear glinted in the corner of an eye, her mouth twisted in false mischief. 'I even know who will conduct it.'

I stared at her in horror.

'Hush!' Gauri scolded her sister. 'Let us not talk of sacrifices.'

'Who is your master?' I demanded. And then locking both their gazes, pointing a finger at them, I stood up. 'Whose Action Seals are you? Who *owns* you?' I persisted.

Finally Gauri raised her flashing eyes at me and said, 'All who enter here are silenced. People are murdered to maintain the vows of secrecy. The head of Religious Articles broke the vow and was killed with mantras of the death code. You should leave now.'

And because I desisted, a high-pitched ululation emanated out of them. It was a tenor of anguish, a lament in song tuned to make the air shiver and the implements rattle. I hastily turned to leave and as I reached the courtyard, their mournful dirge stopped. Instantaneously, Gauri was beside me.

She stared at the courtyard and with her palms clapped on her ears, screamed: 'I see only serpents! Thousands of them! They are everywhere! We are trapped! There is no way out!'

'Gauri,' I softly intervened. 'The courtyard is empty.'

'Run, Siddhartha. Run!' she screamed, 'Leave us and don't look back.'

I ran as fast as my legs could carry me. I paused for breath only when I reached my vihara.

I only had one regret. I had forgotten to check whether their feet touched the ground or whether, like true Dakinis, they glided on air.

Obviously, I rued, Bilwa had more presence of mind than me.

26. *The Sacred Womb*

Never before had I felt so glad to meet my brother. His presence called out my sudden desperate desire for a shared ancestry and the need for my mother. Somehow, Pataliputra seemed full of the light and gaiety that I had once perceived in my own beloved university. Before Mahakala's oppressive demons devoured it in the gaping maw of Time.

But my brother was impatient with all my pleasantries.

'Quickly now, brother, it is already the second watch of the night,' he spoke to me, loud enough it seemed to me for any watchful ears in the amra grove to eavesdrop. 'Let us make haste or it will be light soon.'

His brusqueness saddened me. How often the scriptures remind us about the impermanence of human relationships and how often we forget. *False, false,* the moonless lightless membrane of the sky echoed. *This too is not the truth,* the sky said, thick and deep, a boundary-less state of all-seeing consciousness. *This too is not the truth.*

We had chosen the last watch of the night so we could manoeuvre when the sky was still well-lit and we would not need torches.

Together we jumped over the iron enclosure surrounding the Giant Buddha.

'But, brother,' he said impatiently, 'there is nothing here.'

'Shhh,' I said, moving in a crouching position between the

Buddha's feet. It was dark. In my sanghati I had concealed a small lamp but before I unearthed it, I bent down to touch my head at the feet of the Buddha. The stony skin of his enormous big toe felt warm and reassuring as I begged Him to forgive my digressions.

I took out my lamp and examined the stone roof above me, the lowermost hem of the Buddha's robe. It did not take me long to find what I suspected. A dark line, five feet by five feet, marking out a square, suggested that there was a door of some kind. And sure enough, we spotted an engraving on the stone, of a motif very similar to the one that opened into the core of the Secret Nalanda.

The Dharmachakra Seal.

In triumph I turned to my brother, my eyes widening in shock, excitement and a delicious ripple of fear.

'Do you have the seal?' I demanded.

'Yes,' he replied in dumb amazement, 'I think I do. But I don't think King Mahipala knows that this seal opens other doors.'

'Wait,' I said, holding the light up against the hem of the Buddha's robe. And there it was, clear to the naked eye. The Inverted Palm Seal rubbed out in charcoal. I almost dropped my flint as I turned around to face my brother. His face looked diabolical to me.

'The king has usurped this territory from the Abbot,' I exclaimed.

My brother at least had the grace to wilt under my withering glare. 'I had heard some rumours but I wasn't sure,' he stuttered.

'You lie!' I was raising my voice. 'You just said that Mahipala doesn't know this key opens other doors.'

He capitulated after a pause. 'Okay, so I lied. This area has been sealed off for a long time now. I didn't feel the need to tell you.'

'Of course,' I said, 'you only felt the need to tell me about Inverted Palm territory not in the king's possession so I could help you get access.' My brother did not reply. Judiciously, he waited for my tirade to get over.

'You obviously know what happens here. Why don't you tell me so we can stop this silly charade and I can get some sleep,' I said bitterly. Asita and Tarpa had been right all along about Siroha's territorial control, I thought. Asita and Tarpa were always right, and I always wrong.

'Elder one, on our mother, I swear to you, I've never been inside. I just know that the New Science initiations take place here. Mahipala got them done here, all except the Great Initiation. That happens in the roofless temple I showed you.'

Since my brother held out the seal like a peace offering, and since the anticipation of quelling my curiosity was beyond my control, I diffused the matter by taking the seal from him.

When the seal was fitted into the stone motif and turned, the stone slab slid across, leaving a gaping hole above us, five by five handspans in size. We looked at the darkness inside the Buddha's body and breathed in awe.

'The garbhagriha,' I gasped. The sacred womb. The sacred womb is an architectural term for the sanctum sanctorum of temples. But here the architects of Nalanda had taken the literal simplicity of the term to the heights of unprecedented genius. Of course, in the Twilight Language, it meant other things as well. When I reached out my hand to feel into the darkness, I found an iron rung.

We climbed with some hesitation and much trepidation upwards *inside* the holy body of the Lord Buddha. It seemed deeply sacrilegious to be crawling into the Holy One's innards. I reminded myself this was the same Buddha whom the devout bathed in a thousand buckets of milk every day.

As we ascended, the feeling was so palpable, I knew without asking that Aditya Raj felt it too. The feeling that the world as we knew it was falling away and we were moving to another land, beyond life and beyond death. Again that familiar consciousness-altering sandalwood aroma prickled my nose, reminding me of

Sitavana. In a dream-like state, we reached the first landing, large enough to be a reader's quarter. The light of a small altar lamp showed that it was circular in nature. Across the opening was a life-like image of the divine male and female sitting in each other's laps in cosmic union.

'The Great Seal!' my brother exclaimed. He stopped in his tracks, awestruck.

The female aspect of fair colour wore four masks, her buttocks clenched by the male aspect, who was coloured dark like that of deep consciousness and also wore four masks. They looked so real with such natural flesh tones, that I thought if I reached out and touched them, I would break their embrace.

The room was red in colour and completely mirrored. Near the opening was a seat shaped like a wheel with sixty-four spokes and a triangular centre. I knew that they were sixty-four because I counted. The altar lamp situated right before the couple reflected a steady unmoving flame in all the mirrors.

It was then that I caught the sharp smell of blood and incense. Our eyes simultaneously turned to the sacrificial decapitation block before the divine couple. Next to the sacrificial altar was a skullcap bowl artfully moulded with silver embossing.

It was full of fresh, warm blood. Beside it was the machete, the knife, the thigh-bone instrument, the offerings of the five forbidden meats, just as described in the *Book on the Twilight Language*. Urine, semen, blood, faeces and brain, all the ingredients of alchemy were here. Next to all this were the sceptre and the bell, symbolic again in Twilight Language of the male and female.

The room opened out directly above us through a hole in the centre of its roof and we climbed up by means of rungs on the ladder welded to the wall. We entered a narrow cylindrical tunnel that opened out to another smaller room with its accompanying ritual paraphernalia of a deity statue, a seat and a lighted lamp.

I immediately understood the architecture of the interiors. The narrow cylindrical tunnel was a faithful reproduction of the sahaja central channel of the spinal column, just like the Chinese scholar had explained a few months ago.

Each room was the duplication of an energy wheel located in the sahaja channel. According to my calculations, there would be seven such rooms. I was right. The corridors extending out of the rooms were the spokes of the wheels. Each spoke corresponded to a *nadi* or subtle channel of the human body. A human's subtle anatomy had seventy-two thousand such channels.

If that were so, then the Giant Buddha's innards was a labyrinth. It would be very easy to lose one's way inside the connecting corridors.

'Stay close to the central tunnel,' I warned my brother. 'Do not go into the side corridors.'

'Yes,' came his stifled reply.

Our voices sounded disconnected, as if we had lost our grip on gravity, verily on physical reality.

Some of the rooms were coloured red and some were blue and green and orange, just like their corresponding human energy wheels. Each had a reigning deity. The rooms smelt like the interiors of most well-used shrines. Rancid butter. In the centre of every room was a seat shaped like a wheel. Some wheels were triangular, some were circular, some had eight spokes, some had sixteen. One had thirty-two. Before the seats, inscribed on the wall, were various syllables. Some had the short-ah. Some were inscribed with the letters RAM and some said HUM. I looked closely at the ritual articles in every room. Though from far, they looked innocuous to the undiscerning eye, on close inspection, they were as I suspected. Again the kapala, or silver-embossed drinking bowls made of shining human skulls. Again the trumpet, fashioned out of a human thigh bone. So neat and dry, as if the human bone existed only for this purpose. Every room also had lettering on the wall. I held the lamp up to see clearly. They seemed like the thousand names of a deity.

I did not mention these to my brother who was not noticing the finer details but staring about him in a daze. It would drive him over the delicate balance of bravery and fear that he trod.

Or so I thought.

In this way, like two worms in the gut, we kept climbing inside the Lord's body. By the time we reached the last room, we had counted seven rooms in total as I expected. I climbed the last rung of the ladder knowing that it would surely reach up into the crown of the Lord's head. I was right. The roof was a carved stone mesh of the thousand-petalled lotus, the sahasradhara. In its centre was a circular hole, two feet by two feet in diameter, again corresponding to the antahkarana, the psychic cord. I pushed my face up against the stone mesh of the Buddha's cranium, his kapala. From its giddy heights I saw the great boundary-less vault of black sky.

Aditya Raj, completely stupefied, his mouth loose and comically open, looked at me like a dumb-mute animal.

'Not in any of the battlefields have I felt so much terror,' he bleated like a plaintive sheep. That was the first time any of us had spoken for a while. His voice had an unreal ring to it. Here, the human sound had been rendered hollow, ethereal. I wanted to tell him that it was from the crown of the Lord's head that the wind and air moved through the chambers but did not dare speak, lest the Buddha take away my voice too.

I had better vantage to see the corridors coinciding with the spokes of the wheels down the Buddha's stony spine.

Silently, I motioned my brother to go down three rooms below. There, in the light of my torch, I found what I was looking for. It was the candle wick placed in the scalloped arches coiled clock-wise around the sculpture of the upright letter HUM. I had expected it to be a reproduction of the human anatomy of subtle energy channels and seed syllables described in *The Book on the Twilight Language.* It was exactly so. What I had not expected to see was the burning wick.

We climbed with the sizzling flame, watching it all along. And then we realised that the fire was gradually snaking up the central channel pillar of the corridor to the cranium room that held the letter Om. There, in the Buddha's kapala, coiling clockwise around the melting letter Om, the heat of the burning wick torched with a blue flame the bottom of the upside-down letter HUM, hanging from the middle of the ceiling.

This was a faithful depiction of how the elixir 'amriṭa' drips from the kapala when the tongue, ignited by the Great Goddess Kundalini's fire, rolls back to make contact with the palate.

I reached out and touched the letters. It was an alloy of the softest wax I had ever touched. As the letters melted, they fell in drops on the seat situated at the centre of the room. The sudden illumination emanating from the room and down below made me see the seat in a better light.

'The diamond seat,' I whispered in awe. In sooth, the seat was made of the same precious stone and the thirty-two spokes were uncut jewels of the largest and rarest diamonds human eyes had ever beheld. I put my finger out to catch a drop of the melting liquid. The coolness of the touch startled my skin. It was like fine silk against fevered flesh.

I took it to my tongue, and it felt like ether evaporating its sweetness on the tip of my taste-buds. It tasted a little like the rasa of Baladitya White. Its soothing sensation made my mouth water. Immediately, I felt intoxicated. The shapes of the walls started shifting.

'The nectar of immortality,' I remembered the verses I had read in *The Book on the Twilight Language.* And the jars in the Rasayana laboratory.

The dripping liquid from the burning letters seemed to feed

the fire, but soon, the long meandering wick burned out, plunging us into darkness again. Our last sight was the seat glowing in an eerie blush of blue light, just like the brightening sky beyond the crown of the Lord's head. I took out a flint from my robe and lit my lamp; it had gone out without my noticing.

'Aditya Raj!' I hissed at him.

'Yes?' he looked at me. If I hadn't been frightened, I would have laughed at his plight.

'The wick was burning when we came down,' I whispered.

'So?'

'Someone is here with us,' I whispered back. Seeing the expression on my brother's face, I finally did laugh, even if it was born of hysteria.

I indicated to my brother that we should start our descent, not trusting the otherworldly quality my voice took when I spoke, as if I were possessed.

That was when we heard it. That and the distinct sensation of being followed, nay, hounded. Whispers in a chorus first started out low, then gradually increased in volume till we could hear them clearly. Whether it was one voice or many was difficult to tell. But the voice was female.

'*Now I take your life*!' she whispered from an indefinable direction.

'*Now I kill you!*'

The pitch of the whispering was reaching a crescendo as we descended, and terror made us grope our way more carefully down the rungs. As if we were hanging on to our lives.

It was in the third or the fourth room that a trapped wind travelling down the Lord's crown came hurtling down at us like a ball of thunder. It sped through us and drowned out the whispering. The wind's heavy rolling ricocheted in the round room, making it sound distinctly like the word Om. It lifted my robes and made every hair-root and skin-pore tingle. Then two things happened at once.

Aditya Raj shouted, 'Run, brother, run!' And I saw a fierce and deadly form standing in front of me. In a flash of light she was gone, but one glimpse of her dark, wrathful visage, her red, protruding tongue and hair like a nest of black cobras was enough to stun me into death-like stillness.

I screamed. As I ran from the vision or hallucination or sight, I do not know which, the light of my lamp went out. Stumbling and falling we blundered down the corridors and rooms, some primeval instinct prompting me to stay in the central tunnel.

All we could hear was our own laboured breathing and the blood pounding in our ears. By the time we reached the bottom-most room, the wind had vanished and the room was again spectral and still. Just as when we had first seen it. The ambience was so quiet and meditative that it made me wonder whether the wrathful vision I had seen had simply been a trick of my own fevered imagination. We paused to catch our breath and when my fear was nearly dispelled, I took a moment to light the lamp that I held. I did not realise that I had been clutching it in fear all this time. Just as well, I thought. It would not have been fortuitous if I had left it behind. All those who visited a place such as this would definitely be clever enough to notice this telltale evidence of intrusion.

As we moved to go down the ladder that still remained open, a thought struck me and I turned to my brother.

'Hold the lamp,' I said and placed it in his trembling hands. I wanted to look closely at the paisley design of the bejewelled masks adorning the divine couple and see whether the jewellery matched Uma's nose ring. As I turned towards the couple, cold lightning clapped between my ears and my body froze in shock.

'Aditya Raj,' I said.

'Yes?'

'Do you notice anything?'

'What?' He was too frightened for intelligent communication. 'It's unnaturally cold in here,' he ventured.

'The divine couple, you fool!' I shouted. 'It's gone.'

'O Buddha, O master of the Universe, O great and Divine Providence,' my brother moaned and started reciting the Green Tara couplets.

'They must not catch us,' I said, 'quickly, brother, let's go.'

'Let's, brother, let's,' he whimpered.

We sped down the ladder and ejected out like Buddha's faeces.

In the orchard we collapsed in an untidy heap. It took a few harsh words and a shake of his shoulder for my brother to regain a grip on reality.

'What was that brother?' he kept repeating, 'what was that we just saw?'

And thus I explained. Though it took many clarifications and questions from my brother to understand.

'What we saw was the architectural reconstruction of the central channel of the human spine. To understand the importance of the central channel, one must understand the Great Goddess, brother,' I said and went on to explain it to him.

'The Goddess is powered, moved and guided by the breath. In the New Science, there are elaborate visualisation practices to guide the breath into the central channel of the spine and make it ascend to the various centres. Each centre is marked by a deity and a certain syllable. Each centre is in the shape of a wheel and has different spokes according to its location. Though of course, none of this is visible to the human eye, considering it is made of the subtlest energy. Great meditation stokes the inner fire of the Goddess and she rises up the central channel. When a tongue of its flame melts the syllable HUM in the crown chakra, a drop of nectar is released. It gives rise to the Great Joys. It destroys disease, grants superhuman powers, purifies the mind and leads to Buddhahood.

'The seven rooms we saw were the seven centres of the human body. You can guess what the paraphernalia you saw signifies. The deities, the syllables, the candle wicks, the mirrors, the colours of the walls are all aids for visualisation practices. What I tell you are the most basic tenets of awakening the Goddess. I have no knowledge, experience or interest in this science. And my lay information on the subject is a drop in the ocean of the New Science. Much of it is kept secret from even the scholarly public. But it is quite evident that here it is practised in its most extreme form. Do not ask me what those extreme forms are. I don't want to discuss them.'

I finished in what seemed to me like one long breath. 'This New Science, my brother,' I spat out a sardonic laugh, 'truly flourishes in Nalanda. And no less than all the Abbots would be involved. Who else would build this elaborate architecture?'

'But why inside the sacred body of the Buddha?' my brother whispered. 'What wild heinous heresy is this?'

'Why not?' I retorted. 'Why should the sacred body of the Buddha be unreachable when the transformation of the human body is the ultimate goal of human endeavour? When it is the Buddha you meditate on, it is the Buddha that you will become. When you meditate on his body, your body will become like his body. This too is a form of New Science. A very secret form, as has become quite obvious to us today.'

'There is one more place to visit today.'

'Where?' my brother asked.

'Sakya's library,' I said. 'Quickly. I have to corroborate something.'

As we reached the lecture chaityas and crossed the rows and rows of concentric courtyards to reach the Main Assembly Hall, I couldn't help thinking that Nalanda's movement through time was like the spirals of an ancient nautilus. And when Aditya Raj used his secret and highly official Dharmachakra seal, I felt we were slipping again into a primordial source. The air was thinner and more rarefied, the darkness more consuming, as it should be inside the beginning of all that is. The dust of criticism had not fallen on its uncontaminated knowledge. Here, the mutation of learning had not yet begun. The heart of Nalanda beat with the quiet rhythm of its own certainty.

At the entrance we were stopped by the dwarapalas. They handed us white sanghatis and white hats that I tried clumsily to wear like a mask. Silent monks clothed in white went about their chores in utter humility, unaware that what they did was rare and stupefying. But whether the heart of Nalanda was that of a deadly demoness or a wise sage, I was soon going to find out.

Somehow I expected to spot Rahula in the beehive-like bustle that went about in the deathly quietness of the star-shaped etheric library. His absence came with a sharp pang of suspicion. Could it be that he was innocent? Had I misjudged him? If I hadn't, which sect did he belong to?

Then I saw one of Pandit Dharmapada's students. My confusion gave in to alertness. I pulled the cowl over my head. I did not want to be recognised.

We crossed several monks in the process of transcribing and translating manuscripts in dark and airless halls of the akashic transcripts library. Today, an entire floor was dedicated to cataloguing and collating texts. On our way to the top-most storey above the library, I saw a Metallurgical Science acharya conducting a secret lecture with a class of three students.

Even though this was not my first visit, I was still unable to completely rationalise the events unfolding before me. I decided to concentrate my thoughts on what I needed to find in Sakya's library.

Sakya's musty, secret-most library had not seen light for many centuries. But at its entrance stood a shadow of even more intense darkness. Darker than the dark, it seemed to be waiting for me.

I thought it was Sakya, the Monk Who Never Sleeps, standing sentinel over the secret contents of books that could change the fate of mankind. But it was not Sakya.

It was Siroha.

My brother's reflexes have always been sharp during nefarious activities. Before I could open my mouth, he had quickly moved to talk to Siroha. As they whispered in quiet confabulation, I pulled off a tallow from the wall and, entering the empty library, started searching through the stacks of lovingly bound manuscripts. I looked around at the librarian's low desk. There was no one there. Where was Sakya, I wondered.

I scanned and searched in vain for the book I had found the last time I had been here. On its cover leaf had been an iconographical painting of the terrible female visage I had just seen inside the Giant Buddha. Words in black ebony written on the Buddha's visceral walls had been familiar to me because I had first read them here, at Sakya's library.

It was imperative to hide away the book in my sanghati and pore over every detail. For this book was the missing aspect of the knowledge my brother had so foolishly tried to acquire. The words on the Giant Buddha's walls had helped me put together the pieces of this horrific puzzle. Whoever had been inside the statue today had been conducting the Great Initiation. An initiation that was taking lives. The same initiation denied to Mahipala and Siroha.

The book would be loaded with clues about who had marked the holiest of holy statues in the whole world with their dirty presence. The Abbot or the king.

I quickly started pulling books at random. I blundered and blustered, like a drowning man gasping for air.

And then I found it.

On its cover leaf, the same terrible visage I had just seen. The red protruding tongue, hair like a nest of bees, three flaming eyes. And a nose ring where the nose should be.

The words were in antiquated Brahmi, but I could read them now.

Great Initiation, it said.

The book had been easily and openly hidden because it was written in antiquated Brahmi. But I had seen the Brahmi lettering on the statue walls. That and the iconographical illustration in the book gave it away. I knew I had seen that face in Sakya's library and I had been right.

Inside the book was the detailed account of the New Science formulae for the Great Initiation.

'*The master and the disciple walk on the razor's edge before the initiation*,' one verse said. '*One transgression and utter destruction ensues*.' And then a few leaves later, '*Experiences of the initiations penultimate to the Great Initiation are not always pure*.'

I was suddenly suffocating for air. I hurriedly put the tallow back on the wall and, in the darkness, moving out of the library, I gesticulated to my brother that we should leave. My brother caught my eye and started to finish his diplomatic exchange with Acharya Siroha. I was at the door. My brother paid his respects and bowed to the acharya. From the corner of my eye I saw Siroha walking towards me, smiling, his hand raised in benediction. I had almost slipped out to the corridor when Siroha called out to me. My blood froze.

The darkness spoke in the quiet tones of a charnel ground spirit. 'I see you have found what we were looking for, Siddhartha.'

I looked at his hypnotic eyes and was overpowered by the urge to hand him the text in supplication, like a lamb moving towards its own slaughter.

I do not know where Sakya came from. Maybe he had always been there, observing us, watching our every move. All of a sudden he was between Siroha and me. 'That text doesn't leave this library,' Sakya, the Monk Who Never Sleeps, said, facing me. Siroha stood beside him.

Clutching the *Great Initiation* book to my chest, I glared at all of them.

'Hand over the text, Siddhartha,' Siroha's voice was magnetic, compelling, difficult to resist, like honey for a bee.

'Hand over the text, Nalanda brother.' Sakya was moving towards me, his eyes not leaving my face. I knew it was no longer possible to take the book away with me. I knew I had to choose. And the choice was between appearance and reality, life and death, truth and falsehood, beauty and ugliness. Siroha and Aryadatta.

I took a deep breath, like a diver preparing to jump off a cliff, not knowing how deep the waters ran. The last step of Logic off the precipice of choice and free will. Should I take that leap of faith? Or not?

I made my decision.

I closed my eyes and remembering my master, I made an obeisance to the memory of his sandalled feet. And I knew, in this life or the next, I would never renounce my master. Walking up to Sakya, I handed him the book.

Turning his eyes now to Siroha and without looking at us, Sakya shouted. 'Run! And don't look back!' On cue I fled. So did my brother. At the turn of the corridor, I saw Siroha and Sakya clashing with swords. In another moment, Siroha was running and Sakya was giving chase. And in a trice, everyone disappeared.

'What now?' I panted to my brother. Putting distance behind us, we raced down the stairs to the lower storeys. 'Who will die today?'

He did not reply.

'What did you say to Siroha?' I asked my brother as we slipped out into the echoing silence of the Main Assembly Hall.

'Oh, he was enquiring after the health of King Mahipala,' my brother said, a little too noncommittal. He studiously fussed over the seal and avoided looking at me.

When we reached the monastery compound just shy of my hostel, I asked him, 'Who told you about the Great Seal?'

'What do you mean?' he said, startled.

'You stared at the couple inside the Giant Buddha and like a dumbstruck mule you said, "Great Seal!"', I retorted. 'I learnt about the term after a lot of research on *The Book on the Twilight Language*. Research you are not capable of,' I added, cracking my knuckles, ready for fisticuffs.

'Grandson of a sow, I don't know the word and I never said it!' he swore.

There was a silence between us as ripe as a pregnant woman. And that was when I was sure that my brother was also a secret practitioner like the king and probably Siroha's protégé as well.

I just hoped that a day would not come when I would have to kill my mother's son.

27. *Pataliputra*

I did not get a day's rest after that life-changing night. I received urgent summons the next morning to leave forthwith for Pataliputra. King Mahipala wanted to see me.

I wept at my plight. Here I was, a high official appointed for a diplomatic enquiry as delicate as a murder investigation, and my preceptors had disowned me without even an afterthought. In a university where there was a protocol even for the etiquette of dreaming, I was left unsupervised for an occasion of such importance. A meeting with the king, no less.

My brother had arranged for a horse carriage from the Royal Vihara and I left for Pataliputra without informing anybody. And no one asked. Not even the Disciplinarian who kept attendance. I left, having lost my capacity to consider the consequences of my actions.

I find it difficult to describe the grandeur of Pataliputra even though I was not visiting a royal capital for the first time. I knew I had entered the city as soon as we crossed the timber palisades surrounding the capital. I just remember the inside of the city as a jumble of colours and disorderly crowds—uncultured and illiterate. The people of Vaishali had been less showy. The citizens of Pataliputra looked arrogant, too proud of the glamour created by Magadha's legendary kings.

Although the mansions of noblemen were grand and the bazaars festive, I was shocked to see rubbish on its streets. This was unthinkable in my Vaishali, where the roads and parks were swept every day.

Little else of Pataliputra's sounds and sights and colours registered in my mind. My mind, it seemed to me, was in some sort of a permanent psychedelic haze.

My brother received me at the palace and, in spite of repeated queries, did not tell me why the king wanted to meet me.

Everything connected to the king was accompanied by a great degree of pomp. Who greeted whom first, who was the first to sit and where, with what title was one to be ushered, the details were tedious and endless.

The contrast between Nalanda and Pataliputra could not have been made more stark in my mind. Nalanda was dedicated to a gracious life of rigorous enquiry and contemplation. Pataliputra was dedicated to political power and the acquisition of worldly riches. Pataliputra was chaos, Nalanda order.

But inside Mahipala's lavish palace, it was impossible not to be stricken by the polished columns, the gigantic arcades and the high-ceilinged audience hall. Exquisite stone artisanry perched on wooden beams decorated the entire ceiling. Every courtyard had a fountain and all the slaves were women. And they wore more jewellery than temple priestesses. I tried not to stare at them. After all, I was a Nalanda monk, not a country bumpkin.

The language of the slaves and even the nobility was crude and unrefined. I was quite shocked at the flippant use of colourful expletives and ribaldry amongst the dwarapalas.

A palace eunuch ushered me into Mahipala's private antechamber. This was adjacent to the royal court's chamber of ministers. Quite obviously, I had entered the inner echelons of Pataliputra nobility.

The hustle and bustle of Mahipala's palace was not as controlled or monochromatic as Nalanda's. The cult of eighty-four mahasiddhas had created a bureaucratic democracy in Nalanda.

Here, it was the elaborate showmanship of one man. The king.

Before meeting Mahipala, my brother briefly introduced me to his wife, the daughter of Vasantapala, King Mahipala's brother.

She presented only her silhouette behind a heavily curtained mesh window inside the small audience hall of the royal palace's family chambers and did not speak a word.

I smiled in irony. 'I can see,' I said in greeting, 'that you have adopted the Muslim customs of the West. Of keeping your face hidden, of not being physically present before your husband's elder brother for your entire life, for he is, like all men other than your husband, to be held in caution and suspicion. Times have changed. Such were not the ways of my land. In Vaishali, the beauty and grace of a woman is a daily and overt presence for all.'

She had replied, with extraordinary poise and sagacity, 'Such are the contingencies of time, Elder One. We shall depend on the enlightenment of sages like you to ensure that daughters of the future do not suffer like us.'

Her presence stayed with me like a delicate perfume even while I was being presented before the king.

Mahipala was short, chinless and overly made up. He was pacing the room when I entered and his slave was having difficulty keeping time with his steps to position his smoke holder for a whiff of marijuana. The king's minion kept tripping on the lush carpet. Quite unlike Nalanda, where even the pageboys conducted themselves with dignity. Even Mahipala's throne looked too big for him.

In spite of the elaborate feudal systems of primogeniture that distanced the king from his own brothers, as an extended son-in-law of the royal lineage, custom behooved that I be given some modicum of respect. As a monk from Nalanda, and one fully ordained, even more so. But to see that my cushions were almost at the same level as his chair was a matter of grave concern. This was too much respect. I feared a trap, a preparation for a diplomatic coup of some sort. So I chose to stand throughout the king's audience.

Mahipala cut short the preliminaries of my greetings.

'Have you got the Great Initiation books?' he started with a shocking demand. The aim, I presumed, was to take me by surprise.

'What books are these, O Ultimate One?' I demurred, looking as ignorant as I possibly could.

'The ones that have the instructions for the Great Initiation. Aditya Raj said that you would get them for me,' he pouted.

So I had been set up by my brother again. How quickly I walk into his deployed manipulations, I thought. He had somehow made me seek the book out, a book I did not know he knew existed!

'I tried my best, O Ultimate One, but alas could not find it,' I stalled, my mind racing with thoughts. Had my brother told the King the book was in my possession? Would I be tortured? Had Aditya Raj too, like everyone else, thrown me to the wolves?

I congratulated myself for handing over the book to Sakya. Mahipala's chin trembled, as he brought forth a fine exhibition of a royal tantrum. Quite clearly, this was the torture Mahipala had in mind. Sighing deeply in relief, I looked at him with a great deal of amusement.

'I want the book!' he whined, miserable with thwarted desire.

'Sire!' I tried not to laugh. Mahipala's hunger for sorcery had made him a caricature fit for a good limerick.

'Surely Mahapandita Siroha's magic is powerful enough to get the book out of Nalanda's secret library?'

'Siroha!' He stamped his feet and took a whiff of the smoking cannabis simultaneously, setting his slave spinning out of balance. 'He shall go down in the annals of Nalanda as the most useless mahapandita of all time. All the wealth and power gifted to that washerwoman's illegitimate son has been wasted. As soon as I summon the courage to go against his magic, I shall have his head served at my feet on a platter.'

'In all humility may I ask, O Illustrious One, why is the Great Initiation so important?'

I bowed my head and folded my hands in supplication. Mahipala stopped pacing on his tiny dwarf feet. He calmed down and spoke with as much patience as he was capable of.

'Because it is the apex of the New Science. There are fifteen initiations in all. Seven public and eight secret. I have received fourteen initiations. The last one eludes me.'

I held my silence. I was quite enjoying his plight.

He made a grandiose sweep with his puny bejewelled hands. 'Look again at the glory and grandeur that you see around you. The power of the Pala dynasty and Pataliputra kings comes from Nalanda magic.'

I nodded, still maintaining my stance of supplication.

'And now your masters deprive us of these powers. Secretly, the Tibet Vihar translates all the best books and sends them to the land of snows. This has been happening for many generations. This is so reprehensibe,' he sputtered for words, 'disloyal!'

'For sure,' I concurred, trying to be as unctuous as my brother.

'Masters, grandmasters, arhats, eighty-four mahasiddhas became so after the Great Initiation.' I spouted knowledge acquired over the last few days, as if I had been born with it. He looked at me with hope, as if I was a fully formed gift dropped from the sky on his lap.

'And they deny this knowledge to us. Us! The hand that fed them for centuries!' he finished for me.

I shook my head in empathetic disgust.

'It is a pity the Great Initiation eludes the Most Honorable One. You, of all, are the most worthy!'

Mahipala now pulled himself up to the full extent of his dwarf-like stature and clicked his fingers.

'On my call,' he menaced, 'denizens of the hellish underworlds wait to be unleashed. My armies of Hindu Senas and Muslim Turaskas are at the ready. If the Great Initiation is refused, at the click of my fingers,' and to prove his point, he clicked his fingers, 'first Odantapuri University shall be burnt down. Then Jagaddala! Tell your masters that!'

I hung my head low. I could not tell him that my masters had forsaken me. He probably knew that anyway.

'Would you like to see that, young Nalanda monk? Would you like to see the Odantapuri and Jagaddala mahaviharas burnt down to the ground?'

I did not care about Odantapuri and Jagaddala. They were extreme seats of New Science practices. I was quite indifferent to their plight. But I shook my head in feigned dismay.

'Then get me the Great Initiation book, Siddhartha!' he huffed like a child demanding candy, 'so Siroha can use its formulae to give me the powers denied to me by your masters. Or better still, write it down. Aditya Raj says your masters have imparted this knowledge to you.'

I stared at him aghast. Mahipala was an example of how there could at times be no difference between appearance and reality. He was an imbecile, through and through.

'You have a week.' He turned his back. My audience was over. I bowed out again.

'Remember, Siddhartha! I demand definitive success in all my employments.'

I was glad to be away from him. When I took one last look at him, he was talking to his slave.

'What a lovely word. Definitive,' he was saying. 'I must use that word tomorrow at court.'

The slave was nodding furiously.

28. *The Council*

My brother and I would not speak after my unchaperoned return from Pataliputra. Not because of lack of intention—I did want to personally wring his neck for subjecting me to the abomination that was Mahipala—but because both of us were embroiled inextricably in preparations for the impending council. He on the royal side, and I, for Nalanda.

It had been made clear to Nalanda in no uncertain terms that this had to be the biggest council gathering since the time of Ashoka. All the Buddhist sects from the various monasteries with their royal patrons were to be represented.

Vikramshila, Odantapuri, Jagaddala mahaviharas and even the far reaches of Gandhara and the Southern Islands were sending representation. Nalanda went about the arduous austerities needed for the nominations and elections of the speakers. For the masters, rehearsals of the talks were strenuous and back-breaking. The agenda for the council was read out in a secret meeting among the Nalanda Council members. For those of us outside the walls of the great halls, seditious rumours filtered through. That some of the masters would be held on trial. A new abbot would be appointed, and it would be Siroha. That all the monastic codes, or the pitakas, the vinayapitaka and the tripitakas would be discussed, and digressions noted and acted upon. Many of us wondered whether our particular masters would be put up to trial. They said that certain unorthodox practices, especially

New Science, were to be brought up and frowned upon. That a strong Brahmin contingent organised by a Sena kingdom had already been prepared to rout us in philosophical debate. And that they were the ones who had initiated the event by pinning the first Hinayanist challenge on the Nalanda entrance gate a few seasons ago.

Many thought that the fate of Nalanda and Buddhism in our country hung on the outcome of the council. Unlike the previous councils that had occurred over a thousand years ago, it was not just the purity of the teachings and the Sangha that would be put to test, but the veracity of Buddhism itself.

Ever since my early days, I had known that the winds were changing. The mood of the populace was swinging against the favour of our religion. It was a popular perception that it was the very openness of the Sangha that had proved detrimental to its wellbeing. Heresies, unorthodoxies, misguided and false doctrines had abounded within it for too many centuries. An eventuality the strict confines of Vedic Brahminism had guarded against. The very divisiveness of Buddhist sects proved how far they had strayed from the Buddha's teachings. And that was why Adi Shankaracharya could easily annihilate each discourse with the purity of Vedic Brahminism, our rival doctrine.

Nalanda was nothing more than a corrupt, state-sponsored, religious organisation running for the last so many centuries in collusion with polluted priests and patrons. Many hoped that Mahipala would succeed in doing what no other king after Ashoka had been able to do. Purge Buddhism.

We were told that many senior and powerful Buddhist Arhats were threatening to boycott the Uposatha ceremony of the council, proclaiming that Nalanda was mlechcha, polluted. Behind closed doors, trials and purificatory rituals were held for many masters who struggled with their conflicted souls and consciences.

Students said in awed whispers that Mahipala had organised

a mythical test of fire and many prophesied that it would burn Nalanda to ashes. Among ordained monks too, there were heavy and rigorous preparations. Lists of debating contingents were catalogued and arranged.

All students submitted their walking sticks that contained in their notches the chronology of their time, years of study, monastic service, ordinations, etc.

Accordingly, new notches were made and we were apportioned our tasks. To my consternation, no tasks were deployed to me. My monastery karmadana said that there were no tasks for monks on special duty. He chided me for not wearing my special duty robes. But in spite of the gnawing sensation that something was greatly amiss, I refused to comply and wore my simple monk robes.

Some copiers were instructed to write down the decrees on birch leaves, and others were taught about the locations where they would put the oral discourse down to memory. Scribes and translators were lectured.

The Translation Department was the busiest. Organising translators for all the local dialects was an onerous task, even though most of the discourses would be held in Sanskrit and Prakrit. Arrangement for parchment paper and writing material became a temporary and full-scale industry. After the Translation Department, the busiest were the Trading posts. Merchants of books and stationery did brisk business.

And though Nalanda had always been respectful though slightly aloof regarding the hospitality accorded to royal patrons, this time, care was taken that no opportunity be afforded for a royal flare-up. Seats, cushions, parasols, eulogies, accommodation and food were carefully organised and reorganised.

Finally the appointed day came in the holy month of Baisakh. The gardens and fields of Nalanda and beyond were festooned with temporary pavilions to house the debaters and their listeners. The rules of engagement and code of debating conduct were prepared and re-prepared by readers refereeing the debates. You could not oppose metaphor with analogy. Metaphor must be used for metaphor, and analogy for analogy. The discipline of the art of debating was made more rigorous and exhausting. There were disqualifications for contradictions. Solipsisms and circularity could lead to severe penalties and confiscations. The risk of losing your head and life in the debating pavilions hung over the debaters like a gladiator's gloom.

The day of the council looked less like a religious conference and more like a town fair. Stalls selling fried gram and beaten rice had been set up along the walls of the main pavilion. Some were openly hawking fermented palm juice. Artisans, local sculptors, and painters put up their own small pavilions and trade was brisk. Local masked dancers enacted the chau to an enraptured audience. Fathers from neighbouring villages, their infants hoisted on their shoulders, enjoyed the shadow puppets and the spectacles of fire-eaters and contortionists, while their wives and mothers haggled over low-priced textiles. Political skits were staged, and many revolved around enactments of idiot lay students and tyrannical panditas who combated kings with wooden swords.

Every now and then, a royal retinue would pass through, its pennants waving stiff and proud. When they weaved through the crowded bazaar that had suddenly sprung up like mushrooms after the rain, local pedestrians would part for the chariots and the foot soldiers. Sometimes, a rousing cry of welcome and praise would spring up from the crowds and sometimes, a stinging catcall for lowered taxes.

I walked through the melee and sensed political tension in the air. This did not augur well. My father used to say that festivals marked with political tension usually ended in a bloody revolt of some kind. Some monks had been stoned in the night streets. One had died.

Inside the closely guarded pavilions erected for sophisticated philosophical discourse, where only the scribes and the learned ones sat, the atmosphere was as heated and noisy as outside.

The pavilion where the first Hinayanist challenger debated in a loud and raucous voice attracted the largest laity and acolytes. Everyone wanted to see what he looked like. Everyone except me.

The mood was festive. Local temple art, paintings and dwarapalas adorned the entrance of each pavilion.

Inside pavilions, upholders of popular doctrines of my time, the Mahasanghikas, the Sautantrikas, the Madhyamiks, the Mimamsa vadins and the Vedantins debated and counter-debated their convoluted logic. How much ink is shed in philosophical debate. How many dust storms are raised. Sophisms, tautologies all. Having surfeited on them for four years, they tired me now. It was not there that my interest lay. I wanted to know what transpired in the main tent pavilion presided upon by King Mahipala. Not much noise emanated from its makeshift walls. Here, dwarapalas had cordoned off the unruly masses that were only allowed in the debate pavilions. In some pavilions, only students and masters with seals were allowed.

An entire military contingent guarded the flimsy doorway of Mahipala's tent. There, I knew, rested Nalanda's fate.

I sneaked in after narrating to the mustachioed dwarapala guarding the entrance a long and complicated story about how I was the official scribe who had lost his seal. And there, in a silent ominous gathering waiting for the pronouncement of doom, I stood at the back and listened to King Mahipala's quietly ferocious allegations. Mahipala was much uglier than his statue adorning the Entrance Hall of Nalanda, but the general populace did not know that.

If it were possible, he had become uglier since I last saw him in Pataliputra.

His hairdressers could not prevent his round, chinless face from looking overly hirsute. He looked like a puppet in a comical farce. It was the Buddha's way of telling him that being king was not enough. But he did not care. He expounded in trembling tones on how the Buddha, Dharma and Sangha had eroded under the aegis of the Venerable Ones in Nalanda. His arguments were elliptical and badly disguised with sugary diplomacy, but for me especially it was easy to glean the sinister motive shining through his discourse, like a thief behind a curtain.

The Abbot and my master were present, as were other kings and the abbots of other Mahaviharas, such as Vikramshila and Odantapuri. They sat in a circle before a select audience, each with their personal slaves in attendance and with the rest of their paraphernalia, parasols and flags.

The autonomy that Nalanda enjoyed over the centuries had made it not only arrogant but also defiant of the Buddha's way, Mahipala said. It was the fault of the royal patrons who polluted the purity of scholastic learning by bestowing upon it so much opulence. Nalanda had become so powerful that it was now flagrantly defiant of the very dictates the Buddha had formulated for the functioning of the Sangha. And it had reached a stage where it had become the exact opposite of what the Buddha had intended. It had been brought to his notice that several acharyas were responsible for gross misconduct. It was important to put them on trial and decide the further functioning of this esteemed university. The political hegemony of the Nalanda Council must be questioned. The power of the panditas carefully delineated again. It was just not enough to redefine Mahayana Buddhism, which was taking place in neighbouring tents, even as he spoke. It was important to understand and catalogue the definition of the New Science that had bloomed secretly like a poisonous flower within the walls of this esteemed university.

What is it? Its secrets must be expostulated, the involvement of the acharyas and panditas carefully noted. Its manuscripts, its esteemed designated power must be handed over to its royal patrons.

'It was all very fine that Nalanda had so many foreign departments, translators and emissaries carrying our sacred word and knowledge across the boundaries of our motherland. Politically it had helped us in the past. In trade and in diplomatic pursuits. But such a transmission of knowledge had not always been fruitful. Many of our enemies, in the land of snows and in the lands of deserts, had become powerful, aided by the secret formulae of the New Science. But the royal patrons were kept in the dark about its nature and powers,' the king said.

'I won back my father's kingdom from the Kambuja King in Tibet who had oppressed my forefathers, but my battle against them has been tough. I have been led to believe that they know too much about us. And that is how they had conquered us. The autonomy of Nalanda has created a network of spies that spread a web of deceit against us. We, who nurtured Nalanda as a mother nurtures an infant to its breast. Politics is the rot that destroys a religious institution. And we, the royal patrons of Nalanda, cannot allow this to continue. Nalanda stands on trial today for depravity of the moral, the philosophical, the material and the political. We shall go over the points one by one. And the revered and venerable Abbot of Nalanda and my personal guru, the Most Precious One, shall preside over each point,' Mahipala's monotone went endlessly on.

The Abbot sat in his seat like the moon shining over mountains. He looked more the magnificent monarch than the king himself. He struck me as a most resplendent figure. His eyes still contained the same piercing intensity that I first beheld across the tiny window at the Nalanda Gate. His face glowed with the learned indifference of the sagacious. And his speech was controlled, unlike the spitefulness of the king.

The Abbot, when he spoke, never once let his dignity, stature or sophistication slip. Right from the time of the Buddha's promulgation of the precepts of the Sangha, he said, the viharas and monasteries could not have flourished but for the royal patronage they have enjoyed. Nalanda, like many other monasteries dotting our landscape, has a long and illustrious lineage of royal patrons. And here the revered Abbot digressed briefly to illustrate the various kings who patronised Nalanda.

But, he continued, the very reason the Sangha was started by the Enlightened One was to create a sashana or system that was able to welcome into its fold people from every walk of life, and not only the privileged, as is seen in the Brahminical systems. And so it came to pass that Nalanda grew in stature and kept on growing over the centuries. And as learned ones came within its walls, they brought with them the knowledge of moolanivasis in forests, the low-born in palaces, the outcasts in the streets and the slaves in artisan shops. Not only this, yavanas from around the world and scholars from across the seven seas had flocked there. Many learned ones, persecuted in their own lands, had secreted away to Nalanda manuscripts denounced as heretic by deluded kings and priests in their own kingdoms. Thus it is that every school of learning in this land, nay, the world, had grown and flourished in the lecture chaityas of Nalanda. The power of Nalanda is the power of knowledge. That is where the autonomy of Nalanda springs from.

It seemed to the Abbot that his most illustrious disciple, King Mahipala, hankered for the old Brahminical way the Buddha so stringently abhorred. In the Brahminical system, the secrets of the scriptures rested with very few, passing only from mouth to ear, hidden in the dense foliage of forests and the high towers of palaces. It was kept away from the people. But the Sangha the Buddha created was for everybody. He did not aspire for his religion to be practised in lofty realms. Thus he centralised the knowledge scattered in forests and palaces.

'Is this what my illustrious disciple wants? To go against the basic tenets of the Buddhist Sangha?

'Maybe King Mahipala yearns for a Brahmin guru. A guru who, instead of interpreting the scriptures, presides over his heir's naming ceremony and imparts cunning suggestions to battle court intrigue. Maybe King Mahipala seeks a guru like the famed Brahmin priest Chanakya who would teach him the nuances of statecraft formulated in the Arthashastra.

'But may I remind King Mahipala, as a guru might take the liberty to remind his disciple, that such was not the Buddha's way. In fact, such was the exact opposite of what the Buddha sought. The autonomy of the Sangha is its independence. It is the very life breath that keeps the university alive. Without it, Nalanda will die. The generous endowments of its patrons are the alms that the Buddha's body survived on, as the physical premises of Nalanda survive. But Nalanda's intellect is not controlled by the sensory demands of its body, and may well survive, even if its belly is starved.

'As for the new sects that Nalanda has birthed and nurtured, the course of Buddhism has seen the springing up of many new and conflicting sects, and they have all survived the ravages of time. So will this new school we have come to call the New Science. All I can say of the New Science is that there are no secrets in it that have not existed in the streets and forests of this great land for many millennia. But that is a matter to be discussed by the learned ones in the neighbouring pavilions. Here, I must face the most serious charge of all, that of moral depravity. Let the Enlightened Buddha be present here during the trials and bear witness to the ordeals of innocents. By the grace of the Buddhas, Truth will prevail.'

It was almost as if Truth, all this while, had waited in the wings for its cue. During the course of the venerable Abbot's speech, my brother had entered the Hall, disturbing the air with his unruly presence. But he looked grim, ashen-faced, and by the time he had spoken into King Mahipala's ear and my lord Abbot had finished his speech, it was quite clear that something was terribly wrong.

With all eyes on him, King Mahipala sat in silence for a long time. Finally, with an unfocussed look, he moved to address the audience. The moment had taken on a dream-like quality. His speech was stuttered, and when unrehearsed, his verbal performance was of very poor quality.

'A tragedy has occurred,' he spoke to the gathering. 'An omen of terrible portent. *At the feet of the Great Buddha statue, there lies, my official says, the slain body of a young girl!*'

A universal gasp rose from the audience. My heart clenched. A nameless dread filled my inner spaces.

'It looks like a beheading. Many learned ones here may be unaware of the investigation currently under way in Nalanda. Several murders were brought to our attention many months ago. We...'

The king's words were drowned in pandemonium. Amongst the elderly and young alike rose fierce remonstrations of pious disgust. When my brother reached my side, a cacophony of voices drowned his words. Hair tufts bristled in indignation. Elderly arhats flung their staffs and cursed Nalanda, pronouncing powerful mantras from the scriptures. Others demanded clarifications in heated tones. One in extreme anger pulled a tuft of his hair out and threw it on the floor. A noisome debate ensued over our heads, like the thundering of a coming storm. One voice rang out in catastrophic clarity.

'The council has been polluted. It must be adjourned!' And before the words could register, it was accompanied by a high-pitched wail like that of a witch's. 'At the feet of the Great Buddha, a corpse! Hold me or I shall swoon right here and now.'

I dragged my brother out of the tent to ask him my burning question. 'Who was the girl?' I demanded, my breath trapped inside, draining me of life.

'A village girl called Uma.'

A thunderous noise clapped in my ears. The next moment I exhaled. The wrathful Buddha had hit close, but missed his mark. I felt terror, shame and relief at the same time.

'Who found the body and how?'

My questions came thick and fast, and thankfully so did his answers.

It seemed that the murder had occurred at night, inside the security railing surrounding the Giant Buddha. I presumed that it was last night because a visiting villager was the first one to point it out early this morning when the pavilions were opened. The decapitated body had been lying in the undergrowth and escaped detection by gardeners and monks who may have been working in the area. The news spread quickly throughout the village and inside the university, except in the debate pavilions that had convened early, explaining why the acharyas were the last to know.

The university officials had made a desperate attempt to hush up the news but by now all the neighbouring villages were aflame with the news that an innocent village girl had been brutally murdered in the hallowed precincts of Nalanda University. A revolt was brewing outside Nalanda's walls. Effigies of the acharyas were burning in village squares. The shocked and scandalised clergy declared a collective boycott of Nalanda.

The focus of their peeve remained not the slaying of a young girl but that she had polluted the feet of the Buddha.

Rumours of female sacrifice within Nalanda fuelled outrage in a conflagration of unexpected proportions. Female sacrifices were vaguely known in my time, even accepted among the common folk. But not so from an institution as hallowed as this. A ritual female sacrifice in Nalanda was not acceptable.

This time, effigies of monks were not burnt. Monks in flesh and blood were heckled outside Nalanda, and pelted with stones. One of them was killed. They said his name was Suka. Suka the Stupid Dreamer. How hard we had laughed at his dreams.

Like a gust of seasonal wind, the guests who had filled the fields of Nalanda disappeared from its scenery as suddenly as they had appeared. All that remained was strewn garbage, broken bamboo poles and red silk awnings everywhere.

I sat on an empty dais, facing an empty pavilion, my head whirling, wondering what direction events and the investigation would take.

I looked up to see my brother racing towards me.

In his haste to find me, Aditya Raj knocked down a painting depicting the last Buddhist Council held by Ashoka. Our eyes locked over his misdeed, neither of us beyond the superstition that he had just converted good fortune into bad. The investigation that we were officiating, he informed me, had been taken over by King Mahipala and the Abbot. I sighed, exhaling out of my body months of trauma. I could breathe freely again, and I swore that each breath I took would be purely Buddhist, unpolluted by the worldly contaminations of the last few months.

The elders, my brother said, had convened in the Assembly Hall of the main building. He had been sent to summon me.

The elders had demanded my presence, and I was to be presented posthaste.

29. *The Sacrifice*

The events that would subsequently occur were of such a nature as to preclude the possibility of a predictable human reaction. Let me liken this to falling off a cliff. The experience does not evoke a feeling or emotion but rather suspends it.

It stops the mind, evaporates thought and benumbs the body.

The gathering in the Main Assembly Hall was august and sombre. King Mahipala sat on a platform with the most number of raised cushions behind the exact floor motif that opened out into Secret Nalanda. Many ornate arrangements had been made for the king. His opium smoke holder was most conspicuous as were his footstool and parasol holders.

Beside him on cushions of similar height sat the Abbot. My master Aryadatta was present, as was Acharya Siroha. My masters looked conspicuously austere in comparison to the rest. They radiated knowledge. Other royal patrons sat on the left side. I did not recognise one of them, the other I vaguely knew as a Sena Chief. Some prominent Lichchavi officials and other acharyas were also present at a slight distance from the Abbot and the king. One of them, I surmised, must be my brother's father-in-law, Vasantapala. Behind King Mahipala stood the royal physician, the Raj Vaidya. No doubt he had been summoned to study the corpse. Even Rahula was there. I was shocked to see that he was standing next to my brother.

In the centre of the gathering stood Gauri. Her presence was not surprising, considering that she was the murder victim's sister. She looked completely at ease in the gathering of greats and seemed quite unperturbed by their presence. Her poise and regal bearing in the presence of those who had sometimes reduced me to tears inadvertently made me proud. She looked like a beautiful queen without a kingdom.

I took my place behind my master, as Aditya Raj had taken his behind his king. The investigation, which had seemingly paused on our entry, continued.

'Were you with your sister at the time of the murder?' King Mahipala asked in a belligerent tone of voice.

'Yes, My Lord,' she replied quietly.

'Speak up,' the king said.

'Yes,' she said, a little louder this time.

'And where did the murder take place?' the king asked.

'At the feet of the Giant Buddha.'

'And when did it take place?'

'Yesterday, in the last watch of the night.'

'Do you not know that the university is closed to the laity at night?'

'Yes, my Lord.'

'Then how did you enter?'

'The doorkeepers are known to us, my Lord.'

'And why did you break the stringent rule of entering the sanctum sanctorum, especially in the middle of the night?'

'My sister and I were overcome by a need to worship the Lord Buddha, my Lord.'

'And why did you commit the most forbidden act of crossing the protective railing?'

'We were overcome by a need to worship the feet of the Lord Buddha, My Lord,' she repeated, like a gentle mother to a slow child.

'Have you ever committed such forbidden acts before?'

'On some rare occasions. Yes.'

'And then what happened?'

'The assailant suddenly attacked us from behind and cut off my sister's head with an axe.'

'And then what did you do?'

'Before he could turn to me, I climbed over the railing and fled.'

The king looked towards the Raj Vaidya; it was the cue for him to speak.

'It is obvious by the nature of the decapitation that the assailant was male, possibly a young able-bodied male.'

'Did you see the face of the killer?' the king turned back to Gauri.

'Yes, my Lord.'

'Do you recognise him?'

'Yes, my Lord.'

'Is he present here in this gathering?'

'Yes, my Lord.'

'Can you point him out to us?'

'Yes, my Lord.'

'Then do so.'

Gauri then turned and with all the simplicity and power of a human killing pointed her finger at me.

Two guards had appeared beside me. They hooked their arms around my elbow and led me to the spot Gauri had vacated.

'Do you plead guilty?' the king asked.

I was too numb to register what was happening. All I could see was the king's round, chinless face, and the feverish moving of his mouth that caused spittle to fly out and hang in the air. I looked incredulously at my brother. I have seen different varieties of facial expressions on the one who comes from the same womb as me. Never had I seen him look so inscrutable. I looked at my master Aryadatta. He was smiling!

'We record your silence as compliance. It has been brought to our notice that you were the last person to see the foreign student alive. Because of a lack of other suspects, logic dictates that you must be the killer. Do you agree?'

But then I remembered how much I had slept on the night of Bhim's death and on the following day. Could I have killed Bhim and Uma in my sleep? *Was that possible?* 'Those who walk the path with arrogance, will be destroyed,' kept echoing in my head.

'Your silence implies consent. That leaves Pandit Dharmapada. Why did you kill him and the foreign student?'

This time Guru Aryadatta spoke. 'Your Highness, Siddhartha has been in a very disturbed state of mind for the last few months. Victimised by doubt and negative forces, he has been exhibiting extreme irrational behavior for quite some time. The Abbot and I resorted to putting him in charge of the investigation so that concentration on his responsibilities would keep him focussed. We realise that to be a mistake. It proved to be to his detriment and that of the university. We prescribe the strictest verdict to be passed against him.'

Next, it was Mahipala who spoke.

'Should we behead him? It would be a just retribution to the way he has beheaded innocent victims. Or should we have him trampled by an elephant? You decide,' Abbot. A message must be sent out to the entire Nalanda population,' Mahipala said and then with a flutter of his fingers added, 'but please make it quick, so we can resume the rest of our business. This is taking too much time.'

'Four months from now, at the time of Chaturdashi, he should be hanged,' the Abbot declared. 'The time is auspicious for the expiation and liberation of his unfortunate soul. His head shall be cut off and placed on a stake at the Main Gate of Nalanda. That should be a powerful deterrent to the monk community and should assuage the inflamed passions of the common people of Nalanda.'

'So it is settled then. Take him away.'

It seemed that an inordinate amount of time went by before chains were clamped on my hands and feet. It was with the detachment of executioners that the guards tenderly bore away my huddled body.

When I looked back for a last glance at all the people I had known, cared about, respected, trusted and loved in this short life, not one met my eye.

30. *Demon Shrine*

Since there was no prison in Nalanda, I thought I would be placed in the solitude cells meant for the punishment of young monks.

As usual, I was wrong. There were many dungeons in Nalanda. Rows and rows of black stone structures encapsulating darkness.

But I was not taken there. I was escorted beyond the dungeons through Sitavana to the demon shrine. It was situated in the same lane that ended at Siroha's private vihara. Asita had pointed it out to me from across the Sitavana shrubbery. Maybe he had known that I would soon be incarcerated here.

As I was escorted into its premises, I reminisced the banter with Asita and Tarpa that took place what seemed like centuries ago.

'Have you heard of arbitrary detention?'

'No,' I had said.

'The death penalty?' they had asked.

'No,' I had said.

'Keep it that way,' had been their reply.

And now it was Tarpa who led me to the chamber of horror. Dwarapalas in red and black robes wielded machetes, looking like dull executioners bored of their work. There was no light here, just various shades of darkness. And heavy clanking iron chains hooked on walls. There were no other prisoners. I was alone, except for rats and flies fattened on human body parts. But that was inside the demon shrine walls. Outside, jackals howled for more corpses.

As if in premonition of the horrors that awaited me, anger rose like fire to my throat.

And before the iron gates clanged shut to imprison me in the nethermost of Buddhist hells, I shouted out to Tarpa, the Gentle.

'This was planned, was it not, from the beginning?'

He turned his head towards me and replied without even a change in breath.

'Yes, Nalanda brother, it was.'

Before darkness enveloped me, I let loose a cry of anguish. 'What did I do wrong?'

He did not reply till the last padlock had been fastened. 'You were not ready.'

As darkness descended on me like a cascade, I called out again. 'In whose name do you do this?'

After an eternity, Tarpa's voice emerged from the darkness beyond.

'In the name of She Whose Name Cannot Be Uttered.'

Desperate for human contact, like a dying man clutching at straws, my voice echoed in the thickening darkness.

'I have read the book. I know her name.'

His final sentence rang out like the death knell of the gallows.

'Do not utter it. You are not worthy.'

With that he ended my last contact with the human world.

My cell made the gloomy chambers of the Honeycomb seem like paradise.

It was the entrance to a grim world indeed.

In snatches of dim light I could see it was not unadorned. It was decorated with every known human body part. Amputated hands bleached of blood hung in rows. Human heads, indecipherable of gender, and in various stages of decomposition, were arranged neatly on a vertical stake. Transparent crystal vats stored hearts, livers, floating entrails and other questionable body parts, like tongues and eyes. Bones made an intricate geometrical pattern. Some were made to chime with the wind that flowed from a singular vent. My hands and feet were chained to the wall decorated with amputated hands. If the decor was meant to strike terror into the prisoner's heart, I doubt it ever failed.

Not only was there no place to relieve myself, an arsenal of bizarre weapons, masks and stuffed animals greeted me wherever I turned. Dried human organs, tanned human skin, bones of children were images that persisted in my delirium.

I vomited often.

I was allowed a clay pot of brackish water that aggravated my delirium. It was a room deprived of all sunlight and steeped in the most perverse melancholia. A room where day was night, and night was night of course.

I constantly heard the sound of dead souls being forced through the narrow vent in the room and cut to pieces on a chopping block. It was the first sound I heard when I became conscious and the last when I lost consciousness.

I lost my capacity to calibrate time. There was no water clock in the room. I did not know how or when the hours passed. Did it matter? The illusion of the reality of time is maintained by memories of the past, perceptions of the present and imaginations of the future. When these mental faculties are suspended, eliminating the past and the future, there is no time. Time ceases to exist.

Whether forty-five minutes or forty-five days or forty-five months or forty-five years, when it is over, it is equally over. What does the duration of time matter?

After a while, there were no sensations of terror or fear or anger. There were no syllogisms of reasoning. No premises and deductions and inferences. There was no doubt or absence of doubt. Ordinarily, I would have felt relief at the absence of all this.

But there was no relief either. There was nothing. I was nothing, suspended in the absence of time.

On the eve of my death, I discovered what I had read about, spoken about, learnt about, but never known. I found awareness of the core concept of Buddhism. *Shunyata.* The Void. The absence of existence. And I realised that *this* was She Whose Name Cannot Be Uttered.

Kali.

The destroyer of time.

Time is experience. Time is perception. Time is consciousness. In the present moment of time, old consciousness can be cremated in the great pyres of the mind to create a new consciousness.

This consciousness was a new state of being beyond the mind, beyond thought, beyond intellect, beyond the petty promptings of the individual self. A state of being yogis spent lifetimes searching. Now that She had voluntarily descended on me, I was driven by an uncontrollable need to meditate, steeping into this new state of consciousness.

I do not know for how long I meditated in the chamber of horrors. All I know is that unlike my previous attempts at meditation, this one was not fruitless. I fell into a disembodied trance-like state and had visions of many Buddhas and bodhisattvas. Some that I recognised and many that I didn't. I felt a tingling in my spine, as if ants were crawling up my bones, and I knew that the Great Mother had fully awakened within me. I saw sudden flashes of inner light. I felt the heat of a red unmoving flame between my eyebrows. As I concentrated on it, the heat spread out from the flame and warmed my body. I recognised this warmth as Her again. I meditated on Her and she showered me with her blessings. Lotuses bloomed inside my head and I smelt the unworldly fragrance of ethereal roses. My tongue rolled back involuntarily and at a particular point in the palate, it made contact. There, from the centre of my skull, the kapala, nectar dripped down my throat, filling me with unbearable ecstasy.

One day, I do not know why I opened my eyes. Maybe a vestigial sensation of earthly sound brought me out of my trance. But when my eyes grew accustomed to the dark, Gauri was standing in front of me, fresh as the dewy roses of my visions.

What I had heard was the sound of her opening the door, I thought, the thought moving extremely slowly through my intoxicated mind.

I looked at her wide-eyed like a child. I do not know how and why the metamorphosis occurred, but I had turned into a blank slate. A tabula rasa waiting for her to write on. I do not know how, why and from whom she had wrested the keys to my cell. All I could do was absorb and accept the awesome power her presence generated.

She touched me, and her hands were like flowing water. She led me out of the chamber and I followed like a willing slave.

Outside, the moon was not yet full. I felt I still had a few days and nights to live. Nalanda was quiet, unmindful of everything else, except the opulent beauty of its own night. She helped me wash and clean myself of my filth at the Dragon Pool, then led me to the amra grove.

In the amra grove there were no humans except us. Only the wisdom of plants and trees and little creatures I could not see. In the amra grove there were no words. Words are primitive and full of paradoxes. There was no bitterness. Only the soothing salve of midnight air. In the amra grove there was only touch. Touch that was not a sensation but an awakening. An opening of hidden doors that I had read about in the Buffalo Farms, but did not once believe I could experience. It was the touch of liberation.

When she leaned her body against mine, the smell of sandalwood emanating from her breasts filled my spaces and I started to expand. The more she leaned on me, the more my body dissolved into space. Her space. Soon, my body evaporated altogether and I realised that I was nothing but an inky blue sky of expanding consciousness. I had shed all my inhibitions like crumpled clothes. And with it, all my limitations. I was not Siddhartha, I was not a man. I was not a monk. I had no parents. I had no age. I was only boddhichitta. I was only emptiness so full of awareness that I encompassed the entire world. I grew beyond the amra grove, beyond Nalanda, beyond my country, beyond this earth and beyond the planets and stars. I had become the Universe whose boundaries kept expanding unto eternity. And then I heard a word. It was the word HUM, like the buzzing of an ancient bee. The word that had started at the beginning of time and never ended.

As soon as I heard the word, she kissed me. When she sucked in her breath, I, the Universe full of the scent of a million roses, started contracting. I kept contracting till I became the root syllable of HUM. It was the size of a mustard seed. All this happened in an instant. By instant I do not mean an earthly instant, but an immeasurable instant when an entire lifetime passes by yet not a second does.

She sucked me in through her mouth and I passed through her body and came out from her secret lotus, her bhaga, her yoni. When she ejected me, I lay at her feet, spent in post-cosmic exhaustion. I was back in my body, back in my nakedness and my incompleteness.

She lay down next to me and touched me. She touched me with her eyes, her hair, her mouth and her hands. She did to me what no earthly woman can do to a man, and I did what no earthly man can do to a woman. She was all women and no woman at the same time. She transported me into such cascades of bliss that after a point, the ecstasy became unbearable for my body. Yet she continued till I reached such a height of erotic pleasure that it made me comatose. But my coma was not a state of inertia.

It was a state of lucidity that gifted me such clairvoyance that I could see in my mind's eye the past, present and future. I saw the nature of all things, and the laws of karma and dharma that bind man. Knowledge showered down on me and I knew them as the great blessings of the ten wisdom goddesses. I gasped at the incisive force of their secret truths. Truths that had baffled the sharpest and brightest intellects.

And then I slept. When I awoke, her face was above mine and she was looking at me. Black luxuriant hair framed her face and in the luminosity of her eyes, I saw the most auspicious conjunction of all polarities.

I moved my mouth to form words and they were like hard pebbles, as if I had just learnt how to speak.

'Who are you?' I whispered. I regretted my speech, because it had brought the magic to an end. She lifted her swan-like neck and let loose a peal of laughter. It drove me to mad adoration.

'I,' she said, smiling her mysterious smile, 'am your real master. And you just received all fourteen initiations necessary for the Great Initiation.'

I did not feel surprise at her words. It did not surprise me that I did not feel surprise. Detachedly, I became conscious that my mind was returning to its traditional way of thinking and emoting.

'So why have you been kept hidden?' I asked, voicing a thought that had always been on the fringes of my consciousness, but had never found the confirmation of truth.

'Because,' she replied, 'of the obsessive focus on male masters as bestowers of knowledge.' Her words did not have any humility, neither did they smack of pride. She was beyond both.

'The real masters are human Dakinis. Most human Dakini transmissions are oral and in song. Or in runic symbols. We can't write. Even if we could, polarising languages of dualistic consciousness do not interest us. Though we are women, we are beyond gender. It's easy for us to fly through the air in abandon.

We have transcended morality and all known social and human conventions. The contexts religious leaders operate in don't interest us. But male authors from such contexts cannot accept our reality. Their existence requires our truth to be kept secret. That is why they write in the twilight codes of sandhya bhasha.'

'Explain to me, Gauri,' I reverted to my role of humble disciple without any pangs or qualms that the master who sat before me was a woman. She was the real master, I kept reminding myself again and again. I thanked the Buddha that I was unstained by the vanity of men. 'What is the need for an Action Seal in the path of self-realisation?'

'As you know from your readings of the Twilight Language,' she instructed me like a Goddess imparting her teaching, 'by successfully using the breath technique, the life force in the breath enters the subtle central channel of the spine through the subtle vacuole near the navel. Through this movement, the seven subtle spinal wheels are pierced. But for complete and total enlightenment to take place within the body, an inordinate amount of force is required to propel the breath into the central channel. This can only be done during physical death. Or sexual intercourse. Because the breath mechanism of death and sexual intercourse is the same.'

I was quiet for a very long time, still unable to come to terms with such a mundane requirement in the path of Enlightenment. It seemed that Gauri had read my thoughts.

'Siddhartha,' she said, cupping my face in her hands, 'I tried to tell you before, your notions of chastity are true. Retention of semen is necessary for the male adept. But chastity should not originate in hatred for women, but in supplication to the female principle. In the formulations of the Great Initiation, it takes fifteen initiations to realise this chastity. Transmuting the hatred of women to their worship is the most difficult path for the male adept. The Action Seal sits like an inversion switch at the base of the spine. She can step up the actualisation of a practitioner to his next level of advancement. Through sexual intercourse, she can give and the male adept can take. Through her, he can appropriate the female principle. But even advanced siddhas, still hungry for magical powers, rarely go beyond using the woman to steal her energies.'

I sighed and turned away from her. The possibility of her with other men gnawed at my entrails. She turned me back, forcing me to face her.

'Even though the Dakini is indifferent to a gendered social consciousness, the imbalance has been too skewered for too long to ignore. Efforts to secure dominance have crossed known acceptable limits. Since female authorship is oral and found only in melody, it has been easily usurped as male authorship. In the rare event that a woman joins the Sangha, she is kept disconnected from her spiritual powers. Every ten-year-old girl is the embodiment of the Goddess. But she doesn't know it. She does not know that it will soon be wiped out, if not by rape, murder and abuse, then by shame.'

I looked deep into her eyes and hoped that she could know my wish that there was a different way, a better way.

'Think, Siddhartha,' She held my face and looked back at me, so deeply that I felt myself dissolving into her again.

'For too long, shame has been an unmitigated preoccupation to preserve the prevailing social order. Especially the shaming of our bodily functions has kept us disconnected from our biological powers. Menstruation is the source of our power. Breastfeeding is our source for compassion. Birth for creation. Sexuality for ecstasy.'

I remembered *The Book on the Twilight Language* mentions the generic Buddhist mantra. *Om mani padme hum*. The jewel in the lotus. This twilight code for phallus in vagina was not different from the Vedic purna kalash. The coconut placed on eight mango leaves over a pot full of water adorns every auspicious Vedic occasion. The coconut was the male phallus. The eight mango leaves the petals of the vulva. The pot the receptacle.

What Gauri spoke of was coded in the deepest Twilight Language, where the law of inversion was used twice. The purna kalash and jewel in the lotus were no longer union of male and female. The linga and jewel were no longer a phallus in the yoni or lotus. In the deepest twilight, the coconut in the purna kalash, and the linga in the yoni, were not phalluses but creations of the female birth process. It was a celebration not of union but of birth.

Someone had said that the Kapalika is the pause between the breath of two great religions, and the Dakini holds that breath. I did not understand it then. I did now.

'If I understand you correctly, ego in the deepest Twilight Language is the male social ego.' I gave a small piteous laugh. 'There is no respite for me, is there?'

'No,' she smiled. 'As the generatrix, the Dakini gives birth to the cosmos. Every world or loka, every creation, emerges from her bhaga or yoni. Within her gendered symbol of fertility is absorbed all the magical powers male adepts hanker for. It's buried in her consciousness. It can be appropriated to a certain extent by sexual intercourse with a girl or woman.

'But complete abjection of the male before the female blesses him with access to the creative principle far beyond that taken by brute force. Mahipala has bullied Nalanda into forcefully giving him fourteen initiations even though he has not achieved the most basic prerequisite of the Great Initiation—semen retention. And he will never achieve it.'

'What about you?' I mused. 'Are there no rules for you? No laws, no regulations?'

'No.' I thought she would laugh, like the tinkling of bells, but she explained in all seriousness: 'These rules do not apply to a woman. She does not need to subjugate her ego. On the contrary, she needs to awaken to her powers. Unlike men, who lose power with the loss of semen, sexual intercourse does not diminish the woman. Female sexuality is the substance the Great Goddess is made of. In men the Great Goddess cannot awaken without the retention of semen, even during sexual intercourse. This is because the Great Goddess is the sublimation of male virility, but in women, every particle of her physical existence is the Great Goddess. Once awakened, it cannot be diminished.'

'I understand now the elaborate social and religious practices to cut off women from their source because it could disempower men. I understand why the Dakini is demonised, hidden from the masses,' I said, my thoughts turning to the *Kama Sutra* incident, and I mentioned it to her.

'The *Kama Sutra* was commissioned by a king,' she said, 'and written by a Kapalika monk. The sixty-four acts of lovemaking are for the New Science adept who takes an Action Seal. It is only in the last chapter, in the addendum, that Vatsyayana gave details of its alchemical properties. Lust for magic is the hidden motive of the book. The last chapter is the grain in the chaff, edited out from most copies. I believe only Sakya's library has the real version.'

'Law of inversion,' I said. 'The book written by a monk is now found under every householder's bed mattress.'

'Law of inversion,' she said, 'celibate religious patriarchs wield social power, but their spiritual power rests in the palms of invisible women.'

'Yes,' I complied, 'and finally, the law flips reality into illusion again. Hiding this reality is a necessary illusion. If the truth were to come out, people would flock to the New Science, not for the bliss of enlightenment, but for the mistaken joys of sex.'

'Like Mahipala,' she said, resting her head in the crook of my neck.

'And the sex-crazed, power-mad Vidyadharas and Kapalikas in Nalanda,' I finished for her.

We lay that way for some time till I absorbed and accepted the revelation of not only my most confounding mystery but also reality as we know it.

'There are others like you?' I asked watching above us a mischievous Nakshatra star twinkle between two mango leaves.

'Yes,' she said, 'Nalanda is full of Dakinis like me. And there are many who come from your master's country in Uddiyana, or what we call the Pure Land. Every woman there is a Dakini, every man self-actualised.'

'I hear that none of the eighty-four mahasiddhas studied in Nalanda,' I said.

'Yes,' she said. 'It's true. They came from a secret monastery called Eighty-Four in the Dakini Pure Land in Uddiyana. Again its existence is hidden in sandhya bhasha. The Pure Land is an island in the Prachi valley, where the mouth of the river Chandrabhaga meets the ocean. The Eighty-Four had been sent to transmit the Great Initiation in monastic establishments. All their masters were women. Like my mother, who is your master's real master.'

The mention of her mother brought to my mind the vision of Uma's decapitated body. My breath stilled and I could not move. Sensing that my limbs had stiffened, Gauri brought her face close to mine and forced me to look at her.

'Do you feel remorse at how the events unfolded?' she whispered.

I thought about her question for a long time. Even after all my mystical experiences, I could not find a satisfactory answer to her question.

'No, I do not feel remorse. But,' I blurted, 'I am confused, I admit.'

She rose from her side, her wide hips still resting on the ground. She uncovered her bosom and took out a crystal dagger. The Dakini's phurba, I learnt about it later. When I rose up in alarm, she took the dagger by the hilt and drove it through her heart. Her slim hands opened her chest and in the space within, I saw the events of the past unfold, in moving pictures. I saw all the events that had occurred before my eyes and all those that hadn't. When the spaces closed and her body became whole again, I realised the level of her attainment.

I enfolded her in my embrace and lay down again. I closed my eyes and surrendered to bliss that was of a sweeter, less lofty kind.

'Will I see you before I die?' I asked her.

'Oh death,' she brightened, 'I had forgotten about that.'

She again extricated her crystal dagger from a fold of her robes and turning towards me, drove it into my chest. I gasped in shock even though I felt no pain. When she pulled out her dagger, my heart stopped beating and my breath disappeared. I started floating in a hazy, dream-like state. As my mind started losing its grip on reality, I wondered whether my lungs had collapsed. In my fading vision, the last thing I saw was a ruby red drop of blood on her dagger, her midnight eyes and her white molten smile. Her smile turned into a circle of light and I sank into it at great speed. It was then that I knew I was really dying.

I had read somewhere that one goes down a black tunnel during the time of death and that there is a light at the end of it. I had imagined a dank corridor made of black, musty, rounded stones and the light to be many yojanas away. If I could laugh out loud, I would have. For surely death is a situation full of mirth. The tunnel is nothing but a shift in consciousness hurtling through a different perception and the light nothing but your next level of consciousness. Death is merely another type of wakefulness.

When I received body consciousness again, Gauri was massaging my hands and feet back to life.

'Not only will I see you before you die,' she promised. 'But after it as well.'

And then I knew that death was not a wall from where you jumped off into oblivion but a door through which you could come and go. At will, if only you had the key. They called it immortality. How simple it all was. Reams and reams of verses in the scriptures, nay an entire library full of them, for such a simple truth.

'Put your dagger away now,' I said and she smiled her first girl smile of the night.

When I drew her towards me, she had one more instruction to give me. 'The New Science rests on the story of the musk deer who spends his entire life chasing the scent that lies in its own navel. The secrets of heaven lie within our own bodies.'

'Enough, my priestess, enough,' I gently chided, 'this student has had enough lessons for today.'

'Oh, no. He hasn't.' She tied her hair into a knot and smoothed down her robes. 'Master Aryadatta is waiting for your Great Initiation, even as we speak.' She was full of brusqueness, ready for departure. She held my hand and said, 'While I am very impressed that you did not once ask me how I got the keys to your prison, and it does show a remarkably advanced level of detachment, I shall tell you anyway. It was your master's orders. And now we should make haste.'

But I drew her back for one final moment. We lay down next to each other and looked up at the starry vault of the sky so I could savour for the last time the velvet night of my rebirth into a profound reality. The air was gossamer and the earth was scented. Every pore of my body oozed nectar. In the play of darkness and light around me was only magic and miracle. And between heaven and hell there was only her laughter.

31. *The Reconciliation*

My master waited for me at his residence. Gauri took leave of me at his front courtyard. For the first time in many months, I stepped into his inner quarters without intimidation. His house was alight with luxuriant torches on every wall, transforming night into day, a glowing firefly in the enveloping darkness. For me it was a matter of great good fortune that I could walk through his house without an impending sense of doom.

'How the Nalanda bells had tolled with the admission of four great candidates.' He came rushing to me with open arms and tears flowing down his cheeks.

'When I sent all four of you to the Ten Wisdom College, Asita and Tarpa were immediately absorbed into the high sciences. Bilwa suffered a little, but my most beloved student had to pass through the demon shrine for realisation. How I have wept, watching you walk the razor's edge all these days!'

In his tight embrace I sensed the surge of the purest moment. He looked at my face with so much longing that tears welled up in my own eyes.

'It is an auspicious moment now, Siddhartha, for I liken you to the mahasiddha who sacrificed himself.' My master then leaned forward and whispered the mahasiddha's name in my ear.

'To what do I owe such extreme honour, master?' I asked, choking back my months of utter desolation.

'Your readiness, my son,' he said, full of unabashed pride.

I waited for him to continue.

'Beneath the surface of mental mundanity exists an inner world that only a chosen few know of. There are suns and moons in this inner world, entire planets and constellations. You are unaware of your own maturity, Siddhartha. Even the Abbot understood your advancement the moment he laid eyes on you. But however advanced you may be, and however sharp your intellect, all very important for evolutionary pursuit, your mind was trapped in many dualities. There were many mental limitations, of doubt and prejudice, that needed to be pierced and annihilated.

'It was not by chance that you met Gauri. It was the law of attraction between master and disciple that guided you to her. It was not by chance that you were put in charge of the murder investigation and pitted against your worldly brother who brings up your conflict-ridden complexes. All that too was meant to happen.'

A thought crossed my mind and my master read it.

'My indifference towards you when you needed me most was deliberate,' he said. 'Step by step I forced you to a point where no reasoning, no mental faculty, no logic could work any more. You had no alternative but to take that quantum leap into the unknown.'

I remembered the moment I had handed over the Great Initiation book to Sakya. At that moment I had not felt like a diver plummeting to the ground, but a diver who was flying, who was free at last.

'And the murders?' I felt my chest tightening again, an old familiar suffocation gagged my throat. 'Was I supposed to have committed them too? Did an inner power force me to it, without my knowledge?'

My master gazed at me deeply, full of an implacable compassion that I could not understand. His beatific smile brought up those old dark demons inside my breast. 'Do not fight surrender,

Siddhartha. Take the logical leap away from the last logical step. It is only here that great flights are possible. When you take that calculated leap into the unknown, the mind and intellect, with their limitations, cannot follow you.'

'But why, my master, why?' My agitation was again spiralling beyond my control. 'What if the calculated leap leads to more duality? The dark forces of duality are meant to be shunned. You taught us that! How can it lead to enlightenment? How can you teach me one thing, and then the opposite?'

It was only when he gripped my arms that I realised my extreme state of turmoil.

He forced me to sit down in front of him and placed his hand on my head. At that instant thoughts vaporised into nothingness, like bubbles bursting on the surface of calm water.

'Do not dishonour me, Siddhartha. Trust. Jump, Siddhartha, I shall catch you, however high the cliff may be, however deep the abyss. I never deserted you, even though you deserted me. I have followed you, Siddhartha, and shall follow you, from this lifetime to the next. I shall never let you go. Sometimes, extreme suffering brings us close to the nature of truth. Your ordeal was necessary to break through your mind. But do not worry. I have brought you to your real master, your Dakini, your most personal deity, your ishta. She shall take you to the threshold of siddhahood, where you and only you shall enter. You will find all of us there, when you reach.'

His words soothed and calmed me. His hand on my head was the touch of falling stars. Soon the room was spinning around me and I fell into the trance of the nameless unknowable Void. She Whose Name Cannot Be Uttered.

Shunyata.

Kali.

When I regained consciousness, my master was gesticulating in ecstasy. His laughter was booming around the room.

'What a rare adept!' he exclaimed. 'How easily you accept the force of Her power.'

My eyes were still drawn inwards into the bliss of the nectar dripping deep within my skull when my master sat down to speak to me. So this was what a Kapalika drank from his skullbowl, I thought. The purest ecstasy. This was what being a Kapalika meant.

'My most revered one,' he said, 'a true Kapalika forever tastes on his tongue the intoxicating elixir dripping from within his skull. This is where She roams and sports and flies in the air. She is the Mother and you can dance with Her, in Her space, if She wishes it, if you supplicate Her.'

And when he spoke, he confirmed the realisation that had already dawned unto me. All imbalanced worlds fell back into their axis and there was only light, white dazzling light.

'A true Kapalika is not a butcher for a skull or blood. A true Kapalika will destroy anyone who does this. A true Kapalika would never let the Mother be disrespected. He knows that unlike women, he can never be Kali. But he can be Kali's soldier. That is what a Black Hat is. Kali's soldier. We call them Kalki.'

I listened in awe and a huge surge of hope welled up in me. This was a world, I thought, that I could die for.

'Nalanda is like that,' my master continued. 'In Nalanda, there are other warriors like you. You now have the vision to see that.'

I fell at my master's feet and begged forgiveness for my shortcomings. Blinded by doubt, I had not been able to pierce the veil of illusion. My state of contraction had prevented me from seeing beyond the obvious. Maybe I was still deluded and unworthy of such high teachings. My master embraced me and reassured me it wasn't so. His consolations gave me hope again.

When I had calmed down into a more peaceful frame of mind, my master propelled me into action.

'Make haste, Siddhartha. There is not much time left for your Great Initiation and higher teachings. We have only fourteen moons and fourteen suns left. We must set forth immediately to the Great Initiation site. It is good to know that in the holocaust that Nalanda shall be subjected to, one of its only survivors has no fear of death.'

'What is it you speak of?' I stuttered. 'It fills me with dread. I do not understand.'

And thus my master spake.

'I speak the truth. My words are not based on prophecy, but fact. For long now, the Abbots of Nalanda and the sacred keepers of the Nine Unknown libraries have been under pressure to surrender their power and knowledge. Nalanda has grown beyond the petty confines of ordinary learning. Its secret powers do not bind us to this world any more. The Nine Unknowns are sworn to protect this knowledge forbidden to the unworthy. And though we have imparted the Great Initiation to deserving kings in the past, King Mahipala's hunger for sorcery is far greater than the preparedness of his soul. His overweening ambition has proven to be Nalanda's undoing. For it is our dharma to deny transfer of power of the Great Initiation to those who are not ready.

'King Mahipala has not taken the rejection well. He and an entire cohort of disgruntled royal patrons have joined forces with the rising Brahminical forces to bring about our downfall. The murder investigation and then the Buddhist Council were convened for this purpose. It was to put extreme pressure on us to either grant him the Great Initiation or face the prospect of the dissolution of the university and the final decline of Buddhism.

'The third murder, however unfortunate, proved to be a blessing for Nalanda. Extremists in Nalanda believe that the wrathful deities had been appeased by a human sacrifice. Be that as it may, the most important acharyas and arhats boycotted the council and King Mahipala was forced to dissolve it. We offered you up for sacrifice in the murder investigation and he had no choice but to accept. With the murder investigation resolved and the culprit put to death, we had bartered a longer lease of life for Nalanda.

'But nothing can appease the dark spell the king is under. Our spies in the palace informed us that the king has joined forces with an invading Turkish Army. In a few days, they plan to sack Nalanda, confiscate its properties and manuscripts and raze it to the ground.'

'What then is our plan?' I blurted in dismay.

'Our plan, Siddhartha, is not to hand over one sacred book to the unworthy. Even if we have to die doing it.'

'But master,' I said in growing alarm, 'how can monks untrained in martial combat stave off an army of bloodthirsty infidels?'

'With purity of heart and faith in the glorious afterlife of a Kali warrior,' my master smiled. He added as an afterthought, 'And a cache of arms that previous Abbots had stored away for such an eventuality.'

Somewhere deep within, the Buddha had granted me the capacity to withstand all this information. I sat in stunned silence as my master looked on.

'The decrees of the Buddha never cease to fill me with wonder,' my master said. 'Today, I shall grant the Great Initiation to a monk convicted for murder. The same initiation that so-called benevolent kings have plotted for. The same initiation that like a dagger will be plunged deep into Nalanda's breast.'

'Why?' I asked my master, humbled by the grace that had befallen me. 'Why me?'

'Because,' my most noble master said, 'you are the most worthy. You always have been. Right from the day you first tolled the bell at the Nalanda gate, I knew. It was meant to be. You are destined to protect our lineage.'

'Did you always know it would end like this?' I asked.

'Yes,' his whisper held the finality of fate, 'I always knew.'

'But exactly like this?' I insisted. 'What if my death assuages the king's pride for a while? Then you can buy more time for Nalanda, can't you? And it can change the course of events. After all, you wouldn't have offered my life to the king unless you thought the ruse might work, would you? And that increases the chances of my head being spiked on the Nalanda Main Gate fourteen days from now by more than half, doesn't it?'

'Ah,' my master indulged in a little laugh, 'my ever-doubting Siddhartha. Yes, what you say is true. How the dice will fall is governed by the laws of probability. And we did load the dice against you. But it is also true that Kali is like the potter shaping a clay pot on the potter's wheel. While She applies pressure from the outside, She also supports the pot from the inside.'

I sat quietly, trying to assimilate his cryptic words.

A bemused expression played on his face as he watched me. 'Does it fill you with dread, Siddhartha, that you might possibly be dead fourteen days from now?'

'No, my master,' I replied, 'I seek only to understand the course of events.'

'Hurry, then,' he said, his patience infinite, 'go finish your cleansing rituals for the Great Initiation. In my mind I can hear the clattering of hooves in the distance. The enemy draws near.'

32. *The Roofless Temple*

On the way to the roofless temple, I crossed the Giant Buddha. I looked up at the vast serenity on the Buddha's face and he looked proud as he smiled down at me. Immense happiness filled the distance between us. An equally august gathering waited for me as I made a long prostration to His sacred body.

I walked with my retinue to the Main Assembly Hall where, but a few days ago, my crimes had been read out to me and executioners had borne me away. Today, my master knelt before me to personally open the Dharmachakra seal. We entered Nalanda's secret place. Dwarapalas offered me black robes and a black hat this time. I wore it with utmost care. Monks in black and white robes lined my way to the innermost secret place. They stood with folded hands and bowed to me in obeisance as I crossed them.

When we reached the stone latticed wall running concentrically around Nalanda's core, my master stopped at a small wooden gate and opened it with his Inverted Palm Seal. We entered and immediately started walking under a lantana bower blooming with the most exotic orchids. The bower opened into a pleasure park where white peacocks roamed. We crossed over a small bridge across a rippling brook and entered the roofless Dakini temple through one of its many gates.

Its circular sandy arena was completely flat and shorn of any adornment. But in stone niches surrounding the arena were beautiful statues of the sixty-four Dakini principles. In front of them stood her live human embodiments. They were all there, in a circle, waiting for me.

Kumari virgin girls of the evening worship, old washerwomen, moolanivasi slaves, high-caste Brahmin priestesses, blacksmith wives, women young and old, small and big, fat and thin, rich and poor, high and low stood around me in a circle. They were gloriously and completely naked. They were the highest Dakini practitioners. I saw the forest Dakini amongst them, nursing her infant. I recognised her as my brother's wife and it did not surprise me. For when I had met her veiled and shadowed in Mahipala's palace I had recognised the infant, my nephew, playing in the corner. We smiled at each other in true recognition.

They were the queens of space and time. They were the Initiation goddesses. Silhouetted against a rose-tinted sky and an ephemeral crescent moon, they were the source through which the powers of the universe flowed.

In the centre waiting for me, as the symbol of the overarching principle of all Dakinis, stood Gauri. She stood smiling beside the four-faced lamp. Gauri, my real master. Gauri, my chosen deity of worship, my ishta. She put on the mask of the three red eyes and the protruding tongue.

She was Kali, the one whose name is not uttered except by the most adept.

Kali, the creatrix of the universe.

Kali, the giver of the Great Initiation.

Kali, known only to the most worthy.

Kali, the manifestation of Shunyata, the Void, the highest Dakini principle.

Kali, the Great Mother.

In a smaller circle around me were the couples. The Abbot with the Chinese scholar, my master with Gauri's mother. Asita, Tarpa, Sakya and Bilwa with women my brother had probably seen fleetingly through his eye piece levitating off the ground.

The niches were festooned with pennants. The sacred geometrical diagram of the Great Initiation mandala was artfully coloured with indigo pigments. As soon as I walked into the mandala, the chanting of the thousand names of the goddess began.

Her eulogies rent the air in a crescendo of devotion. She was the creator of the doctrine. She was the initiator of revelation. She was the cause of all actions. She manifests all that moves and all that doesn't move. She was the founder of the New Science. She was the mother of the eighty-four mahasiddhas.

My master stepped forward to lead the chorus with verses from the Great Initiation book.

Women are Heaven. Women are Dharma. And women are the highest penance. Women are Buddha. Women are Sangha. And women are the perfection of wisdom.

When she is naked, kneel and worship the goddess. When she is clothed, obey the great mother. When she is angry, unsheath your sword to avenge her. When she flies, know that she comes from the Pure Land and brings auspiciousness.

We changed the names of the eighty-four mahasiddhas, and exhorted them as Kali's warriors, the Kalikas and Kali's tribe as the Kalika tribe.

The chanting stopped. My master introduced me to the Kalika tribe and informed me about the Kalika lore. I was taught that the female masters had knowledge so profound that it was beyond the reaches of chauvinistic limitation. I was told stories of how the female masters of the Kalika lineage became enlightened. Though they were sworn to secrecy, how they rose out of their sexual slavery as Action Seals to achieve moksha. How they transcended the adversity of their circumstances to become more powerful than all the acharyas across all the lands.

I was taught how to pay homage to my real master. I was told never to dominate her, or enlist her energies by appropriation.

I was warned that whoever offends her incurs the wrath of the Great Goddess. My relationship with her was that of a devotee to a deity. I must always remember that she need not render me any service. I was taught how to remedy my ordinary views of a woman so she would be perceived accurately as the embodiment of the divine. The powers that flowed through her should not be stolen but received at her will.

I was taught the etiquette on how to approach her, give her tributes, pay obeisance. How to worship the dust of her feet.

I was taught the secret signs of the Kalika family, and consigned its vocabulary to memory.

The Kalika tribe wore red dots between their eyebrows when they met in secret gatherings. I memorised the sixty-four secret locations where the family met and the dates and time. I learnt how to find the Dakini Pure Lands because it was not accessible to the unworthy. *Om mani padme hum*, in our Kalika code the jewel in the lotus, was the Dakini paradise island hidden inside the eight snowy lotus waves of the ocean.

Lastly, I was taught how to be her warrior, her Kalki. I learnt the codes of chivalry, courage, duty and honour.

With this I was welcomed into the Kalika family, and formally made my offerings to my master. My real master.

With constant incantations of this new awareness, Gauri, my real master, accepted me and her warm breath whispered our future reincarnation lineage in my ears and embedded it in my consciousness. The whispered lineage of the Dakini's breath would become a part of my breath, through death and birth, through many consecutive lifetimes.

I took another step into the Great Initiation mandala and Gauri sealed my consciousness. My body shook with the divine force she unleashed on me, like a thunderbolt. The descent of grace was like rain falling on parched earth. Like a stream flowing over a dry riverbed.

We sang songs of realisation that intoxicated us to unprecedented heights of ecstasy. Together we gazed at the stars and the sky, lost in the merged spaces of inner bliss.

My third eye flew open, and for a long time after, wherever I looked, I saw only golden light. For fourteen days, I went through many purificatory rituals and cleansing ceremonies. I fasted and spent long hours in solitary confinement and contemplation of my new awareness.

On the fourteenth day, even as monks were given their last lessons on the art of sword fighting, my master Aryadatta took me to a quiet spot under the Bodhi tree by the Dragon Pool and gave me his final instructions for the protection of the Dakini lineage.

When the frenzied tolling of the bells at the Nalanda Gates warned us about the assault, a lone heart-shaped Bodhi leaf started a slow downward journey to fall on my lap.

My master took it as the sign of the great mistress of linearity, Mahakali. It was time.

Almost in the time it takes for a Bodhi leaf to slowly fall to the ground, an entire world was wiped out. I remember each unfortunate moment in detail.

Two of these are indelibly imprinted in my memory. After the annihilation of Nalanda, these memories have not lingered so much as they have damagingly refused to be wiped out.

The first had a significant bearing on my personal destiny, the second on the destiny of humanity.

33. *Heart Blood*

These incidents occurred just before the sacking and burning of Nalanda. All bells were tolling in panic at the same terror-stricken time. News of the destruction of the celebrated seat of Jagaddala Mahavihara had reached us. Tales of extreme atrocities meted to its inhabitants filled our ears and resulted in an unprecedented outpouring of fear in the monasteries.

Monks had been made to kneel in rows and beheaded, they said.

An army, they said, of Muslim mercenaries and fifteen thousand elephants was heading towards us.

I had risen from my meditations with the gift of clairvoyance. I walked lightly on the ground, hardly touching it. Scintillating sparkles of light shimmered wherever I went.

My night was full of awareness and devoid of sleep. This was the time the Vidyadhara Kapalikas of Nalanda, dressed in bone ornaments, usually stepped out in pursuit of female flesh. For some reason, subliminally, I was out looking for them.

I inadvertently walked towards Sitavana and before me in the dark night, Tarpa came into view walking in the same direction. Strange how in the panic-stricken mahavihara, he alone walked without urgency.

I was about to call out to him when I clearly and lucidly saw the Great Initiation text strapped around his body. In a small section at the end of the book were the detailed instructions of the Great Initiation rite. I did not know what had happened to the book after I had handed it over to Sakya.

Who had given him this book? Where was Tarpa taking it? Where was Master Aryadatta?

Through the university gateway, I followed Tarpa into a silent Sitavana using the sound codes. In spite of the chaos around us, there was nobody inside the Honeycomb. Except for an old, bent moolanivasi monk tying bales of straw behind Nagarjuna's gold mint, there was nothing else.

The gold mint was dark, cold and deserted. Iron channels with empty barrows lay overturned at the mouth of its dimly lit caves. This was the first time I had seen the mint open. I was surprised. Nagarjuna's mint was the one place in Nalanda that was the most magical manifestation of the root of all human desire. Gold. Yet, it showed no signs of plunder or attempted loot. Involuntarily, I laughed. Here was a place where mud was turned to gold and so few knew about it. It is true then, some secrets never come out. The Nine Unknowns were surely very accomplished in their tasks.

It was true that Nalanda was in the grip of fear and hysteria. And this was not the best demonstration of Buddhist mindfulness, Bodhichitta. But it was also true that not a single incident of theft and burglary had erupted amongst the monks or laity.

I followed Tarpa down the Honeycomb cells that turned left and ran alongside the murmuring river. Tarpa crossed the river and I did too. In a few moments, I saw him walking beyond Siroha's Vihar and entering a cemetery. So did I.

The river flowed quietly, detached from the destruction it witnessed. In its corner the perpetual funeral pyre blazed. Its fire sputtered where it found human fat. I was startled by a slight drizzle of rain falling on my skin.

On the left side of the burning pyre was an unlit pyre. I knew immediately that what lay on top of it was the dismembered corpse of a young woman. She had been used in a sexual rite and killed thereafter. Around the pyre were the diagrammatic markings of a mandala. I did not need clairvoyance to know what had happened. The ritual articles that still lay strewn on the mandala and the way her chest lay open indicated that a heart blood sacrifice had been conducted with great precision. Very soon, fumes of her spirit would rise from her body and wait for the ritualistic formulae that could control and contain her transition into a ghost. She would then be useful in the spirit world as well, in ways that assigned more power to her executioner. Surrendering her life heart to her conqueror was not the end of her suffering. She must now forever be in his service.

But that had yet to happen. When I saw her, she was just a dismembered corpse. Her head, hands, legs and torso were neatly arranged on top of the pyre, like timber for kindling. The four truncated limbs of action had been sawed off according to the faithful enactment of the ritual that 'dismembering her body is dismembering samsara.' The rites for sexual cannibalism, when her body would be eaten, remained.

I take your life.

I kill you.

I heard it clearly now, the disembodied female voices. Their whispering incantation wafted around us, like toxic smoke, rising in pitch with every horrific moment. At the other times too, there had been no telling where it came from, this haunting melody of unstruck sound. It may have come from the rustling wind in the trees, or the brooding river, or unseen women, or the darkness of our own perversions. The words were always clear, the chant always rising to a crescendo, but never reaching a climax.

Over the woman's corpse, on either side of the pyre, were my master Aryadatta and Siroha, standing face to face in mortal combat. I had seen this scene before. Run, my master had screamed in that deja vu, you are not ready. And I had fled.

But not today. As soon as Tarpa entered the cemetery, my master called out to him.

'Place the book on the funeral pyre, Tarpa. We shall burn it today with this unfortunate woman.'

'Hark! Desist!' Siroha hissed, his bone accoutrements billowing in the wind, drops of rain glistening on his beard. 'You don't own this knowledge, Aryadatta.' Turning to Tarpa, his voice lashed out across the rain and the wind. 'Hand the book over to me, man from the land of snows. You who have come to our land to steal our knowledge.'

My master raised his voice too, but without rancour or bitterness. 'The way you steal a woman's fluids.'

Siroha's teeth flashed in his monstrous face. 'That is how the Buddha wills it. If enlightenment is fated for her, she will be lucky to be born a man in her next life. She died with gratitude. My compassion has released her from her low birth.'

And from somewhere a sword appeared in Siroha's hand, gleaming with power.

'Spare me your pious arguments, Aryadatta,' he said, preparing for combat, 'You are no stranger to ruthless compassion.'

Even though Siroha held within him enough will and dexterity to behead my master in an instant, my master did not move, nor turn a hair.

'You disrespect the Sacred Mother, Nalanda brother,' he said quietly. And paused.

During my master's pause, rain fell with the softness of a whisper. Again he spoke. He was friendly, as if conducting a debate between friends. 'I want to tell you a secret,' my master smiled, 'and the essential difference between you and me.'

Siroha glared at him, waiting. And in his waiting lay his weakness.

'Try as you might, you can never become She Whose Name Cannot Be Uttered. But you could have been her soldier. A brave warrior like me, a Kalki. But you can never be a Kalki because you do not have the courage to face the truth. The truth that it is your Action Seal that holds the power of enlightenment. Not you. You have the power to cut her to pieces, but you can never have what she has.'

'You blaspheme the Buddha, infidel!' Siroha was now slowly, handspan by handspan, lifting off the ground. 'You blaspheme the One who subjugated the daughters of Mara with one finger pressed to the ground.'

'Since the Buddha's time, the Honeycomb was used for austerities,' my master said, lifting off the ground too. He was keeping time with Siroha, in an unnatural, unforetold synchronicity. Between them drops of rain fell on the brutalised remains of the woman, like mercy. Her face still remains etched in my memory. A calm, unperturbed face. A face so much like Uma's.

'Until you let Mahipala turn it into a place where even ghouls fear to tread. You usurped the Nalanda I loved, but I will not let you usurp this woman's spirit.'

They were now circling the pyre like eagles in confrontation, their feet floating off the ground. A whirling gale of dust and dead leaves followed their movements. The clouds hung dark and low.

'Poison kills poison!' Siroha thundered, gnashing his teeth like a villain in a Baisakhi play, flashing his eyes. 'The law of inversion. I shall rise by what makes me fall. And if that logic doesn't hold, then she and I are both always the Void. It's all an illusion.'

'But was what you did for the good of all sentient beings? Would the Buddha have allowed it?' my master asked, a rousing accusation at not only Siroha but many siddhas and mahasiddhas.

Before my master could finish speaking, Siroha was swooping down at Tarpa the Gentle who in a flash slid across the caves of Sitavana and vanished into Nagarjuna's mint.

I ran after them, and was pleasantly surprised to see that my feet lifted off the ground and I could be airborne too. I lost track of them and when I came racing out of the caves of the mint, I saw them flying overhead above a Honeycomb courtyard.

My master had a sword too, and Siroha and he circled each other in mid-air, clashing in a magical martial battle that shook the three worlds.

Tarpa was beside me now, and we both looked up to see my master circling in the air and swords dancing the dance of death. Rain fell on our faces as we watched, and I sighed.

'I do not want you to take our text, Tarpa,' I said.

His voice was sweet, as if inviting me for a friendly stick race. 'Will you fight me, Nalanda brother?'

Proof that I was not yet fully enlightened came to me with a sore and inappropriate temptation to fight. With my new powers and clairvoyance, I resisted the desire to conjure a sword from the air.

In a trice my master was before us. His hair and beard were drenched, rain stuck like crystal beads on his skin. He was not even breathing heavily.

'Yours is not to reason why,' he said to both of us. 'Yours is to fulfil the roles the Dakini lineage has decided for you.' Like Mahakala, he pierced through our very beings with his instructions.

'Right here and now, Kali bear witness, I pronounce both of you the Dharma Protectors of two wisdom books,' he said.

'You,' he said, looking at Tarpa, 'will take the Great Initiation book. Keep its wisdom alive in your land and never let its flame extingush.'

'And you,' he looked at me, 'will find the wisdom book that you must hide in the darkness of time and all humanity. For eternity.'

With that he disappeared in a flash. We looked up to see them still circling each other, like two stars before collision.

Siroha was never seen after that night in the cemetery. Whether he was killed or disappeared into oblivion, nobody knows. Legends and myths were silent. For a very long time.

I shall never forget Tarpa's parting shot to me. As we walked away from the Honeycomb in the pouring rain, I looked longingly at his departing form, so solid and ever reliable, like a rock. I thought this was the last time I would see or speak with him.

'You are fated to always be the last to know,' he stated as he turned away at the main entrance of Sitavana. He said it simply, as a matter of fact. His arms were crossed at his waist, protecting the dripping red silk of the Great Initiation text from the downpour. He looked as if he was holding his bleeding gut.

I shook my head in bewilderment. 'What is it that you say?' I quizzed him.

'You have not understood the Nine Unknowns,' came another cryptic response.

Those were his last words to me. Wise words of a great sage. Wise words of a mahasiddha. History bears witness to his mighty deeds.

34. *The Last Flicker*

Even after the infidels scaled our walls, all the eighty-four mahasiddhas, some dead, some alive, were visible and manifest. They sat or stood on pedestals and gave instructions for the future to monks and masters alike. For almost an entire day, their soothing presence could be seen crossing our paths, like moonbeams across a face.

Secret Nalanda was so busy that when I reached the Main Assembly Hall, the Dharmachakra seal had been left open. The vows of secrecy were broken and awry-gaited monks, some of whom had not even been ordained, moved out of the hole in the floor, their backs bent with laden books.

Burning with urgency, I made my way inside to the Meditation Wall. In the past few days, all the secrets of Nalanda had opened up to me. The knowledge that lay in the heart of known reality had been revealed too. But I did not know enough of the Nine Unknowns. Who were they, and how I would find their wisdom book, nagged me. Tarpa's words had made their impact.

Overwhelmed by curiosity for this last piece of knowledge, I sat on the listening side of the wall of perpetual meditators. They had not been moved. This was unusual, since all of Nalanda was evacuating everything of value.

On the other hand, scribes were hurriedly noting down, one last time, all the words the meditators emitted. Either by rambling, or muttering, or in some cases, shouting the knowledge that came from deep within other realms.

I sat before the old monk in transition inside the last cave because he was the only one unattended. His attendant had left to fetch ink. I took this opportunity to reach out into the stone and whispered.

'Who are the Nine Unknowns?'

Miraculously, he spoke, but he did not answer my question. His voice was tired, inarticulate, but it was speech nevertheless. Clear for me to hear and understand: 'Nine Volumes. First. The secrets of the human race. Second. The science of creating cholera and plague-producing colloids. Third. The most dangerous of all sciences. Psychological warfare. Moulding mass opinion to govern the world. Fourth. Physiology. How to kill a man by touching his nerve impulse. Fifth. Transmutation of metals and the science of alchemy. Turning base metals to gold. Sixth. Study of all communication, terrestrial and extra terrestrial. Seventh. The most exhaustive cosmogony known to mankind. Eighth. The science of light. Ninth. The rules of evolution of societies, and foretelling their decline.'

The Broken One had already given me this information what seemed a long time ago. All nine subjects were taught at Nalanda, probably with the same layers and codes of secrecy used in the New Science. I was certain that if I knew where to look, I would find it in both public and secret libraries. But there was no time now.

The holy one in transition was talking about the magical properties of the Ganges, whose water remains eternally pure, when in a trice my master stood before me. In a way that still took me by surprise, he appeared before me a moment after I heard his voice.

'Quick, Siddhartha.' He grabbed my hand and took me out of the cave.

'I need you to not leave my side till you get express instructions from me. Bear witness, be mindful. Do as I say.'

'Yes, master,' I said.

In quick steps he led me down a corridor that I had not seen before. It opened into a courtyard littered with overturned manuscripts. A moss-lined corridor in its corner led to the stone-latticed wall. We were moving into the roofless temple. My master led me through the lantana bower. The heavy undergrowth easily gave way to the touch of a hand, disclosing the wooden bridge over the rippling brook. Ahead of us, a seven-feet mahasiddha walked with his sandals clanging. As I gazed at his magnificent gait, the music reached me. Like waves rising and falling in some wondrous ocean. The thousand names of She Whose Name Cannot Be Uttered. Except by the most adept.

A few monks lead by Vallabha the Long Nose ran ahead of us with instruments for musical accompaniments. The dholak and cymbals tinkled and clashed as they ran.

The pathway opened out into the sandy arena of the roofless temple where I had received the Great Initiation. A secret conclave was already in progress. My master was the last to arrive.

Already in raptures, arms interlaced in a circle, they sprang up amid the dust of the sacred dance with their feet on the sandy ground. Older monks, students and some laity chanted in an outer circle. Gauri's mother was a conspicuous presence swaying to music at the centre. So also danced the Abbot and the Chinese scholar, like a married couple, cavorting in domestic bliss. Leading everyone was my brother's wife, a Dakini of outstanding beauty, head lifted, hair falling down to the waist, her throat swelling like a coveted bird of paradise.

My master took his place in the moving circle. I swung on the outside, within my master's eye level, in case he needed anything. I was already intoxicated by the heady chant and also the shock of impending doom. I saw Asita and Tarpa keeping perfect beat and rhythm in the inner spiral. Sakya and Vallabha were all smiling at the fortuitous occasion. Even the dead Suka was present. There were at least a hundred of us, men, and women, and many were disembodied like Suka. I felt no discomfort in their presence. Only Rahula stung me with his painful absence.

I turned to see Gauri singing next to me.

Looking at my master, the Abbot and the Dakinis twirling like dancing flames in the spiralling circle, I saw greatness illuminating together. It seemed to me the essence of all the knowledge contained in this world was burning brightly one last time before dying out.

For it was true, it was true, it was true, seemed to whisper the cool wind blowing through my body. Buddhism had brought a depth and culmination to knowledge in my land not known until now. And never would such a miracle occur again.

As I chanted and danced in ever-expanding Dakini circles, I realised that I had safely crossed the most dangerous terrains of my precarious practice. Doubt.

I had conquered the four most difficult stages where the master-disciple relationship breaks down. Disgust in the first stage is recompensed by an enhanced surrender to the master in the second. This gives the impetus to confront social dogma, and loss of faith again, in the third stage. When this invisible and treacherous stage is crossed, it finally leads to reconciliation of the self and master in the final stage.

I did not know then that the path to enlightenment never ends. And that doubts over my master Aryadatta's integrity would come up even at the end of my life, during my conversations with Rahula. I did not know that even mahasiddhas could be tainted.

I was startled out of my reverie by the rising crescendo of music. Gauri's mother was leading the climax.

As her neck throbbed with song, the outline of her generous body emanated a strange glow.

'The Nine Unknowns carry their message to you.

They say:

The wheel of dharma is going to soon stop turning.'

The crescendo ended with these words. Her voice was mellifluous now, serene. All of us infected each other with immobility. Nobody moved.

'Their time is done here,' she finished, 'and we have failed, our lives short-lived.'

She looked everybody in the eye as she spoke. Big though she was, and old, she was the intensity of lightning. She was the power of the Earth.

In the intense interlude that followed, my brother's wife picked up a eulogy of the Nine Unknowns. The ode turned to the Nine Kalkis, soldiers of the Nine Unknowns. Each of Kali's soldiers, the Kalkis, were named and praised. I listened carefully but most of the names were unfamiliar to me. But soon my ears picked up some familiar ones—Asita, Tarpa and Bilwa—and I was filled with an unnameable pride.

'We now have our ninth Kalki of the Ninth Unknown,' she sang, as the sacred dance slowly picked up pace again.

'Siddhartha. The able Kali warrior also guards the tribe of Kali, queen of the dakinis.'

'Kali's tribe, the Dakini trust lineage, the Great Goddess family, will come back to turn the wheel again.'

I joined the chorus wishing I knew what she meant, but I didn't. I looked askance at Gauri. She inclined her head; keep your peace, it suggested, the truth will be revealed.

'This lineage will annihilate the forces that ended Kali, the
queen of dakinis.
When Kali's name can be uttered again, the end will have a
beginning.'

As our steps picked up pace with the rising notes, we held hands and raised our faces to the clear blue sky. Some women had started ululating and clashing drums; their feet raised a storm of fine sand. Dust hung, like frozen auspiciousness, in the air.

Gauri's mother was looking directly at me. But I did not have time to dwell on her because my master led the chant next.

'Soon this time will be past,' he started and he paused after the prelude. Everyone waited with so much calm, as though we were celebrating just another annual Baisakh for the Buddha's birthday.

'Those who survive the holocaust,' he picked up, drumming his words to the gathering beat of drums, 'go to Uddiyana and the Pure Lands. The place of eternal twilight. The place where Kali's tribe dwells.'

Gauri picked up the melody after him, stepping lightly amongst us, her cymbals chiming in rhythm.

'The vows of trust among Kali's tribe never break,' she sang.

'Our work is silent, sacred and secret.' Another old feminine voice picked up the musical note.

'For a thousand years Kali waits.'

It was the Chinese Dakini singing now. And all joined the exulting chorus.

'For a thousand years Kali is mistaken as the power of destruction.
For a thousand years she is vilified as a flesh-eating demoness.
For a thousand years she sticks her tongue out in shame for overstepping her role.
For a thousand years she will be defined by her husband.
For a thousand years Siroha will flaunt her vilified image to the social order.'

It was at this moment that I realised that this was the form Siroha was creating in his private laboratories. By presenting Her as a horrible ogress, a husband can control and shame into submission, Siroha would bury Her reality in full public view. This was how he would accomplish a thousand-year curse. Kali's curse. I had underestimated him.

'After a thousand years,' the Chinese Dakini sang,

'Woman realises that Kali does not stick out her tongue in shame,
But to invert it.
And turn it inwards.
So she can taste the nectar dripping from the centre of her skull,
Because that is what the tongue is made for.
That is the way of the true male Kapalika.
That is the way of the true female Kapalini.
The woman who realises this will be released from bondage.
The man who realises this will be released from bondage.
The law of inversion will reveal the path of liberation for her.
The law of inversion will reveal the path of liberation to him.
The wild beauty of the inner worlds will lie at her feet again.
The wild beauty of the inner worlds will lie at his feet again.
And never again will she stick her tongue out in shame.'

The Chinese Dakini roused us into another rhythm. She faltered a little when the pandemonium outside penetrated our entranced defence. The armies had reached Nalanda. The assault was at hand. There was no more time.

'Uddiyana and the Dakini Pure Lands will hide in the mists of antiquity. Never to be found again.' She stopped abruptly. Gauri's mother picked up the fallen note, unhurried, as if there was all the time in the world.

I still remember the last words of the chorus before the masters slowly dusted their robes to get up and disperse.

'The couple stands at the edge of eternity,
Looking down at an abyss of intense darkness.
And so they shall remain for a thousand years.'

Finally the music stopped. And then the dancing stopped. And then there was silence.

35. *A Craggy Face*

When the bloodcurdling screams of infidels scaling over the university walls reached our ears, dusk was setting in. It was the twilight time between this world and the next. The threshold between life and death.

Muslim barbarians descended on us like an army of hungry ghosts.

My master had just finished a quiet confabulation with the Abbot at the Dragon Pool. Against the din of elephants trampling down the giant doors of the gates, he was calm and unhurried, as if on his way for the evening worship.

'This is the key to the secret tunnel from your monastery to the outskirts of Nalanda,' he said to me. 'Flee now, and never return. There is no more time.'

And as simply as that, my master turned and left.

Four years, I had sat at my master's feet and learnt from him. Four years, where time lay strewn around us like unguarded wealth. And now that we were impoverished, deprived of our greatest luxury, all that we had left was dignity. My eyes lapped up the sight of the last glimmer of his receding figure and my heart filled with an unbearable sadness.

Meanwhile, hell's minions had already broken loose of its chains. I could not help but watch in transfixed horror the rape of my beloved university. For four days, teachers and students had tried to evacuate as many manuscripts as was humanly possible.

The Buddhas had laughed at their panic-stricken attempts, for they had failed miserably. Two days were wasted in bitter acrimony over which books should be saved. On the third day, many bullock carts of randomly selected books were dispatched out of the university. On the fourth day, a large bulk would have left had the attack not happened earlier than expected. We thought that the messengers of death would come at midnight. They didn't. They came at dusk, when the libraries were still three quarters full.

It was a bloodbath. I could not flee. I stood rooted to the spot and stared. Unshaven, unwashed, dark-clothed men gripped gleaming swords. Swords whose capacity for blood never seemed to be sated. The soldiers burnt whatever they could and desecrated whatever they could not. They ransacked the kitchens and pissed on what they could not eat. Hordes descended on the servant colonies and killed whatever livestock and cattle remained. They hunted for women and not finding any, fell upon the novices. Fresh young boys who had still not grown down hair on their upper lips.

All the time the swords whistled through the air, animated by an independent life. The pungent smell of sweating horseflesh trampling on muscle and bone hung in the air. The soft sounds of limbs breaking, of organs puncturing, of decapitated heads falling gently to the ground. Amid all that was the collective semi-human roar of fragile men building themselves up to a frenzy. Aiming to kill. When there was nothing left to hack, they fell upon our beautiful statues and took to cutting off their limbs and fornicating with them.

All eighty-four mahasiddhas were present during the sacking. They bore silent witness to the desecration of this holiest of places.

As a monk and as Nalanda's son, I was duty-bound to defend my mother. Hot tears of fury rolled down my cheeks and a cry rose out from within me, as if it came from the very bowels of the earth Nalanda stood on. Every inch of me straining against hysteria, I picked up a sword from a fallen monk. Even though my hands shook as I hurled it at the back of an unsuspecting soldier, the blade found its mark. He hurtled full face on the ground, so easily dead. Blood rushed to my head and sword in hand, I looked around for more adversaries.

All around me were fallen monks, like trampled blossoms, like crumpled paper. Many bodies were lifeless, and those barely alive wailed and whimpered, calling out for their mothers and begging for help. Some recited their sutras and prepared for a braver exit.

Those that were still on their feet were soft and easy targets for the barbarians.

They cowered before the ruthless assassins, their swords dangling limp in their hands. Some fell at their attacker's feet and cried shamelessly for mercy. Some stood before the invading soldiers like sacrificial lambs, bowing their heads for the slaughter. But some fought, and fought bravely.

They gathered in groups at the gates of the three libraries. At Ratnanidhi, Sakya had succeeded in staving off the hordes by spurring the regrouped monks on to courage. Sweat and blood poured into his eyes. He was the first friend I had made in Nalanda. Today, destiny was exacting the strictest dues from his task as doorkeeper. He seemed ready to pay to the fullest. I saw the Broken One fighting on his side. And Baladitya readers too, and pageboys alongside masters, equalised in the face of death. Bilwa and Vallabha fought together, their swordplay unwieldy and clumsy, but enemies no more.

They looked beautiful to me, these brave monks, grim-faced and serene in the face of certain death. Burning brightly one last time before the final snuffing out of life. Some were using their powers of levitation to fly, but these were paltry defenses against the enemy's thirst for blood.

Among the infidels, I noticed one striking figure. He appeared to me to be the general. One undamaged eye shone shrewdly out of a craggy face. Though one hand hung useless on his side, he used his sword-wielding one with great dexterity. His leadership was evident in the way he mobilised and ordered his troops. I noticed that he kept exhorting his men for the most important task that he seemed to have in mind. A systematic and orderly collection of the manuscripts. Though dauntlessly focused on the libraries, he bestowed on the defending monks some grace.

'O monks! You have fought courageously and deserve a glorious death,' he shouted at Sakya. 'Fear not, I am sure jannat awaits you, and the doors of paradise for the bravest will reserve their most special charms for you.'

With that he fell upon our band of university soldiers, their training only fourteen days old. I saw my friend Rama in battle. The sandal-keeper, the head washerman, my monastery cook, the moolanivasi water carrier were by his side, paying their last tribute to Nalanda.

It suddenly struck me that there were very few panditas at the battle scene.

Though I was loathe to abandon my imperiled friends, some hidden force made me leave the scene. It was fate again that had intervened, for if I had stayed, I would surely have been killed with the others that day.

Amidst the flame torches that were jettisoning into the gathering night, I made my way to the Main Assembly Hall. Again it was fate that I saw a monk entering the Dharmachakra door, for if I had not followed him, I would not have been able to enter, since I had lost the seal my master had given me.

When I emerged from the tunnel into the inner courtyards, a strange and unreal sight awaited me. More than two thousand meditating panditas and mahapanditas sat cross-legged in the various nooks and corners of the secret core of the Nalanda observatory. They looked exactly like a flock of eagles reposing on the edge of a mountainous cliff. The sonorous hum of their incantations rolled against the stone pillars in wave after animated wave of constructed sound. I sensed the exudation of so much power in the courtyards stretching out vertically above me that it seemed enough to explode a mountain.

I whirled about me at the grandeur of it all. Student monks were receiving final instructions from their masters and preparing for departure. Before each pandita was placed a platter of flowers, incense and the paraphernalia of worship. Disciples rearranged the clothes on their masters one last time. Some bowed and took leave gracefully. Some succumbed to inveterate weeping in front of statue-like panditas lost in the vortex of the highest meditations.

And then the realisation of what was happening felled me like an axe. I sat down on the stone steps and held my head in my hands. I saw from the periphery of my vision the hem of approaching robes and when I looked up I saw the Abbot and my master.

'What are you doing here?' the Abbot demanded.

'You are jeopardising all that we planned,' my master said.

I looked up at my master and implored him through the mist of my crushing grief.

'Has it come to this? Master, surely there is another way.'

'No, Siddhartha. There is no other way. The Nine Unknowns will never allow forbidden knowledge to reach the masses. Now go. You should have been far away from Nalanda by now.'

My master looked me in the eye. 'Since you are still here, it is a sign that you are meant to know about the Three Betrayals that are about to follow. The mental hardships caused to you by my indifference during the death investigation have established your wisdom. Let it be your guiding principle during the Three Betrayals of family, sangha and self.'

Even though I would go over these words again and again in

the future, at that time all I was aware of was that I would never see my master again.

After I emerged unseen from the Dharmachakra door, the masters securely fastened the seal behind me. Outside, Nalanda burned. The frenzy of screaming had died down to a low-pitched wail. Somehow peace had descended on me, washing away the bloodlust that I had experienced only moments before. And when I hacked away through the army of brigands, I did it with the precision of a practised dancer. It was as if a supernatural power inhabited my body and wielded my sword. My senses were extremely heightened. My breath was slow and controlled. My skin felt soft and supple. I had stopped sweating.

I accidentally knocked off the turban of a fallen soldier and saw the vermilion marks on his forehead. I exclaimed to my brother monks fighting next to me.

'Brahmins! Disguised as infidels!' I yelled in disgust.

'And Hinayanists too, brother. Buddhists too.'

I knew then that the two brothers—the Brahmin Vasantapala and Buddhist Mahipala—had made peace against a common enemy. Nalanda.

'Vile treachery is upon us,' they shouted and while many fell back at the imagined magnitude of the enemy, many were reinvigorated to continue fighting. Again I saw many whirling in the air in a last bid to summon all their miracle-making siddhis.

A righteous anger filled my soul and I made sure I unmasked those I injured, so they would be face to face with betrayal. As if to test this anger, the Goddess of chance made sure that the next face I unmasked was my brother's.

'Aditya Raj!' I recoiled from the force of this treachery.

My brother picked up his fallen sword and stood up to face me with a whimsical smile.

'You wretch!' I screamed and lunged at his throat. He parried me easily, warding off my swerves with the hilt of his weapon.

In the slowest of speeds my surroundings receded into the distance. The burning shrines, the littered corpses, the coagulating blood, the smoke-filled night fell apart and away. Sounds of screams and neighing horse, of last pleas for mercy and the crescendo of the shriek before the falling axe swerved away from me and veered into a smudgy blackness. All I could see was the glint of steel and the chest dancing before me that I needed to pierce. All that I could feel was the reassuring heaviness of my sword. My only premonition was my brother's next movement.

We did not know when our thrusts and parries, our macabre acrobatics of death took us beyond the battlefield that was once the most beautiful university in the world. We found ourselves beyond Nalanda's gates, beyond the Reject's Colony, down to the fields where I had first looked down at the valley with my first alms bowl.

There in the green fields of my youth, under a star-studded sky where the moon looked down at us in complete impartiality, steel clashed against steel and I dismembered my brother's finger. It lay on the grass like an ugly wanton creature of no particular purpose. The night was suddenly very still. For the first time my brother panted and fear glinted in his eyes.

Fear, because he thought he had mastered swordplay better than I ever could. And also because the only unevenness in my breath was a slight sighing sound. I had tired him. Even though I was the elder, he had always been bigger and stronger than me. But now we were standing in a moment when I would not even give him time to recuperate. With a four-step advance, a parry and a thrust I pierced him through the shoulder and forced him onto the ground.

'Submit,' I said from within a well of quietness I had found inside me. My brother was mortally wounded. Watching him, it felt as if it was I and not him, who felt the pain of cold steel slicing through nerve and tissue. I pulled out the sword so the wound would be clean.

'Would you kill me if I didn't submit?' his pride struggled against fear of impending death. His hand lay bleeding on the grass.

'You remind me of flowers before a graven image,' I said. 'They never bloom. But you won't understand.'

'Only the Buddhas can judge me, brother,' he said lifting his hand from the grass. 'Our paths are different.'

'A path of cunning and deceit,' I mocked, 'aimed at more power and more glory.'

'And you, brother? At least I have been faithful to my masters. What flowers made your doubting bloom?'

He took the point of my sword with his uninjured hand and pushed it into his neck. 'Kill me if you will, for my death will be an honourable one. For, brother, history shall bear witness that tonight we cut off the dead wood of a dead and decaying religion.'

I drove the sword point deeper into his neck till the skin broke and his vein swelled against the blade. 'Grand words, brother, grand words,' I spoke between my teeth, 'history is a shortsighted crone who will never know what really happened. She will never know who the heroes really were and what compromises were really made. She will never know of the inner battles fought and lost, or the pettiness of the human spirit, or the immortality of a real martyr. History will never know that tonight, brother shed the blood of his brother because it was his dharma.'

This was when my brother started talking. He spoke in a sleepwalker's monotone and I did not know whether it was deliberate pretense or something else.

'My master placed a drop mixture of his semen and her blood on my tongue and showed me the technique of accepting an Action Seal,' he said. 'After fucking her I offered her to my master.'

My body went limp. So did my sword. I took a step back. 'What are you talking about?' I was suddenly feeling weak and deflated.

'In one of the initiations I melted into a drop and was swallowed by the master. I came out on the top of my master's penis and was transferred to the vagina of my Action Seal.'

I staggered, feeling dizzy, overpowered by the desire to sit down. 'You've been initiated? Who was your Action Seal?' Powerless, I did not even realise how much he was now in control.

His smile was slow and twisted. 'I've had twelve initiations. And my Action Seal was the best in Nalanda!'

With both hands I drew my sword up to bring it down his neck, but I was too slow and he had already side-stepped me. 'Don't you want to hear the rest of it, elder brother?' He was prancing around me and my thrusts and parries were as futile as a blind person's. Don't you want to know your role in the plunder of the beloved university that is taking place right now?'

I stopped dead in my tracks, as if my brother had turned me to stone. The sword dangled uselessly by my side. I could only stare at him.

'You were never privy to the interviews of the murder suspects and detailed death investigations. And you never suspected. Siddhartha the Doubter was so childishly tied to the worldly ties of family that he couldn't doubt his own brother. I knew who killed Dharmapada the minute I saw his body. After the exhumation I immediately informed the king that I had found the culprit. I knew who killed our most skilful and loyal Dharmapada and we swung into action to tighten the noose around Nalanda's neck.'

I must have looked so foolish to him, with my mouth agape.

'After Bhim's death when you told me that Bhim had mentioned the words "action seal" and "real master", we immediately knew who killed Bhim. You practically handed us the culprit on a platter.' He was smiling at my plight, slowly rising from the dewy kusha grass.

I shook my head to bring myself out of my stupor. But there were no thoughts in my head, no feeling in my heart.

'You thought you were interviewing Siroha? In actuality we were interviewing you. And you walked right into our trap. You even wanted to change your master to Siroha!' He laughed uproariously here, giving me an insight into the duplicity he had been practising all along.

'Thanks to you, we could plan Uma's beheading with much precision.'

'And the night of the Giant Buddha?' I asked. But I was not thinking about my brother. I was thinking about my master's last words.

So this was my first betrayal. Family. Brother against brother.

'That was the only time I was speaking the truth,' my brother said, relating his tale with much relish. I thought he might give me a friendly slap on my shoulder, and he actually did. 'That was scarier than all the sex rites, all the cannibalistic feasts and all the decapitations I've witnessed there. Mind you, Uma was sacrificed there, and it was not a pretty sight.'

I could feel the touch of my sword again. It was cold and smooth. I felt the strength coursing through my veins again. I lifted my sword, but my brother started talking again.

'There was that horrible chorus of whispering voices as soon as we entered the sacred womb. You didn't seem to hear it. And this terrible face with three eyes and a protruding tongue seemed to watch me wherever I went. But I was the one who started the wick burning, while you were busy admiring the night sky from the crown of the Giant Buddha's head. I did it to distract you. The plan was to kill and sacrifice the Action Seal that night. But because of your insistent visit the killing could not take place.'

All I knew was that I did not want my brother to utter a word ever again.

I was dispassionate again. Light on my feet again, I corrected my stance.

It was when I was about to use the touch of death on my brother, a technical move taught to us by the martial arts masters many moons ago, that a great mortifying sound rent the firmament, like a giant whip cracking open the flesh of the earth. The ground beneath us trembled, and in utter stupefaction I dropped my sword and looked towards the direction it came from, my beloved mother, Nalanda University.

The sound of the explosion was so great that it must have reached the heavens. A cloud of smoke billowed where Nalanda once had been, and a gigantic white monsoon mushroom rose up like a venomous flower. And then I knew that either the Abbot or my master had used the *Brahmastra*. The acharyas, mahapanditas, panditas and Arhats, nestling in the mother's heart, were dead.

That was it. In an instant it was all over. Nalanda was gone. It ceased to exist. A unified cry, half human wail and half shattering earth, floated up to us. My body lost its power. I sat down heavily on the scented kusha grass. In the face of so much instantaneous destruction I could not kill anymore. Not even my brother. Neither could he.

Inner core legends would speak of a last congress of mahapanditas. And how they read out the last instructions.

Their work was done here. They had to move on. Disperse into the milky way of galaxies once again. And await another time to fulfil their timeless vows. To meet again, to lead again, to teach again.

Legend says the Nalanda libraries burnt for three months.

They were wrong.

The Nalanda libraries, all its secret places and its secret masters burnt down instantly to the ground.

What burnt for three months was the legend that was Nalanda.

Afterwards, for those who know, Nalanda still lived on.

36. *The Remembering*

All the years and the layers of forgetting could not erase the sound of the explosion that night. It still remains inside me somewhere, like an unpollinated seed. It is only during my highest meditations that I have managed to leave it behind. It has taken many practices of detachment to slough off, cleanse and wash away the dirt that had stuck to my soul during the last days of Nalanda and, in many ways, Buddhism's decline.

I had found Gauri waiting for me in the valley that day, her belongings tied in a small cloth bundle. We walked on foot many leagues away from Nalanda and set down our roots near a little temple close to the Mahabodhi tree in Bodhgaya. She had wanted to join her sisters in Uddiyana, especially since her mother and Uma had perished. But I could not leave Nalanda so far behind, and she relented.

In a small village near Bodhgaya I conducted my practices to the letter, obeying each of my master's last instructions. I never wanted to take the risk of disobedience again. When my eyes were closed, he was always there, guiding me through my visions and dreams. When my eyes were open Gauri was always there.

She was clever, my Gauri. She was shrewd, self-controlled, and industrious. She cared for the family, worked the fields, supervised the livestock and fought with the neighbours. She was my guru, my consort, my wife, my sweetheart. It was her breath that gave life to my body. It was she who stoked my inner fires. Together we mastered the Kalika practice. Together we became the God and Goddess performing their eternal play.

I heard that my brother's wife, thwarting my brother's wishes, took over her father's kingdom. Her name was Madhumati. She was a good ruler and shaped the course of Magadha. So widespread and powerful did she become that my mother offered her Vaishali's throne, and she accepted. Mother sent an envoy to escort us for the coronation, with a personal message.

'I'm so glad you didn't go to Taxila,' it said. My mother recieved the Great Initiation, and both women ruled both kingdoms, ably and well.

My brother, I heard, spent his time sulking in forest retreats, trying to regroup Kapalika brigands into writing texts in the Twilight Language.

My name would take time to spread, but soon followers collected around me and from Siddhartha the Doubter I became Siddhartha the Debater. I wrote a few texts, and people started calling me a mahasiddha, but it would take me two more betrayals to become completely enlightened.

I measure old age with the creeping coldness in the bones. And now my bones are so frozen that no warm bath can thaw them. People say I am more than a hundred years old, but I do not know. The years have been so many that I sometimes forget. Even mahasiddhas forget, I like to chide my students. I had heard from a wandering minstrel that a master still survives in Nalanda. One who has sworn to leave only after he finishes his teachings to a small core of students. The news piqued my curiosity. I wondered which survivor of the great fire and sacking of Nalanda still chose to stay behind. I could not deny that even after years of renunciation I felt a wrenching in my gut, for the image of Nalanda brought back a flood of memories.

Much against Gauri's remonstrations I collected a small group of disciples and decided to make one last journey to my beloved university.

I arrived on a palanquin. It had taken me through the deserted village square. The Reject's Colony where my thesis on Buddhist imperialism had once been proudly pasted on its main pillar was devoid of habitation.

I walked across the broken and charred entrance gate and looked at the expanse of waste where once flowers of every season had bloomed. The giant bell that candidates had tolled sweating in excitement was split from side to side, completely silent.

Nalanda was a pile of rubble that had not been moved in almost a hundred years, a carcass nobody wanted to clear away. There was a layer of soot that stuck to everything, like a miasma. The wells were dry and unused. Everywhere bleached stones, the colour of denuded skeletal bones, greeted us. No dulcet melodies of koels or bulbuls followed us. Only the raucous skirmishes of crows. The unscalable walls of the monasteries were all broken. I walked into my monastery.

Till the end of the boundary wall all I could see was one compartment of rubble leading to another. Nalanda was so alone, so deserted that a fleeing cat seemed like too much life. Only the silence of the past lived here. And forlorn empty pulpits remained where once mahasiddhas appeared from other dimensions to bless throngs of students and masters.

In the distance, by a shrine beside a broken monastery, a lone bell tolled. It was the plaintive resuscitation of a heartbeat. A faint pulse in Nalanda's long-deceased body.

We moved towards it, and on approaching saw an embarrassingly small group of students huddling down to a lecture before a shrivelled old man.

'Who is he?' I asked one of my students.

My student went about making his enquires and returned.

'They call him Rahula Shribhadra,' he said.

'Ah!' I thought. So it is he.

When Rahula was informed about my arrival he came up to meet me. And I came face to face with my second betrayal.

In our bony emaciated embrace we palpitated with the memory of a fleshier youth.

'Look what ancient relics we have become,' he laughed. 'And yet time does not let us go.'

He took me to his quarters where makeshift walls had been constructed and the roof patched up. When a bowl of fruit was offered to me and the disciple dismissed, we sat down, hesitantly, to talk. With much caution we began to speak of Nalanda's last day. We spoke of the monks who had fought and died. And those that were slaughtered. And those who had stuffed books under their sanghatis and fled. We enquired about their whereabouts and learnt how many were now in Kambuja, some in Kalinga, and some in neighbouring islands. I told him that Asita and Tarpa were doing well in the land of snows. He said that Siroha too had started his lineage somewhere in the near east, under the auspices of Sena Kings. I knew this, for I kept close track of Siroha's whereabouts, but I kept my silence.

We talked about the self-destruction of Nalanda and its mahapanditas. Rahula spoke of how Mahipala's mercenary soldiers died like flies during the holocaust. How their nails and hair came off, how their bodies filled with terrible heat. They tried to wash off the malaise in the streams and rivers, to no avail. Where the hidden observatory and the Giant Statue of the golden Buddha had once been there were only black holes.

'The Abbot exacted a terrible price for the safety of Nalanda's knowledge,' Rahula said. The Nine Unknowns' knowledge, I thought to myself.

The conversation turned to the unfortunate murders that had brought on the wrath of the underworld and Rahula, distracted, took to staring at two swans swimming in the only pond not yet dry. Two white birds still as graceful, still together, as Rahula and I had once been during happier times in the monastery.

'Be at peace, Nalanda brother,' I told him. 'I always knew it was you.'

'Really?' he asked, consumed by a curiosity greater than his shame. 'How did you know?'

'My master told me,' I said. 'Just before the Great Initiation. He did it to remove the last film of doubt that clung to me. I was in a state of half-crazed self-delusion that I had committed the murders, in a trance maybe, without any knowledge that I had committed them. That was an intense period of doubt, brother. There were times I doubted my own shadow. I did not only mistake the rope for the snake, I thought I was the snake. It was on purpose that our master had immersed me in such dark depths because sometimes we can see light only when darkness envelops us completely.'

'But,' Rahula interjected and I detected a glimmer of his old peevishness again.

'You talk as if I were responsible for all three deaths. That is not strictly true.'

'Does that make your crime any lesser?' I asked him. But he avoided my question.

'I have often wondered how your master always knew of an occurrence even before it occurred. It was uncanny, as if he had eyes all over his body,' he said.

'A true siddha, and a true master knows the past, present and future,' I said. 'It is true that they could project visions in the collective minds of students. Sometimes I had felt that my master could read a thought before it occurred in my head. And also let us not forget that Nalanda always had a sophisticated network of spies.'

Rahula observed me keenly when I spoke, as if he were trying to find some elusive object. I too could not help doing the same. Like me, was he also wondering what a hard taskmaster Time was.

'But our sect was so secret that it was impossible for an outsider to know about it,' he opined.

'I respectfully disagree,' I said, 'for the intelligent the trail was an obvious one to follow. I always suspected you, Nalanda brother. Master Aryadatta only confirmed my suspicions to put me out of the misery of self-doubt.'

'You had always been the more intelligent, the more favoured of the two.' He smiled bitterly, 'Will you not tell me about the trail I so stupidly left behind?'

I ignored his sarcasm and recounted what I knew so he would see the full face of the ugly truth. I did it to preclude the possibility that he might be avoiding his past.

'It was Pandit Dharmapada who started enlisting innocent students into Siroha's secret, most extreme and reprehensible of the Kapalika cults. You and Bhim were Siroha's disciples, undisclosed to us. When I think of the three of you, you were all over-ambitious seekers, in a hurry for results, with too little knowledge. Just like King Mahipala. It was a dangerous trend that Pandit Dharmapada had started, enlisting immature monks ignorant of the significance of the practices. I do not know whether this was a legacy bequeathed to him by Siroha or a direct order from Siroha. There was a master before him who was expelled for his extremism. Sex rites, female sacrifices, cannibalistic feasts in the cremation grounds are not easy to keep secret. But this was not their only problem. The thorn on Siroha's side was the rampant and uncontrolled awakening of the Great Goddess among masters, laity and students. All practices were without the guidance of a real master. This was what was dragging Siroha's sect into the dark depths of the nether worlds.

'Since time immemorial, the Buddhas and the sutras, the sages and scriptures have warned us not to awaken the Great Goddess without an enlightened master. It leads to death, disease and insanity. Why did you not heed this fundamental advice, Rahula? Was the thirst for supernatural powers so strong?

'Why did you not stop your practices when Pandit Dharmapada died? He sat down under water in the well to hold his breath and control its movements within his body. But the breath currents within his body were already imbalanced and he fell into an involuntary trance and passed into oblivion. He drowned.' Memories of the investigation scorched by anguish came rushing back, but I knew I spoke without resentment.

'My suspicions were aroused by the fact that the well was closed, that he had drowned in four feet of water without any signs of struggle.' At this point I wasn't even observing Rahula's reactions, so engrossed was I in the telling of my tale.

'My suspicions grew stronger when Bhim died. His death too was not natural. He had not burned. He had self-combusted. One side more burnt than the other. I did not know much about the New Science practices then, but I knew that when the Great Goddess rages in the wrong channels, she can burn one side to cinders. I also noticed that both these victims were unwell before their deaths. A sure sign of the New Science practices gone wrong.'

Rahula interrupted me here, his gaze faraway, his voice distant: 'Also, the five great winds of the body had obviously fanned the body's inner heat to fatal levels. The same five winds that kept the three worlds balanced on the fulcrum that was Nalanda.'

'For sure Nalanda's fulcrum was off-kilter,' I said staring at him.

He did not reply. Nor did he meet my eyes. I continued speaking. 'But even though the first two deaths were not murders, you, my Nalanda brother, did commit the third. By the time Bhim died, I knew about Action Seals. And you knew about them even before me. I had seen how you looked at Uma during the evening worship. You were partners. You were in love with her as much as I was in love with Gauri. And the night my brother and I entered the Giant Buddha, the divine couple was missing on our way out. It was you and Uma dressed in masks and Kapalika paraphernalia. And even then I would not have known had it not been for the inordinately large feet I saw. Your big feet gave you away, Nalanda brother,' I paused, expecting him to respond. He didn't.

'You had planned to kill her that night. But you couldn't because of our unsolicited presence. But you got your chance the night before the council. I first presumed you sacrificed her. Her beheading looked like a Kapalika ritual. But that was not why you killed her. You killed her out of jealousy. And my brother watched.'

Here I paused to take a deep breath and sigh, for I remembered how jealousy was the most difficult travail for me to cross too.

'An Action Seal by definition cannot belong to any one man.' In my pause I felt again the pain endured for this knowledge to reveal itself. This knowledge itself was enough to slough off mortality like a snake sloughs off its skin.

'The imbalance of the Great Goddess principle in your body,' I continued, 'did not give you the dispassion required to understand this profound revelation. Moreover, the beheading was sacrilegiously done at the feet of the Buddha. You murdered her out of jealousy and tried to expiate the sin by offering her head at the feet of the Buddha. Hypocrisy, I knew, had always been your tragic flaw.'

Rahula was silent, and remained so, till dusk came and the swans glided away.

The clepsydra would not turn the hour today. The Department of Religious Articles would not bustle with preparation for the evening worship. The famous black Mahasali rice would not be cooked specially for the masters in the numerous kitchens. No young acolyte sat under a tree, swaying while memorising a sutra. There was no commotion in the shrines, there was no sweeping of the pedestal seats. From a distance no parasols of approaching panditas caught our eye. Our ears did not pick up any accompanying fanfare. The chants that resounded throughout the lands of Nalanda had been arrested mid-syllable. Nalanda would chant no more.

'A lot of this,' I brought my mind back to Rahula, 'I understood in the dark cell of my incarceration while I waited for the hangman's noose. And though the reasoning of my mind was flawless, a battle raged in my heart. I thought that perhaps the dark mental states of the unconscious netherworlds had driven me into committing the crime. And even though this is known to happen, such was not the case. Our master allowed my incarceration for various reasons. One of them was also to protect you. My capacity for endurance was far greater than yours, for you were born with a very weakened state. It is such an irony, Rahula, that our master had allowed you into his secret fold much before me. My master transferred your service to his own department so he could keep an eye on you. Yet, you strayed. All the cowries you spent on midnight oil. You were not studying at night. Your impatience, the darkness of your soul, had dragged you to Siroha. Dark pulls the dark. And however intense my tests and doubts had been, it was I who was finally ready for the Great Initiation.' I knew I was sounding vain, and it pleased me to see a vein throb on Rahula's shrivelled temple.

'The turn of events have shown that the Buddha's words are never wrong. The golden mean is the lifeline one grasps when one dives into the unchartered terrain of the esoteric. My doubts kept me on the path of moderation and continued to purify my soul. I justify this with our master's words: "In the path of enlightenment give up doubt but not logic."'

'You on the other hand...,' I hesitated, not wanting to hurt him further.

'Had such an overarching desire for sorcery that I swung like a pendulum to the other extreme,' he finished. 'There is a story in the Panchatantra, my Nalanda brother, of the tortoise and the hare. My felicitations to you, because you are the tortoise and you have won the race.'

'Enlightenment is not a race,' I muttered as I lifted my ageing body to embrace him. 'Think not ill of me, Nalanda brother, for we walk the path in different ways.'

Our embrace was warm this time because of the burden of truth we both had shed.

He told of the last instructions our master had given him—to continue teaching the scriptures till his last breath. 'Teach the scriptures, till you finally understand them. Keep the glory of Nalanda alive till you die,' he had said, 'for you helped end it once.'

'A noble task indeed,' I said.

He brought me his shawl and draped it around my shoulders. Dusk had brought in a wayward coolness that made me tremble slightly. It would be winter soon.

He asked me whether I had met our master recently and I replied in the affirmative.

'He had told me to find him in the Pure Lands. I went there some years ago and looked for the village he had mentioned but could not find it. And then I called out to our master and he came.' The memory came back to me with all the freshness of a lucid dream.

'He hasn't aged at all. His demeanour is more pleasant and glowing than it had ever been on earth. He led me to his village, a little valley in the island snuggled between a ring of snowy ocean waves, lost to the most discerning boatman. A crystalline moat surrounds the village and it is reached by means of crossing a draw-bridge. I met many siddhas from here and beyond, and the departed panditas gave me their blessings. My lasting memory of his village is of its permanent twilight. A gentle bluish aquamarine reflection of the light of the numerous meditations of many, independent of the sun and moon.'

'And so he had told me too,' Rahula replied. He was crying

softly, eyes averted into his beard which was as white as the Himalayan snow.

'To seek him in the Pure Lands of Uddiyana. I too had looked for the island beyond the snowy ocean waves. I was unable to find him. I wonder why?'

It was my turn to be silent.

'The Buddhas and masters choose only the bravest of the brave,' he said.

'Look!' I said in an attempt to distract, 'the twilight of Nalanda! So similar to the one I spoke of. Hiuen Tsang the Chinese traveller's twilight. The meditation-inducing twilight caused by the conjunction of the sun and moon at their closest. It is you who taught me its scientific basis once. During twilight the sun and moon channels converge at the mouth of the central channel, at the base of the spine. It is the time facilitating the easiest meditations. But in Nalanda the twilight is ever present, facilitating meditation at all times.'

He looked reproachfully at me for a while and then smiling shook his head. 'All right, Siddhartha, I submit. Paradise exists here as well, for those who can see it. Through my teachings I shall find it, hopefully before I die.'

And so I took leave of him and embraced him for the last time. When we parted our long years fell away and we both looked at our life's end with equanimity.

'Let not death destroy our friendship, Siddhartha,' he called out after me.

I lifted my staff to the sky and said, 'With the grace of the Buddhas and our master, it shall not, Rahula. It shall not.'

'I hope you forgive me, for all that I did that you know. And for all that I did that you do not know,' was his quiet reply.

I waited patiently, receptive, full of the endurance that Nalanda had taught me.

'That night at the Giant Buddha. It was not Uma who was my Action Seal.'

I turned to wave goodbye to Rahula. Like my last meeting with my brother I did not want Rahula to utter another word. And he didn't.

And so I took leave of Rahula, my last friend. And my second betrayal. The betrayal from the Sangha. I had had a lot of time to become used to the treachery. Rahula's betrayal did not cause me as much pain as my brother's. Maybe because with Rahula I had more time. The wound was not fresh like it had been with my brother.

Before leaving Rahula painted my name as a mahasiddha on the gates of Nalanda.

'The paint will not wear off for at least a few centuries.'

'But I am not yet a mahasiddha,' I chuckled as I picked up my walking stick to find my path again.

And so I took leave of Nalanda, mother of all knowledge. I turned to go back to Gauri and take my leave from her. And from there, where my soul rends asunder from hers, I would make my way to Varanasi.

Varanasi, close to the place of my birth. Varanasi, my chosen place of death. Varanasi, where the Goddess Ganga flows with the secrets of the Nine Unknowns. And there, by the banks of her river, where sins are washed off and pure souls achieve salvation, I would wait, for the next instruction to reveal itself.

After my meagre belongings were packed on the bullock cart I tarried just a few moments more with my still youthful wife.

'My most beloved,' she said embracing me, 'you say we will never meet again in this lifetime. But before we say goodbye we should accept all the truths we have kept hidden from each other.'

I found myself distancing myself from her. 'I know,' I said. Try as I might I couldn't look at her. 'That night in the Giant Buddha, it was not Uma who was Rahula's Action Seal.'

She took my face in her hands and forced me to look at her. Just like she had first done at the amra grove. I have to admit that it disturbed me that there was no expression of shame or guilt on her face.

'Rahula has admitted to killing Uma,' I told her, gently trying to free myself.

'Yes,' she whispered still holding my face. With a feather touch she kept me captive, my woman.

'But I still have to admit to killing Dharmapada and Bhim,' she said.

Now I looked at her. Every sight, sound and sensation faded away into the background. All I could see were her deep twilight eyes.

'The Dakinis have a wrathful side, my dearest. The Buddhas call it ruthless compassion.'

It was she who first let go of me. She stepped back against our humble mud wall so I could get some distance from what she was about to say.

'Mahipala and Siroha's atrocities were beyond the pale. They needed to be punished for the good of all sentient beings. Since Siroha was killing all the poor helpless Action Seals advanced enough to give higher empowerments, Siroha's magic was suffering. He needed enlightened Dakinis to progress. During an Action Seal practice with Rahula I spread the rumour that I was available. Poor Dharmapada became really excited that he had been approached by a real master.'

Images of my wife with other men rose from the depths of denial to the surface. I had trouble concentrating on her words. For the first time in decades I sensed the faint stirring of anger.

'I even taught him a few breath-holding techniques in the village well a couple of times. The third time, however, I killed him. I killed him by water, the second primary element. All I had to do was press the nerve of the moon channel on his left groin. It opened like the floodgates, and he drowned in four feet of water.' As I gazed at my wife, I was unable to see the Dakini. All I could see was the Dayani witch.

'Both Dharmapada and Bhim died in the sitting position. Not because of the Great Goddess wreaking their subtle anatomies like you surely think but because I was intimate with them. When word spread in Mahipala's sect that Dharmapada has finally found a good quality Action Seal, Bhim tried to change his master from Siroha to Dharmapada. That is how desperate they were for real masters. I lured him and killed him through fire, the third primary element. I pressed the sun channel on the right side of his groin, and he burnt to death.'

I tried not to think of the heart exposed through the rib cage. I focussed my thoughts on my master. He would guide me through the betrayals. He had promised. Or had he? I wasn't so sure anymore.

Your true love is where your heart resides. The Chinese scholar had taught us that when you point to yourself you point to your heart. The betrayal of the Self. The third betrayal.

I wished she would stop talking, but she kept on and on and on. 'I was there when you had your last conversation with Bhim,' she said.

She had no shame, this woman. She would not even look away. I was the one looking away. 'I had come to know that thanks to your clumsy disclosure of Bhim's mention of the "real master", and with the disclosure of Dharmapada's desecrated member during the exhumation, Aditya Raj and Rahula had understood that the Action Seals were killing the men of their sect. A report had already gone to Siroha and Mahipala. The sitting position and the desecrated male member was obviously the sexual act gone wrong. Both disclosures took place thanks to you. Siroha had made sure that the corpses were buried and not cremated like the Abbot wanted. The Abbot had been forced to honour the Alchemist's agreement for burial instead of cremation. When Aditya Raj arrived, thanks to your sanction, the mystery was solved even before it began. Disclosing Bhim's confession about the "real master" to Aditya Raj was the final damning evidence that Mahipala used to bring the Black Hats down to their knees. Can you imagine our frustration at your childish naïvete, Siddhartha? That night, at the Giant Buddha, I had enticed Rahula with promises of the Great Initiation. By pressing his life nerve at the perineum I would have killed him by Earth, the first primary element. I wanted him to be found in the morning buried at the Buddha's feet. If you had not given the Great Initiation book to Sakya, if you had given it to Siroha, I would have destroyed you by Air, the fourth primary element. I would have sucked your life breath out of your mouth. For we have taken Mother Kali's oath. Those who walk the path with arrogance will be destroyed.'

The female chant of unstruck sound was starting again. Again I did not know where it was coming from.

Now I kill you.

Now I take your life.

'But Kalika was protecting me that night at the Giant Buddha because she sent you earlier than the appointed hour. And even as your brother distracted you with the burning wick, Rahula and I made good our exit. But poison kills poison. Such is the law. Vengeance was wreaked on Uma a few days láter. It was so easy to lure silly, simple Uma with dreams of eternal love because she was besotted with Rahula. She willingly allowed him to sacrifice her.'

After her long stream of words, there was finally silence between us. It was an empty silence. As empty as the bare room I was leaving behind. After a while I became a little conscious of my surroundings. I heard cow bells tingling in the distance, and from somewhere a hawker selling his wares of toasted gram. The artful designs my wife had made on our mud walls with so much dexterity came into view. But my wife was still not finished.

'With your brilliant powers of deduction you must have realised that all the deaths took place near water. The water tanks near the Giant Buddha, the village well was to keep the Dakini mothers close to me. The nature of the female principle is to flow. Women follow the rhythm of the lunar cycles and seasons. The Dakini resides in the essence of the moon, water. We know how to communicate through the flow of its movements. I was never alone. They were always with me. Kalika was always with me. Notice how dried up the lakes around Siroha's vihara was. He had murdered the Dakini principle.'

'Stop,' I said, 'not another word shall pass through your lips again,' I said turning my back to her.

'Those who offend Her will incur the wrath of the Great Goddess.' Her voice followed me, like death follows life. 'I was always there, beloved,' she wept.

'I was there when you first tolled the bell of Nalanda and the masters knew the one they had been waiting for had arrived. I watched you from the samadhi shrines on the night of the exhumation. I was there in the roofless temple when you entered Secret Nalanda. I was there when you reached the cemetery after crossing the Sitavana forest. I was the one lying on the pyre that day, beloved, the man facing your master was Siroha. He had instructed Rahula to drag me from my village and bring me for the heart blood sacrifice. Your master saved my life that day. I was there when you haunted the nights of Nalanda tormented by terrible thoughts. I am your dakini, always protecting you. Kali was always your meditational deity. I am Kali, the granter of the Great Initiation. And I have already forgiven you for not forgiving me.'

'Is what you did for the good of all sentient beings?' was

the only question I asked her. That was the question my master asked Siroha when that dismembered corpse was lying on the funeral pyre.

And she responded just like my brother did when I had confronted him. Neither gave me the right to judge them.

'Our intentions are judged, not our actions. I shall leave the judgements to Kali, and the Buddhas. You too should let the Buddhas judge you. After all, you killed brethren during Nalanda's sacking.'

I walked away determined to never set eyes on her again.

I made my way to Varanasi, and there I found a Bodhi tree by the banks of the sacred river Ganga. The Ganga, the sweetest, kindest dakini I know, where the Dakini principle flows uninterrupted, since eternity. There, another Bodhi leaf made a slow downward spiral to my lap. The sign of Mahakali.

It was time.

Time for the full enlightenment of a mahasiddha. For fourteen days my three betrayals sloughed off my mentalities till my whole body expanded in the clear light of bliss.

I understood the Buddha's four great truths. I understood the nature of suffering. I understood the nature of life and death. I understood the nature of consciousness. I understood the nature of Self.

I knew now why the Buddha said the Self does not exist.

To be is to be perceived.

I exist only when the other exists.

I exist only because the other exists.

The individual is the illusory reflection of a social consciousness, raised and nurtured by suffering. The Self's very nature is to suffer. Suffering defines the Self.

The Self's first individuation occurs with the cry of anguished separation from the mother. The second for needy acknowledgement from its peers. It finally matures through a pathological desire for oneness with its social order. The Self turns this wheel lifetime after lifetime, chasing this illusory oneness. Oneness always eludes. Oneness can never reconcile emptiness. Because emptiness is the goal. What we are running away from is the goal. Shunyata. The Void. The wheel stops turning with this realisation. Then the Self ceases to exist. This cessation of Self is nirvana.

Birth is death. Death is birth.

I realised then why the Nine Unknowns since Ashoka's time had always been women. Or the weak and infirm. Humanity does not look for power in the powerless, or light in the invisible, or strength in the weak. Because to be is to be perceived. The weak, the infirm, the marginalised are either in the fringes of perception, or not even perceived. They are invisible. They don't exist.

That is how the Nine Unknowns have always hidden from prying eyes. Eyes that looked for men. The Nine Unknowns are never perceived as women. The power of their invisibility protects the light that shines on wisdom humanity can never know, because it cannot perceive. That's how it must be, through the far reaches of time. Still for those few who are meant to know, the Nine Unknowns can be found. I can leave a small clue, just a little hint. Look for them in the cryptic symbology of the ten wisdom goddesses. Mindless, young, widowed, ugly, poor and destitute. The symbols of the wisdom goddesses are also the symbols of the Nine Unknowns.

I realised that my wife was the Ninth Unknown. She had humoured and indulged me by being my wife, even as I failed all her expectations. I had forgotten that she was not my wife, she was my master. My real master, my chosen deity. She was my Kali. I was her warrior. It was not her I needed to forgive, it was me.

I knew this is how the Dakinis challenge all the mahasiddhas, and they fail, again and again. And will continue to do so, till it is time. Mahakala's time. Nay, Mahakali's time.

Until I perceived this unity, I too would be a tainted mahasiddha.

Images of mahasiddhas are always shown in union with their dakinis as consorts. Thus, I saw the Dakini consigned to the lowest social title a man can give a woman. Consort. In the Brahminical pantheon that would soon superimpose Buddhism I saw the same palimpsest.

The creatrix principle is usurped by an old bearded creator. The sacred feminine is consigned to the role of his daughter. In other Vedic symbols, the creative principle rises like a lotus from His navel, while the sacred feminine, his wife, presses His feet. In the one instance the divine feminine is shown as a mother, She remains within the domestic confines of patriarchy.

When tears flowed down my cheeks, as if to meet the river Ganga, my worship of Kali was complete. I was worthy of uttering Her name. Because I had become the most adept.

That was when Gauri came back to me, and I prostrated for a long time before her feet. We wept together. We wept for us. We wept for humanity seeking oneness.

She gave me her wisdom and dictated the Ninth wisdom book. For those who know, this is called the *Book of Light*. It holds within it the scientific principles that govern time and space. I was taught everything I needed to know about Uddiyana and the Pure Lands and received instructions on how to make sure that humanity never finds it.

And then, after dictating her final instructions, she left. There was no remorse in our parting, because birth, death, separations and meetings are for the ignorant. Ignorant are those who cannot stop the wheel from turning. Unlike us.

There are no goodbyes for us.

People have started collecting around me again. They want to hear the teachings. But I am tired of this world of inequalities. Tomorrow I shall voluntarily leave my body. I shall walk into the sacred Ganga and walk out not in this world but in the Pure Lands where my master awaits me. There I shall guard the wisdom book and wait for further news. And for the sign of the Mahakali. When it is time again.

And thus is this book completed, according to the instructions of my master. I have been unable to recount the tale with the prodigious and divine talent some of the great literary writers of my time have. Like Shudraka. I am but a poor logician of limited writing skills. I have only tried to recreate honestly and faithfully the story of my time. So the truth be told.

And thus the ending starts a new beginning.

And I wait. My master shall come to take me.

She promised.

The Jewel island in the Lotus pond.

Om mani padme hum.

Epilogue

Dorge Nhagmo Tulkuma does not sit outside in the courtyard this time, but in the Abbess's private rooms.

All the ritual paraphernalia has been arranged for her to receive Bilana in a very personal audience.

Behind her hangs a thangkha of a naked Goddess with three eyes and a protruding tongue. She holds a kapala in one hand, and the curving knife in the other.

Bilana enters in ceremonial attire. An elaborate headdress adorns her tonsured head. Her outer robes are threaded with gold, silver and gems. She carries a bell and sceptre. She bows low before Dorge Nhagmo and hands her the manuscript wrapped in red silk and silver embroidery.

Dorge Nhagmo says she is extremely happy with the book, even though she has not read it.

She says that it is important for Bilana to know that she is a terton, a person who reveals mind treasures. She says that this book is terma, a mind treasure. It is hidden in the consciousness of time and revealed by a terton when it is necessary.

The Abbess tells Bilana that the terma has lain in the womb of the Dakini lineage for a thousand years. She says that the terma was waiting for the right time to evoke the revival of the sacred feminine.

And that the time has come.

It must be. Because Bilana is the first female terton.

The trust lineage of the Dakinis is ready to be transmitted.

Dorge Nhagmo leans over and puts her hand on Bilana's head in blessing.

'With the blessings of Tarpa, the great mahasiddha of our Kalika lineage of Black Hats, I make this prayer.

'For the Great Awakening, may the woman inside every man, and the woman in every family, and every woman, and every feminine aspect of the material world awaken to correct the course and righten mistakes made by those who walked the path with arrogance.

'May all sentient beings then Follow the Law and turn the wheels of Dharma, guided by Buddha's light, the bodhichitta.

'May the couple now step back from the edge of intense darkness.

'*Om mani padme hum*.'